THE MEN OF WELLINGTON'S LIGHT DIVISION

THE MEN OF WELLINGTON'S LIGHT DIVISION

UNPUBLISHED MEMOIRS OF THE 43RD (MONMOUTHSHIRE) REGIMENT IN THE PENINSULAR WAR

Gareth Glover

&

Robert Burnham

FRONTLINE
BOOKS

ff

The Men of Wellington's Light Division
Unpublished Memoirs of the 43rd (Monmouthshire)
Regiment in the Peninsular War

First published in 2022 by Frontline Books,
an imprint of Pen & Sword Books Ltd, Yorkshire – Philadelphia

Copyright © Gareth Glover 2022
ISBN: 9781399099080

Printed and bound by CPI Group (UK) Ltd, Croydon, CR0 4YY

Pen & Sword Books Ltd incorporates the imprints of Pen & Sword Archaeology,
Air World Books, Atlas, Aviation, Battleground, Discovery, Family History,
History, Maritime, Military, Naval, Politics, Social History, Transport,
True Crime, Claymore Press, Frontline Books, Praetorian Press, Seaforth
Publishing and White Owl

For a complete list of Pen & Sword titles please contact:

PEN & SWORD BOOKS LTD
47 Church Street, Barnsley, South Yorkshire, S70 2AS, UK.
E-mail: enquiries@pen-and-sword.co.uk
Website: www.pen-and-sword.co.uk

Or

PEN AND SWORD BOOKS,
1950 Lawrence Road, Havertown, PA 19083, USA
E-mail: Uspen-and-sword@casematepublishers.com
Website: www.penandswordbooks.com

MIX
Paper from
responsible sources
FSC
www.fsc.org   FSC® C013604

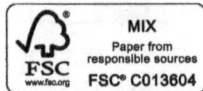

Dedicated to the memory of Captain Nicolas Frank Haynes,
Royal Green Jackets 1951–2021

Contents

Foreword

Having spent the last two decades scouring the archives for unpublished letters and journals of soldiers who served in the Napoleonic wars, I have not particularly concentrated on the regiments that formed the Light Division in the Peninsular War because I was aware that due to their fame, many memoirs from members of these regiments had already been published and it was therefore highly likely that there was little left to publish.

However, a steady trickle of further memoirs by members of the Light Division have been published in the last twenty years to add to the already impressive total, showing that the mine is far from fully exhausted. These include those of Captain George Miller,[1] Lieutenant James Gairdner[2] and Rifleman George Walton[3] of the 95th Foot, Sergeant Samuel Harrison[4] of the 43rd Foot and Captains George Ulrich Barlow,[5]

1. Published as *The Making of a Rifles Officer: The Life and Letters of Colonel George Miller CB FRS (1786–1843)*. Elizabeth Laidlaw. Edinburgh: Burngrange, 2019.
2. Published as *The American Sharpe: The Adventures of an American Officer of the 95th Rifles in the Peninsular & Waterloo Campaigns*. Gareth Glover. Barnsley: Frontline, 2017.
3. Published as *George Walton 1796–1874: the Journal & Diary of a Rifleman of the 95th who Fought at Waterloo*. Peter Coleman: Studley: Brewin Books, 2016.
4. Published as *The Peninsular War Journal of Sergeant Samuel Harrison of the 43rd Foot 1796–1812*. Gareth Glover. Godmanchester: Ken Trotman: 2017.
5. Published as *A Hellish Business: the Letters of Captain Charles Kinloch 52nd Light Infantry 1806–1816*. Gareth Glover. Godmanchester: Ken Trotman, 2007.

Charles Kinloch,[6] John Ewart[7] and Lieutenant Charles Holman[8] of the 52nd Foot.

I also received a request from my good friend Robert Burnham, who resides in Hawaii, to help him search the archives for any unpublished material by members of the Light Division still existing in the British Library, the National Archives at Kew, the National Library of Scotland, the Royal Green Jackets Museum (now held by the Hampshire Record Office in Winchester) or in the Soldiers of Oxfordshire Museum at Woodstock in Oxfordshire, as part of his thorough preparation for his excellent book on the Light Division in 1810[9] and for his further projected volumes. This search unearthed a virtual treasure trove of material that astounded both of us. There was simply more than we could have possibly imagined there; indeed material was discovered that some of the museums didn't even realise that they had themselves.

From this was spawned the idea of producing a book on each of the three regiments that formed the core of the Light Division, publishing the masses of material unearthed, much for the very first time or at most only appearing previously in obscure and very rare publications. This, the first volume, covers perhaps the least known of the three regiments and certainly the one with the least number of memoirs published, that is the 43rd (Monmouthshire) Regiment of Foot. Some eight individual memoirs have emanated from this regiment to date and half of these are rare, whereas the 52nd Foot have fifteen published and the 95th Foot no fewer than seventeen; it was therefore felt that the voice of the 43rd Foot needed to be enhanced most urgently. The others will, however, get their turn in subsequent volumes.

The three infantry regiments of the Light Division in the Peninsular War maintained quite different characteristics from each other. Captain

---

6. Published as *The Peninsular War Diary of Captain John Frederick Ewart, 52nd Light Infantry, 1811–1812*. Gareth Glover. Godmanchester: Ken Trotman, 2010.
7. Published as *A Light Infantryman with Wellington: The Letters of Captain George Ulrich Barlow, 52nd and 69th Foot, 1808–1815*. Gareth Glover. Solihull: Helion, 2018.
8. Published as *52nd (Light Infantry) Eyewitness accounts of the Waterloo campaign*, Gareth Glover. Godmanchester: Ken Trotman 2020.
9. Published as *Wellington's Light Division in the Peninsular War: The formation, campaigns & battles of Wellington's famous fighting force 1810*. Robert Burnham. Barnsley. Frontline, 2020.

John Cooke of the 43rd Foot explained not only the brotherhood of regiments, but also their subtle differences at the end of the war in 1814:[10]

> Though among the regiments that composed it there existed an unanimity that was almost without a parallel in war, yet there was a shade of difference between them, a something peculiar to each corps distinguishing it from the others, which was the more remarkable as amongst them there was a sort of fraternal compact, and it has occurred that three brothers held commissions at the same time in the 43rd, 52nd and Rifle Corps.
>
> The 43rd were a gay set, the dandies of the army; the great encouragers of dramatic performances, dinner parties and balls, of which their headquarters was the pivot.
>
> The 52nd were highly gentlemanly men of a steady aspect; they mixed little with other corps, but attended the theatricals of the 43rd with circumspect good humour and now and then relaxed, but were soon again the 52nd.
>
> The Rifle Corps were skirmishers in every sense of the word; a sort of wild sportsmen and up to every description of fun and good humour. Nothing came amiss: the very trees responded to their merriment and scraps of their sarcastic rhymes passed current through all the camps and bivouacs.
>
> In this way the brothers of the three regiments met together, each being the very type of the corps to which he belonged.

Some of these attitudes are clearly borne out by the memoirs and letters of the men of each regiment.

This volume is, however, far from all the material we found on the 43rd Foot. There is in fact so much material from this particular regiment that four very large accounts will also be produced individually in stand-alone books via Ken Trotman Books in the next year. These will be published in the following order: the letters of Captain William Freer 43rd Foot; the journals of Major John Maxwell Tylden 43rd Foot, the journal of Lieutenant Henry Oglander 43rd and 47th Foot, and Major John Duffy 43rd Foot.

With so much new material to be studied, it is inevitable that a great deal of new evidence will be discovered that will change our

---

10. *A Narrative of Events in the South of France*, Captain John Cooke, London, 1835.

understanding of many aspects of the life of the troops, the military operations and even their thoughts on their fellow officers and seniors at the very time that incidents occurred.

I hope that you the reader will be as intrigued with what we have unearthed as much as we are.

Acknowledgements

A work of this kind cannot come to fruition without the help and advice of a large number of people, but before I make the customary thanks, I must mention one person in particular.

I met Nicolas Haynes, an ex-captain in the Royal Green Jackets, banker and keen researcher on the Light Division, a few years ago, as he wanted to publish the Waterloo journal of Lieutenant Holman of the 52nd Foot. He was determined to see it through and was so dogged that he achieved it, with my help, against some strong opposition. We became friends through our joint passion and I know he had a similar, if distant, relationship with Robert Burnham, as he constantly encouraged us to continue the work of bringing the Light Division material into the public domain. His untimely and unfortunate death was a shock to both Robert and I and we have dedicated this book to him.

I must then thank Robert Burnham, whom I am pleased to consider a close friend, for his help in transcribing the numerous accounts from their original handwriting. He has now been bitten by the bug and has been fully ensnared by the dark arts of transcribing, helping me to prepare these volumes for publication. I have to also thank John Grehan and Martin Mace of Frontline Books for believing in this project when others were not perhaps so keen.

I must also thank the staff of many of the archives around the country, who have cheerfully and patiently dealt with my incessant requests and queries. I have received every help and courtesy from the National Library of Scotland, the National Army Museum, the Hampshire Record Office and the British Library.

I must particularly thank Peggy Ainsworth, Collections Manager/ Deputy Museum Director, for allowing me to literally ransack her archives at the Soldiers of Oxfordshire Museum in the search for material and her unbelievable helpfulness in arranging for copies to be made of literally thousands of documents.

I must also thank Ron McGuigan, with whom I have only ever corresponded by email, but who is the font of all knowledge and finds information on the most obscure subject or person you can ever imagine and rarely fails.

I am also very grateful to Paul Ridgeley and Rory Constant for bringing the Meyricke papers to my knowledge and kindly allowing me to publish them.

Gareth Glover
Cardiff

Chapter 1

History of the 43rd Foot in the Peninsular and Waterloo

Raised in 1741, the 43rd (Monmouthshire) Regiment of Foot had originally been the 54th for ten years before becoming the 43rd. They served extensively at the capture of Quebec, in the American War of Independence and in the West Indies. The skeleton of the regiment returned to Britain in 1795 and spent the next two years recruiting up to strength and forming garrisons at home, before they were sent out to Martinique in late 1797. They remained in the West Indies until 1801, when they returned to Britain again, remaining in Guernsey for three years.

On 17 July 1803 the regiment was designated as Light Infantry and on 12 January 1804 they moved from Guernsey to Ashford. In June they moved to Shorncliffe and were brigaded with the 52nd and 95th. So many volunteers wanted to join the regiment that on 25 November 1804 a second battalion was formed at Bromsgrove but this only consisted of four companies by June 1805.

The brigade remained at Shorncliffe protecting the south coast from the threat of invasion until finally the first battalion was sent on their first expedition abroad, joining the force sent against Copenhagen. There they engaged a Danish force at the Battle of Køge, which eventually saw the entire Danish fleet captured. They then returned to Britain.

In 1808, a large force was ordered to the peninsula under General Arthur Wellesley to attempt to drive the French forces out of Portugal. The 2nd Battalion of the 43rd were part of this force and were heavily engaged in the Battle of Vimeiro, driving in the head of a French column with a determined bayonet charge. The 43rd lost six officers wounded, forty men killed and seventy-three men wounded, of which forty-eight subsequently died. The Convention of Cintra saw the fighting come to an end and the regiment encamp at Queluz.

In late October, the army began to march into Spain under the command of Sir John Moore, the 43rd advancing via Coimbra, Almeida to Salamanca in torrential rain. The army finally concentrated in the vicinity of Sahagún in late December 1808.

1809

The first battalion, having returned from Copenhagen, were ordered to join a force of 10,000 men under Sir David Baird, which landed at Corunna and marched to join Sir John Moore, which was achieved at Mayorga on 20 December. The 1/43rd, numbering 817 men, were in Brigadier General Robert Craufurd's brigade, while the 2/43rd, numbering 411 men, were in Major General Beresford's brigade. Forced to retreat in the face of overwhelming French forces under Napoleon himself, the 1/43rd formed part of the rearguard at Ponferrada.

Craufurd's brigade separated from the main body, marching off towards Vigo and not followed by the French, while the 2/43rd marched with the main body for Corunna. Arriving at Corunna, the army was forced to stand and fight while awaiting the arrival of the fleet to evacuate them. The 1/43rd were not particularly engaged during the Battle of Corunna, but they formed part of the covering force during the subsequent embarkation, parties of the 43rd being some of the last to embark. The losses of the two battalions during this campaign were heavy, almost all the deaths being caused by fatigue and sickness and many of the sick being made prisoners of war. The 1/43rd lost one captain (Carruthers) and sixty-six men dead or captured, while the 2/43rd lost much more heavily given their smaller numbers, losing 183 men, some 45 per cent of their total. Returning to Britain, the two battalions rapidly recruited their numbers, the 2/43rd being augmented by no fewer than 500 men within a week of their arrival at Colchester Barracks.

The 2/43rd were sent on the Walcheren expedition, sailing on the 17 July 1809 from Deal with 662 men. The battalion saw little action but suffered severely from the fever raging through the army. Only eight men were left at Walcheren but almost all of the 654 men who returned to England were severely weakened by the fever and 126 eventually succumbed to it. The second battalion now remained in England and sent regular drafts to reinforce the first battalion in the peninsula.

The British effort on the peninsula was reinvigorated by the return of Sir Arthur Wellesley to command the army still holding Lisbon and the arrival of large reinforcements. The 43rd were represented by a single company in a battalion of detachments in Wellesley's first success in crossing the Douro and defeating Marshal Soult's troops and driving them out of Portugal.

On 29 May 1809 the first battalion was ordered to embark as part of this major reinforcement in Portugal, sailing from Harwich with 1,072 men, and they arrived at Lisbon on 28 June. The 1/43rd were formed into a brigade under Robert Craufurd, again with the 1/52nd and 1/95th, forming the Light Brigade, which also included light cavalry and horse artillery. Hearing that Wellesley's had marched into Spain and that there was likely to be a battle soon, Craufurd rushed his brigade on the march, but they arrived just after the Battle of Talavera had ended. They joined the difficult retreat that followed and suffered equally from the prevalent fevers, losing 110 men to an epidemic by the time they went into quarters at Campo Maior. In December they retired further into much more comfortable quarters at Coimbra.

1810

The 1/43rd were marched up with the Light Brigade to the Portuguese border in January, arriving at Pinhel on 3 January. On 22 February, the Light Brigade was reinforced by two battalions of Portuguese *caçadores* and the Light Division was officially announced, with Robert Craufurd retaining command, despite his lower rank. In March the division was pushed forward to the River Águeda, where they would act as a corps of observation as the French Marshal Masséna brought his troops forward to besiege the fortress of Ciudad Rodrigo. The eventual surrender of Ciudad Rodrigo after a stubborn resistance by its Spanish garrison meant that the French could now contemplate an invasion of Portugal via the northern corridor. Wellington (Wellesley had gained the title for Talavera) maintained this defensive screen in front of Almeida, but urged extreme caution on Craufurd, his division being deployed with the Côa River in its rear. The advance of the French to besiege Almeida in July forced Craufurd to retire, destroying Fort Concepción and retiring under the walls of the fortress, but stubbornly maintaining his troops in front of the Côa, with only one narrow bridge in his rear for them to escape. Attacked by an overwhelming force from Marshal Ney's corps on the morning of 24 July, the division was forced into a hasty retreat over the bridge and only escaped total destruction by a whisker.

Wellington had banked on Almeida resisting a French siege for weeks, but one day into the bombardment a lucky shot, or an accident, caused the huge powder magazine to explode, killing dozens of the defenders and destroying a number of guns. Almeida promptly surrendered. The British were forced to continue to retreat towards Lisbon, with a far superior French army in pursuit. To slow their progress Wellington offered battle at Busaco and successfully defended a steep ridge line against all attacks. Craufurd's troops comprehensively defeated Loison's division, driving them back down the slope in great confusion at the point of the bayonet. This was achieved with the loss of on one officer and eight men wounded in the 1/43rd. The following day, the French found a way round the left flank of Wellington's position, forcing him to resume the retreat. At this point, Wellington's army filed into the secretly prepared defensive lines known as the Lines of Torres Vedras, which were a pleasant surprise to his own army and a great shock to the French. Marshal Masséna deemed the lines too strong to be attacked and found that much of the resources of the country had been destroyed in a 'scorched earth' policy. The French therefore sat down before the lines, awaiting reinforcements and quietly starved, forcing them eventually to a defensive location at Santarém, desperately holding on until the promised reinforcements arrived.

1811

With no reinforcements or substantial supplies arriving, Marshal Masséna skilfully retired from Santarém on 5 March. The Light Division led the pursuit and they were involved in a number of combats as they harried the French out of Portugal, Pombal on the 11th, Redinha on the 12th, Casal Novo on the 14th, and Foz de Arouce the following day. The regiment lost during these actions one captain and one ensign wounded and forty rank and file killed and wounded.

The retreat continued with constant harassing by the Light Brigade until Sabugal on 3 April. Here Masséna stood his ground and sought to push his pursuers back. On a foggy morning, an ill-co-ordinated advance left the 43rd facing heavy attacks, having crossed a bridge without support. The 43rd stubbornly held their ground and even advanced against the French, but were thankful for the eventual arrival of their supports, causing the enemy to retire hastily. Despite the severity of the action, the losses of the 43rd were one officer and thirteen men killed, with five officers and forty men wounded. This drove the French out of Portugal and Almeida was besieged, while the Light Division resumed their old haunts watching Ciudad Rodrigo.

On 3 May Masséna sent his army forward once again in an effort to succour Almeida, but Wellington placed his army in the way at Fuentes de Oñoro and a general action took place over three successive days. During this action, the Light Division was obliged to retire in squares across a wide expanse, which offered the French cavalry a superb opportunity to attack. However, their disciplined manoeuvring saw them successfully march across the plain without serious mishap, although their troop of horse artillery was fortunate to escape destruction. The following day the French retired and that night the garrison of Almeida blew up the works and escaped through the British lines to safety, much to Wellington's fury. Further movements of the French caused the light troops to move constantly and in late June they were stationed near Campo Maior when the 1/43rd received a draft of sixteen officers and 357 men from the second battalion. The battalion returned to the banks of the Águeda in early August.

A further French advance to send a supply column into Ciudad Rodrigo in late October caused small affairs at El Bodón and Aldea de Ponte, but the 43rd were not seriously engaged at either. This brought this year effectively to a close.

1812

The Light Division were abruptly ordered out of their cantonments and began the investment of Ciudad Rodrigo on 8 January. That night two companies of the regiment participated in the attack on the outwork of St Francisco, the 43rd only losing a handful of men wounded. The Light Division was one of four allocated to the siege of the fortress and as such they took turns in rotation to man the trenches for twenty-four hours at a time. Two breaches being reported practicable, one hundred volunteers from each regiment of the division led the assault on the lesser breach on 19 January, while the 3rd Division took the heavily defended greater breach. The Light Division successfully took the lesser breach and turned to clear the ramparts towards the greater breach, finally allowing the 3rd Division to enter successfully. Losses in the 1/43rd were one officer and fourteen men killed and two officers and thirty-seven men wounded. General Craufurd was mortally wounded during the assault and died on 24 January.

Having successfully captured the key fortresses commanding the northern access to Portugal, Wellington now turned to the southern access route controlled by the fortresses of Elvas and Badajoz. Elvas was already in his possession but Badajoz would be a very tough nut to crack. The bulk of the army marched south and Badajoz was invested on 16 March. By 6 April two practicable breaches had been formed and the orders to storm were issued. The Light Division furnished one hundred volunteers per company again but their assault on the breach was to be much harder than at Ciudad Rodrigo. The storming parties being decimated, the Light Division advanced against the breach but could not effect an entry despite all attempts and huge numbers of men were cut down. Luckily 'diversionary' attacks at other points, by the 3rd and 5th Divisions, succeeded in gaining a foothold and French resistance eventually collapsed. The loss of the 1/43rd was the greatest of any regiment involved in the attack, amounting to four officers and seventy-eight men killed, and seventeen officers and 257 men wounded.

While Wellington's troops were engaged at Badajoz, Marshal Masséna made an advance into Portugal in his absence, causing the army to march north again without delay. Marmont retired to Salamanca, but the two armies of near equal size now manoeuvred for advantage, the troops of both armies often marching within cannon shot of each other for days. Marmont overextended his line of March on 22 July and Wellington pounced, ordering his concentrated force to break the van and centre of the French army. The Battle of Salamanca was a huge victory and made everyone in Europe aware of Wellington's name. The Light Division saw little action in the affair, but were involved in trying to cut off the enemy's retreat over the River Tormes. However, they were disappointed when the French escaped using a ford that Wellington mistakenly believed was defended by a Spanish force. The 1/43rd had two officers and fifteen men wounded in this action.

The army now marched on Madrid, which they entered on 12 August. A reinforcement from the second battalion arrived at Lisbon containing sixteen officers and 200 men, but at the end of the march only six officers and twenty men arrived, the rest left sick along the road. Wellington now took his main force northwards to besiege the fortress of Burgos and left a covering force in front of Madrid, which included the Light Division. When the attack on Burgos failed and with the threat increasing from French forces, Wellington ordered a retreat, which included the troops at Madrid, the two forces forming a junction at Alba de Tormes on 8 November. Wellington offered battle on the old Salamanca battlefield but the French troops refused and sought to turn his flanks. The retreat was therefore continued to the Portuguese border, but the commissariat failed and the troops starved on this march. Finally the French left off their pursuit and the 1/43rd settled for the winter at Gallegos.

1813

The military situation had altered dramatically following the disastrous retreat of the French army from Moscow and the subsequent large-scale movement of troops out of Spain, which meant that Wellington began the campaign with superior numbers. Just before the campaign commenced, a further draft of men arrived from 2/43rd consisting of seven officers and 186 men. The campaign began in the middle of May with the Light Division advancing on Madrid as a feint, while General Thomas Graham led the main advance around the French right wing, forcing them to abandon their defensive positions without a fight. On 27 May, the 1/43rd entered Salamanca having found that the French had retired. The Light Division now marched northwards and joined the main advance near Toro. As the advance continued, the entire army was relieved to witness the French blowing up the fortress of Burgos rather than defending it.

On 18 June the Light Division on the march suddenly stumbled into two brigades of General Maucune's division also on the march. An action of encounter saw the French scattered, their baggage captured and a huge amount of medical supplies. Continuing their march, the army discovered the entire French army drawn up for battle in front of the city of Vitoria. At the Battle of Vitoria, which took place on 21 June 1813, the Light Division was initially placed opposite the French centre awaiting the order to charge over a defended bridge at Villodas. However, a local guide advised them that the neighbouring bridge at Trespuentes was not guarded. The first brigade including the 1/43rd soon crossed here and established a bridgehead on the enemy side of the River Zadorra. Within an hour the French line had retired because both wings were under threat and the Light Division advanced to drive the enemy from the village of Ariñez. After some hard fighting, the French resistance evaporated as a flank movement by Sir Thomas Graham threatened to cut off their retreat. The Light Division marched a league beyond Vitoria before halting. The 43rd lost only three men killed and two officers and twenty men wounded.

On the following days the division marched past Pamplona towards Vera, having some skirmishing with the enemy en route that cost them twelve men wounded. The division eventually encamped on the heights of Santa Barbara overlooking Vera. The Light Division were not involved in countering the attacks made by Marshal Soult with the aim of relieving Pamplona. However, the enemy advance having been halted and driven back with loss during the two battles of the Pyrenees, the Light Division was ordered to advance in an attempt to cut off the retreat of the French. Following a tremendous march, the first brigade came up with the French as they crossed the river and retired through the Pass of Echalar (or Etxalar). Firing on the fugitives, they managed to capture

7

many prisoners and much of their baggage. The division resumed its position at Santa Barbara.

The initial storming of the Fortress of San Sebastian having failed, volunteers were sent from the 1st and Light Divisions to bolster the next attempt. The storming took place on 31 August and after very stubborn resistance the attack succeeded; of the detachment of the 43rd numbering thirty-three officers and men, six were killed (including one officer) and twenty-two wounded. A French attack on the heights of San Marcial, which was repulsed by Spanish forces, unfortunately encountered a detachment of reinforcements from the 2/43rd and Ensign Folliott and four men were killed before they had even joined the battalion.

On 7 October the division took part in the crossing of the Bidasoa River into France. The Light Division attacked the heights above Vera and eventually succeeded in driving the French off after some very bitter fighting. Of the 1/43rd, seven men were killed and twenty men wounded.

On 9 November, as part of the Battle of the Nive, the Light Division was ordered to take the heavily defended summit of La Petite Rhune. The works were captured after extremely hard fighting, the 1/43rd losing four officers and nine men killed and five officers and fifty-eight men wounded. The first brigade of the Light Division were placed in the church and chateau at Arcangues and the village of Arbonne.

On 9 December the passage of the River Nive was forced, but this led to a strong counter-attack on Arcangues on the following morning. The pickets were driven in but the threatened assault on the churchyard did not materialise. The fighting continued over the next two days but never became more than heavy skirmishing. On the 13th Soult altered his attack to Wellington's right on the opposite side of the river but this was defeated by Lord Hill, bringing the battle to an end. During this fighting the 1/43rd lost one man killed and thirteen wounded, while another twenty-one men were recorded as missing.

1814

The army rested through the worst of the winter until the Light Division moved to La Bastide-Clairence. However, having been ordered to march back to Ustaritz to receive their new uniforms, they only caught up with the army at Orthes, where they learnt that they had missed a severe battle. They joined the advance to Toulouse, experiencing very little fighting on the way.

On 10 April the Battle of Toulouse occurred, but the Light Division were hardly involved. Two days after the city fell, a further detachment arrived from the 2/43rd consisting of nine officers and 201 men. They arrived when the fighting was over. Peace was announced and the army marched slowly towards Bordeaux, no doubt hoping soon to be back in Britain. The 1/43rd were embarked in HMS *Queen Charlotte* and *Dublin* and they disembarked in Plymouth between 23 and 25 July, where the 2/43rd joined them from Hythe Barracks and all of the fit men exchanged into the first battalion.

However, after three months' recuperation, the 1/43rd, numbering 1,050 men plus officers, were ordered to join a reinforcement sailing for America, the war with the Americans not having been concluded. They embarked in three transports on 10 October and joined the British fleet off New Orleans on New Year's day.

1815

The 1/43rd were landed on 5 January as a part of the force designed to capture New Orleans, but the Americans under General Jackson had received plenty of warning and had built some formidable static defences barring the way. On 8 January a party of 200 men from the 43rd formed part of an assault column on the right of the American lines, but it was destroyed by a murderous crossfire from the American batteries. The attack failed despite a handful of men successfully taking the Crescent Battery at the end of the American line. Seven companies of the 1/43rd lay within 600 metres of the American line in relative safety simply awaiting for the order to advance, which never came. The 1/43rd lost two officers and thirteen men killed and one officer and twenty-one men wounded with another officer and seventeen men made prisoners.

By 18 January the troops had re-embarked and were landed on Dauphin Island in early February, where they encamped until the 1/43rd were embarked on 8 April for England. They landed in early June and went into quarters at Dover and Deal. Reinforced by a strong draft from the second battalion of 214 men, they mustered on 16 June with 1,100 bayonets. They were immediately put on board transports and sent to join Wellington's army in Belgium. Landing at Ostend, they reached Ghent on 19 June, when they received news of the Battle of Waterloo. They marched towards Paris, joining the army there on 4 July. The 1/43rd were to remain in France as part of the Army of Occupation until the end of October. The 2/43rd were disbanded on 3 April 1817, seven officers and 168 men transferring to the first battalion.

Chapter 2

Lieutenant Colonel Charles Macleod–Letters

Taken from MS 15381 at the National Library of Scotland and letters from *Life of General Sir William Napier*, by H.A. Bruce, London, 1864. Charles Macleod was a major in the 43rd Foot, his rank dated from 28 May 1807 and he became a lieutenant colonel on 16 August 1810. He served in the 1st Battalion of the 43rd Regiment during the Siege of Copenhagen and the Corunna campaign, then returned with the battalion to the peninsula from July 1809 to December 1810 and again from May 1811 to April 1812. He served at the Côa, Busaco and the sieges of Ciudad Rodrigo and Badajoz, where he was killed. He led the battalion at the last three of these actions and was awarded a gold medal for them, also being mentioned in dispatches at the siege of Ciudad Rodrigo. He was one of four brothers serving at the time; George served in the Royal Engineers, and Henry and James served in the Royal Artillery.

His first letter to his father described the retreat to Vigo during the Corunna campaign.

To Brigadier General Macleod &c Woolwich, Kent[1]
HMS Hindostan 8 o'clock [at] night Vigo Bay 23 January 1809

My dear father,

A cutter on her way to Guernsey has just brought up under our stern for some assistance, as there is every probability of her arriving in England

---

1. Lieutenant General Sir John Angus Macleod was Deputy Adjutant General of the Royal Artillery from 1795. He was involved in the Walcheren Expedition and was later appointed Director General of the Royal Artillery. He died at Woolwich in 1833.

before us, even if that should be our destination. I chose not to lose the opportunity of letting you know that I am well and that we are *all well* (as far as this small division of the army goes) *out of the scrape*. We are under considerable anxiety for Sir John Moore, however I need not waste my time in conjecturing about what you probably by this time have certain information of. I only hope things may turn out better for him than we expect, as for ourselves, after marching in the most exemplary manner from Benavente to this place over the most abominable roads (I cannot call them roads really), I must call them as in Spanish chaminos [*caminos*], which I am sure means roads and in the most desperate bad weather, we arrived and embarked here on the 12th. We attempted to sail the day before yesterday, but the wind became so unfavourable by the time that the transports were under way, that all they could do was to get about 7 miles ahead and were obliged to come to anchor, near the Bayones, in such bad anchoring ground that in the gale that came on in the night, only one ship besides the agent's rode it out. All the rest lost their anchors and cables without exception, five of them stood out to sea not knowing what else to do I suppose and according to the opinion of all the Navy people have eventually gone to pieces on the rocks, which with the wind as it was, they say it was improbable they could have weathered. They have hopes that one of them run into Pontevedra, where, by running upon the mud the crew may have been saved. I hope it will be found that more than one has adopted this plan; three of them are horse ships and two with part of German Legion. We having orders to bring up the rear remained at anchor the whole time where we were and where we now are. Another signal was made to sail this evening at sunset, but notwithstanding several shots to enforce the execution of the same, not a transport moved and the purpose is abandoned until tomorrow again. We sent some boats ashore this morning to bring off some stragglers of the division, consisting almost entirely of Germans. During the time that the boats were ashore, the mob assembled in a tumultuous manner, understanding the French were approaching; calling for arms and ammunition. The officers on shore were witness to several houses being demolished, the governor's among them, whom they dragged out and made prisoner, under the idea that he was in the interest of the French; and the chief magistrate whose crime was that of having married the daughter of a French consul about *thirty* years ago, was murdered by them in the street. It is thus they intend to resist the French, but when they begin in this way by upsetting every sort of order or authority, I have not much confidence in anything they may do, it appears to me that they have quite enough to do to settle these quarrels

12

among themselves, without talking of the French, who will march quietly in and soon bring them to order. The people here are certainly very much in favour of the English, today even in the midst of this disturbance they hollowed out universally to our people as they passed. Viva Ingleterra! &c but then there are not three armed peasants together in the whole country. Whose fault this is, if the people were willing to resist is another thing, but it is too late now. The game I believe is completely up, we are to sail tomorrow morning if the weather will permit, to Corunna in the first instance w*e believe* by the bye. The division that is here consists of the

1st & 2nd flank brigades

1/43rd, 2/52nd, 2/95th

1st Light Infantry KGL, 2nd Light Infantry KGL

We have lost considerably by sickness. Believe me my dear father, your most affectionate Charles M[acleod]

PS They are firing small arms at this moment on shore, whether it is the arrival of the French or merely settling their own disputes we do not know. If it is the former, we shall soon be informed of it by a few shells I presume.

The next letter we have finds him on the Portuguese border watching the frontier near Ciudad Rodrigo.

Portalegre 17 June 1811

My dear father,

The last letter I wrote to you was from Espeja on the 5th I think, on the 6th as we supposed we were routed out of our cantonments in the vicinity of the Azaza [Azaba], by the appearance of the enemy with a large force of cavalry, with guns and about 4 or 5,000 infantry. The latter we never allowed to near us, for had we been detained by them in that open country, with the inferiority we laboured under in cavalry we might have been made an example of. The army (that part of it under Sir Brent Spencer)[2] drew in that day to a position near Soito, but finding I suppose to his great regret that it was nothing more than show in that quarter, while they were moving their greater bodies by Almaraz. We continued our route to this place, where we arrived the day before yesterday. The Guards & General Nightingales Brigade,[3] followed

---

2. Major General Brent Spencer commanded the 1st Division until July 1811.
3. Major General Miles Nightingall commanded the 2nd Brigade in the 1st Division.

us in yesterday and another division under Campbell[4] is expected immediately, today or tomorrow. Our further movements depend upon those of our enemies. Marmont who succeeded Massena at Salamanca is supposed to be at Almaraz, with an intention of moving upon Merida. If he does I suppose we move to join Lord Wellington. The division of ours, General Dunlop's[5] remains on the northern side of the Tagus, about Castel Manes & Nona Maroz[6] I believe. The last we heard of Lord Wellington he was in a position at Albuera, where they said he intended to engage Soult, or even to move on to attack him. Ross[7] the engineer left him in this situation some says ago. Sir B Spencer is here and of course has much more recent news and it is now whispered that His Lordship intends to take a position on this side of Badajoz, abandoning that place for the present; the siege of which has been undertaken with inadequate means, but as this is all report, I must refer you to your mess and your own ideas upon the subject. We have twice been foiled in attempting to take the fort of San Christoval by approach and the Spanish guns employed on the bombardment have been rendered unserviceable from running.[8] I have heard nothing of George or James lately,[9] they must both have had their hands full.

Therefore my best love to my mother who I have literally not time to write to this post. Your most affectionate Charles Macleod.

The weather is extremely hot, but I am much better than I expected to be.

Martiago 28 August 1811

My dear mother,

I must thank you for your letter although I believe I have very little else to say, however as this is precisely the way you began your letter and as there is notwithstanding, *more* in it than in any ten letters I have received for months, I may have better success than I imagine. As for my father,

---

4. Major General Alexander Campbell commanded the 6th Division.
5. Major General James Dunlop commanded the 5th Division.
6. I have been unable to identify these villages, but it is certain that Dunlop's 5th Division was encamped in the area around Sabugal at this time, but were ordered south soon after.
7. Captain George Charles Ross Royal Engineers was killed at Ciudad Rodrigo.
8. This presumably indicates that the carriages of the cannon had been rendered unserviceable by the constant running in and out of the guns whilst firing.
9. Two of his brothers.

he always takes up two or three lines, no inconsiderable proportion of the whole, in telling me that I have forgotten to date my letter, which I am sure he makes a point of saying whether I do, or do not. I am very glad nonetheless that he is getting over the effects of his awkward, *own* way of mounting his horse. If Caroline thinks that a few lines intermixed with yours, just so as to make it difficult to read either, will go for a letter and will coax an answer, she is *quite* mistaken. You may tell her I do not value her correspondence a *straw*. I will get the beauty and favourite to write to me and abuse less and tell me of all her particulars. I had a letter from George the other day from Almeida. His good Portuguese boy had been away with his horse and a mule with some odd articles of his baggage. I wrote him [to] hold back [and] not to be impatient and I dare say his boy would soon come back and bring his baggage behind him, with two he! he! at the end of it and a SKETCH face, meant to be funny.

James is starving in the neighbourhood of Castelo Branco, I forget the name of the place somewhere near Belmonte. I did not hear from him myself but an officer in the troop of horse artillery in this division, a friend of his, had a letter from him to that effect. We are extremely well off here and at present nothing else to *do* but to eat and drink. We have fruit in abundance and wine enough to swim in, if we chose to take such a fancy.

William Napier[10] I am sorry to say, is sent to Lisbon on his way to England for ill health; he has an ague which he cannot get rid of in this place and besides feels some bad effects from his wound, the ball not having been extracted [and] I fear may give him some trouble hereafter. The doctors say not, but I *never* believe a word they say, *particularly* your great friend *Dr Blane*. Must leave off for the letters will be a-going. George Drummond[11] has got the gout not bad, but such a pleasant little fit in his foot which for one day was swelled as big as two larger feet and he could not put it to the ground, but yesterday he could walk about. This is a proof by knowledge that we are not starving, when people are given to gout. Colonel Barnard[12] is come up to join this division of the army, he appears to be an acquaintance of your ladyships, boats, masts, sails &c. He enquired particularly after you all, so I thought I might as well mention it so that all at present know. Your affectionate son, Charles M[acleod].

---

10. Brevet Major William Napier, 43rd Foot. He was absent from the peninsula between August 1811 and April 1812.
11. Second Lieutenant George Drummond, 3rd Battalion 95th Foot.
12. Lieutenant Colonel Andrew Barnard 95th Foot, commanding the 3rd Battalion. He took command of the 1st Brigade of the Light Division in December 1811.

In his next letter, written to his friend Major William Napier, he told of the aftermath of the storming of Ciudad Rodrigo.

La Encina,[13] 21 January 1812

My dear Bill,

I have just been over to see your brother;[14] he was asleep and therefore I did not go into his room. Rob[15] and all the surgeons who have attended him say that he is going on well and that altogether he has supported himself better than anybody they ever saw in the same situation. I was with him yesterday for some time; he talked very composedly and seemed to have made up his mind to his misfortune. I am truly sorry for him, which I need not tell you, but taking into consideration the service he was employed upon, one could hardly expect him to come off with whole bones. He has covered himself with glory, will be made a lieutenant colonel[16] and be as well as ever he was for health and society; the pain he will suffer in the interim is the greatest part of the ill; he is in a comfortable quarter in the suburbs of Ciudad and will not be removed until he is much recovered from the effects of the operation. I am writing this as if you had accounts of him before, knowing that much had been written to you by the officer who carried the dispatches, but find I have left you to guess what the wound is after all. He was hit by a grapeshot in the arm, the same as he was hit in the *time before* the two last times he was wounded and the bone so shattered that the surgeons were all of opinion that it was impossible to save it and George determined at once to have it amputated, which was done the same evening by Dr Guthrie[17] who is a clever man and I have no doubt has performed the operation in a way that will prevent his feeling any inconvenience hereafter. Poor Colborne's[18] wound was at first thought to be slight, but today the surgeons say that they fear it will be very troublesome; the ball entered his shoulder and was lodged deep in [it] and they are afraid to try to extract it. Craufurd is very bad, his life is almost despaired of.

---

13. 8km south of Salamanca.
14. William's brother, George, who was a major in the 52nd Foot, had been severely wounded commanding the storming party at Ciudad Rodrigo.
15. Surgeon John Robb of the 95th Foot.
16. He was Gazetted a lieutenant colonel on 6 February 1812.
17. Staff Surgeon George James Guthrie.
18. Lieutenant Colonel John Colborne, 52nd Foot, was severely wounded at Ciudad Rodrigo.

The ball passed through his arm into his body and has either lodged in his lungs which is inevitable death, or has passed through and settled in some less vital part; but at all events his lungs are injured and the best that can be said is that there is a *chance* of his recovery.[19] All our own are likely to do well; Brummel[20] is the only one there is any doubt about; his wound is near the femoral artery. Ferguson[21] behaved beautifully; he is turning out one of the best soldiers extant. I am glad to find by your last letter that you are doing well; we were under great anxiety about you for some time. The siege of Ciudad was certainly carried on with great good management and achieved in good style; it was well begun and well finished. The governor ought to have been killed if he had not *preferred his life to his honour.* I do not believe he was near the breach, although he says the contrary; he would have surrendered the next day they say. I am in ill humour and perfectly knocked up. Yours very affectionately, Charles Macleod.

A second letter to William Napier told further of the human cost of the recent action, particularly to their friends in the Light Division.

El Bodon 4 February 1812

My dear Bill,

When I wrote last I was in so great a hurry that I am afraid I gave you a very wild and unsatisfactory account of your extraordinary and inimitable brother; he beats you all out and out, to use Dalyel's distinguishing appellation for the family, in *Tandyism.*[22] When I saw him last, three or four days ago at Gallegos, which is a distance from hence that prevents my seeing him so often as I wish, he had just finished a letter to Lady Sarah[23] with his left hand, which I directed and sealed &c for him, in order to give him an opportunity of eating his soup which

---

19. Major General Robert Craufurd, commanding the Light Division, was mortally wounded at the storming of Ciudad Rodrigo and he died on 23 January 1812.

20. Actually Lieutenant John Brumwell of the 43rd Foot. He died of his wounds on 27 January 1812.

21. Captain James Fergusson, 43rd Foot, was severely wounded at Ciudad, but recovered to be severely wounded again at the storming of Badajoz.

22. Possibly linked to Napper Tandy, who was found guilty of trying to foment a revolution in Ireland.

23. Lady Sarah (née Lennox) was George and William's mother.

he was very impatient for and which he devoured with an appropriate quantity of toast with a most excellent appetite. He was perfectly free from all fever, slept very tolerably and in as good spirits as I ever saw him, talking upon all sorts of subjects and admitting as many people as the surgeons would allow, which very probably are not near as many as he wished. I believe he will not remove from Gallegos for some time, until he is quite able to bear the journey without pain. Colborne's wound is still giving him a great deal of pain, but I hope from what I heard is going on as favourably as can be expected; the ball had worked its way towards his elbow from the shoulder and they have by this time, I dare say, extracted it; when this occurs his case will be easy. Ferguson and Patterson[24] are both going on well; the latter was made a terrible figure of by the explosion of some gunpowder, whether placed there purposely or not is not easy to determine, but it was certainly a large quantity to have been left there accidentally. This scorched his face and one hand very badly and he had scarcely recovered his astonishment at this summersault over the wall, when he received a pretty deep graze from the splinter of a shell or a ball in his *counterpart*, but he is likely to recover completely and be as beautiful as ever. Poor Jim Fergusson is wounded nearly where you were, by a musket ball, as near as it could be with any safety to the backbone and it is uncertain whether the ball is in or out, but the surgeons say it is of little importance which; he is recovering, which I am truly glad of, very fast. Poor Brummel died of his wounds about a week ago. With the exception of Uniacke, who also died of his wounds,[25] all the officers of the light division are doing well. Having now given you an account of all your maimed friends and acquaintances, I suppose I must make some remarks upon the siege for your amusement. It is reckoned a brilliant operation. It was certainly unexpected by the French and the place is of importance to them in their future designs upon this ill-fated country, as commanding the great road and the only good bridge of the Agueda; they must therefore retake it with a loss of time and men before they can invade by this route again. In short, they are now evidently worse in this quarter than they have yet been, and we know that they threw away 80,000 men before, in similar circumstances, without effecting their ultimate objects. How it will end admits of a doubt, but let it end either way it may, the defence of the town

---

24. Lieutenant Cooke Tylden Patterson, 43rdFoot, had been severely wounded at Ciudad Rodrigo, but did survive.
25. Captain John Uniacke, 95th Foot, was blown up by a mine at the storming of Ciudad Rodrigo and died of his wounds on 27 January 1812.

as far as it has gone does infinite credit to the military skill and talents of viscount and baron and knight and conde. They talk of taking Badajoz, but that preparations cannot be made to begin sooner than April. Stewart I am told, is going to send me back your horse, which I am sorry for, because I do not think you will find him to answer. I want horses very much and mean to write to my father to send me out one or two; my own are all dying. We are in bad quarters, particularly for the men, who are obliged to go leagues to cut wood and bring it home on their shoulders in the worst weather; and if Dr Pangloss[26] was here and was to tell me that all was for the best, I should infallibly knock him down. Adieu my dear Bill. I hope you are getting well, but sick enough to keep you quiet for some time. C M.

The next letter home came from his brother, James (serving in the Royal Artillery), regarding the tragic death of Charles.

Elvas, 9 April 1812

My dear father,

I wrote to you yesterday previous to my coming in here & therefore before I had seen George. Our meeting you will imagine and although I tried & before I saw him felt convinced I was master of myself, yet I found it was impossible. However, the interview over, George[27] is more perfectly easy in his mind about everything, having been [and] done for our dear Charles, [all] that could possibly be. George bears it with more fortitude than I dared to expect in his present weak state, but now I am here, he cannot bear me to leave him. The doctor wishes me not to be there much, impossible. I did yesterday as he wished & only staid [sic] half an hour, the 1st meeting. But he cannot understand our feelings & as George does not suffer, nor has he the least degree of inflammation or fever, it eases his feelings and he is much quieter when I am with him.

You will get these I trust & hope, before you hear any reports of the death of our dear lamented Charles. Even bad as I am sure my letters will be, they will be better than your feelings being shocked by being cold & casually hearing it from a stranger. I have made an excuse to George for being half an hour away from him, but he has sent poor fellow, to beg I will come to him. I assure you my dear father, there is not the slightest

---

26. Doctor Pangloss was a character in Voltaire's novel *Candide*.
27. Brevet Major George Macleod, Royal Engineers, was seriously wounded at Badajoz, but survived.

danger of his [not] doing well, the leg is perfectly united & in a few days I hope to take him to Lady Emily Berkley's at Lisbon[28] & if I can persuade him to go home for a little time I shall. For 2 months to come he will not certainly be able to do active duty or he will run a great risk & I think it will be a comfort to you my poor dear mother & Caroline.[29]

I must again my dear father, for a time pain your feelings, but I think that it will consequently be a consolation. Our poor Charles was carried from the breach by his own regiment, determined to carry the breach & at any rate save their wounded & among whom they trusted to find their colonel. Dreadful was the contrary [sic] & horrible the slaughter, but they found even in the dark, the body they had loved so much & bore him to the camp. A third time with vengeance did they swear to revenge him & a third time were they obliged to give way, leaving the breach covered & the ditch full of their fine fellows. 'Twas an utter impossibility, chevaux de frise of pointed swords & bayonets & half musquets buried in the ground, double rows of shells & the ramparts lined with infantry each [with] 20 loaded musquets, defended this breach.

Barnard & myself followed his coffin, followed by Major Duffy,[30] his remaining officers, Jenkinson[31] & Smyth.[32] Duffy was Charles's most beloved friend & his grief, his feelings so keen, he could hardly attend us, he was not singular, the very privates who bore him sobbed aloud, 'twas a scene of grief indeed, yet for worlds I would not but have attended him, they said it would be too much for me & wished me not to go. 'Twas a melancholy duty but I owed it [even] if I had sunk under, to the most virtuous, affectionate, beloved brother & as a soldier to the memory of one of the most gallant soldiers. Of Duffy I cannot say enough, he *would* write to you, but he has many poor families to pay that duty to; but when his feelings are a little more composed he will write. He had given a sword to Charles & which he had on that dreadful night, I gave [it] to Duffy & who will only give it up with his life unless you wish to have it. I have another of our dear brother's & which shall be sent to you. God grant my prayer, may he give you all fortitude to abide by his will. I will write to my mother by the packet. I must go to George, he has sent

---

28. Admiral Sir George Berkeley was appointed to Lisbon to help organise the chaotic supply system for Lord Wellington. His wife Emilia (née Lennox) was in Lisbon with him.
29. His sister.
30. Brevet Major John Duffy, 43rd Foot.
31. Second Captain George Jenkinson, Royal Artillery, A Troop RHA
32. First Lieutenant George Smyth, Royal Artillery, A Troop RHA

again, but I dared not trust to write in his presence. He is a fine fellow, struggles with his fate like a man. He knows not of half of his friends, Latham[33] whom is killed, Nicolas I fear cannot live but no more.[34] The Gazette, if you can read it, will tell you a tale of horror, my dear father let us hear from you, I shall be again with the army before your letters reach Lisbon. I never was better. God Bless you all. George I shall not let write for some time, my mother, my dearest Car[oline], Georgy & Emily, exert yourselves for each other's care, we shall follow, we shall meet again my dear father, your affectionate son, J[ames] A[lexander] Macleod.[35]

Barnard begs his remembrances to all the family in the kindest manner.

From Frederick Duke of York, dated Horse Guards, 12 November 1813

Sir,

The Prince Regent having been graciously pleased to command, in the name and on the behalf of His Majesty, that the officers present at the Battle of Buzaco [sic] and the sieges of Ciudad Rodrigo and Badajoz, should be permitted to bear a medal commemorative of those brilliant victories, I have to transmit to you the medal[36] which would have been conferred upon the late Lieutenant Colonel Charles McLeod of the 1st Battalion 43rd Regiment of Foot; and which the Prince Regent has been pleased to direct should be deposited with his family, as a token of the respect which His Royal Highness bears to the memory of that officer. I am Sir, yours Frederick, Commander in Chief

Letter from his father to the Duke of York, St James's Park 9 December 1813

Sir,

I have received the honour of your Royal Highness's letter conveying the medal which would have been bestowed on Lieutenant Colonel Macleod of the 43rd Regiment and which per the gracious consideration of the Prince Regent is deposited with his family, with the *conveyancing assurance of its being a token of the respect His Royal Highness* bears to his memory.

---

33. Second Captain William Latham, Royal Artillery, was killed at Badajoz.
34. Brevet Major William Nicholas, Royal Engineers, was severely wounded at Badajoz and died of his wounds on 14 May 1812.
35. Lieutenant James Alexander Macleod, Royal Artillery, is missing from the Challis List, but undoubtedly served in the peninsula.
36. He was issued a gold medal for commanding his regiment at Badajoz.

I receive with envy & fervour and acknowledge with all gratitude, this mark of benificent attention bestowed by His Royal Highness on *him*, as *one* of the family so situated. Proud as I was of my son, I am not less alive to his memory and whatever other sensations the sight of it has, and *must* ever call forth, I can never but properly appreciate a testimony so honourable to it.

To your Royal Highness, with every sentiment of respect and regards, I beg to subscribe myself, Sir, Your Royal Highness's most observant & most faithful, your servant J[ohn] Macleod.

Chapter 3

Lieutenant Colonel
Edward Hull–Letter

Edward Hull had been appointed a lieutenant colonel in the 43rd Foot on 8 September 1808, commanding the 2nd Battalion. He had served in the Baltic in 1807 and then served at Vimeiro and Corunna, being mentioned in dispatches at the former. He was appointed to the command of the 1st Battalion in July 1810 and proceeded to the peninsula to take up his post. He arrived at the Côa just as the French attack developed and was killed soon after.

This letter refers to an incident that occurred during the retreat to Corunna. Sergeant William Newman was given an Ensigncy in a West India Regiment as a reward for his bravery, but was embarrassed for funds to equip himself. Colonel Hull sought for funds for him successfully.

To the Committee of Management of the Patriotic Fund

Gentlemen,

I beg to state for your information an instance of gallantry and conduct in a sergeant of 2nd Battalion of the 43rd Regiment of Foot, which I believe has seldom been exceeded by one in that rank. On the retreat of the British army through Spain, Sergeant William Newman was left at a village about four miles from Betanzos, to collect and bring in some stragglers and sick of the regiment, at which time there were about four or five hundred of that description belonging to different corps in that place. Some time after the troops had marched, an alarm was given that a party of French cavalry was approaching and the men were all endeavouring, in the greatest confusion, to make off as fast as their weak state would admit, when Sergeant Newman pushed on a little way to a narrow part of the road, where he continued to stop nearly one hundred of those not able to march, and sent on the rest to join the main body.

These men so collected, he formed into one corps (there being no officer present) and withstood and repulsed repeated attacks of the French cavalry; regularly retiring and facing about for four miles, when they were relieved from their perilous situation by the rearguard of our cavalry. The officer commanding the cavalry reported the behaviour of the sergeant to General Fraser,[1] who commanded the division, and who, having ordered an enquiry to be made, and finding the circumstances proved as before stated, recommended him for promotion. The Commander in Chief has been pleased to appoint him to an ensigncy in the 1st West India Regiment. As however, there must be a great expense in fitting himself out, and preparing for his voyage, I beg to recommend him in the strongest manner to your favourable notice.

I am gentlemen, your most obedient humble servant, E. Hull, Lieutenant Colonel, 43rd Regiment, commanding 2nd Battalion.

Extract from the Proceedings of the Committee

Resolved that the sum of fifty pounds be presented to Ensign William Newman, in testimony of the high sense which the committee entertain of his gallant and meritorious conduct.

---

1. Lieutenant General Alexander Mackenzie–commanded the 3rd Division.

Chapter 4

Lieutenant Colonel
Christopher Patrickson

Born in 1780, Christopher Patrickson originally entered the
Army as a cornet in the 9th Light Dragoons in March 1794 and
was promoted a lieutenant in June of the same year. He then
became a Captain-Lieutenant in the 23rd Light Dragoons in March
1800 and a captain in the 40th Foot in August 1801. He became
a captain in the 43rd Foot in May 1803, major in September 1809
and brevet lieutenant colonel in May 1811 which was made
substantive in June 1813. He saw service at Copenhagen, Vigo,
the Coa, Sabugal (wounded), Fuentes d'Onoro, Vitoria and
Toulouse. He became a brevet colonel in July 1821 and retired
in 1826. He died in Dublin in September 1856.

Letter dated 1845 [?] from Patrickson to Sir Alexander Cameron,
95th Foot, regarding the action at Sabugal, 1811, and the Côa on
24 July 1810[1]

My letter to you about Sabugal was simply to ask you if you
recollected the circumstances of your company joining the 43rd
Regiment during the affair, as I perfectly recollect your bringing
up your company to join our left flank during the fight.

You are quite right in saying all these old stories should be allowed
to sleep after upwards of *34* years have passed, but Colonel Gurwood,[2]
I understand, has published a pamphlet among *his friends* stating
that the 52nd came up towards the close of the business, and took the

---

1. Reference the Museum of the Oxfordshire Soldier SOFO 2081 D/1035/2.
2. John Gurwood was a Lieutenant in the 52nd Foot in 1811.

howitzer at Sabugal, which is all a farce. They hardly lost a man, their first battalion three men and their second battalion none at all. *You need not mention it* but I was so annoyed that I wrote to *the Duke*, who gave the howitzer to our brigade in his Despatch of 6 April 1811, to ask his opinion, which he declined giving, as he says he is not the editor of the work, entitled 'The Duke of Wellington's Despatches', and that he thinks, as you do, that after 34 years the thing ought not to be alluded to; and further he says, that these two regiments that have received the thanks of their superior officer so often, and particularly from *the Duke himself*, should not dispute about such a trifle. I am glad I wrote to him; it is the first letter I ever had occasion to write on the subject.

I am sorry, my dear Cameron, that Napier[3] should have written anything to annoy you, or contrary to the fact of the defence of the bridge of the Coa near Almeida. I have a perfect recollection of your being there, with poor dear Jasper Creagh, who was killed.[4] I lent my horse to carry his poor remains to the bier. Colonel Hull of our regiment, the 43rd, was killed at the bridge also,[5] but I think Napier is only wrong *in placing* the men of our brigade. Your companies were *nearest* the bridge, ours above them. You may remember the attempt the French made to take the bridge. Colonel Hull had a wing of the 43rd Regiment with *fixed bayonets* ready to oppose them, but your men shot them down so completely that they were never able to cross the bridge. Captain Lloyd[6] of the 43rd was wounded in the head near the bridge, our two regiments were the principal sufferers that day. I commanded the left wing of the 43rd when the enemy attacked and our *two regiments* covered the retreat of the remainder of the division across that narrow bridge, which we should not have had in *our rear at all,* with an enemy so strong in our front. I will take care and let Napier know your objections as he is an ardent admirer, and always has been, of *the old 95th.*

---

3. He refers to William Napier's *History of the Peninsular War*. Napier had himself been a 43rd man.
4. Captain Jasper Creagh of the 95th Foot was severely wounded at the Côa and died of his wounds on 25 July 1810.
5. Lieutenant Colonel Edward Hull, 43rd Foot, was killed at the Côa.
6. Captain Thomas Lloyd, 43rd Foot, was returned as slightly wounded at the Côa. Soon after he gained a majority in the 94th Foot.

Chapter 5

Captain Henry Booth Letters

The Booth family provided three brothers to the Light Division; Charles in the 52nd Foot and William to the 95th Rifles, but the youngest, Henry, was gazetted to the 43rd Foot at the age of 15 on 6 March 1806 and he became a lieutenant on 11 June 1807. He served at Vimeiro on 27 August 1808, Corunna, the Talavera march, Côa and Busaco. In December 1810 he became seriously ill with fever and was sent to Lisbon to recover, where he was tended by his brother, Charles. He was sent home in February 1811 to the 2nd Battalion. He returned to the peninsula in May 1812 and was gazetted a captain on 25 June 1812. He saw further service at the Battle of Salamanca, retreat from Burgos, San Millan, Vitoria, the Pyrenees, Bidasoa and the heights of Vera. He became a major in 1822 and a lieutenant colonel in 1830. He commanded the 43rd in the Canadian Rebellion of 1837–38. He died on 6 May 1841.

We have a few complete letters from Henry (National Army Museum 6702/33/1) and excerpts from others published in the Regimental Chronicle of the Green Jackets[1] but unfortunately all attempts to discover the current location of these letters has proven unprofitable. Henry's early letters to his elder brother, Thomas, centre around his constant need for financial help and clearly led to admonitions of extravagance and promises to be more frugal.

Brabourne Lees July 1806

Expenses

Tea Caddie 4s
Regimental queue and curling irons 5s
Toothpowder 2s

---

1. Published in the 1932 and 1933 editions.

I believe I have now got everything Charles thought necessary[2] except shaving apparatus for which I have no immediate occasion.

I will never be induced to go out on the sea again in a row boat and with unskilful pilots. [Henry and a few other officers had apparently hired a small boat to Dungeness, about 14 miles from Hythe by sea].

22 October 1806, Brabourne Lees Barracks

My dear Thomas,[3]

I feel very much obliged to you for your wishes and interesting letter which I received a few days ago with the enclosed £20. I am certain if you knew what pleasure it gives me to hear from you, you would write more frequently. Your letters will not only be a pleasure, but a great advantage and of infinite service to me, especially as I cannot for the present enjoy the benefit of Charles's, being so remote from each other.[4] Therefore, the good advice and instructions of an elder brother must and will be highly beneficial and acceptable to one young and inexperienced.

Henry had become a lieutenant on 11 June 1807.

Hythe Barracks 22 November 1807

My dear Thomas,

Before I touch on the real subject of this letter, allow me first to return you my most sincere thanks and warmest gratitude, which I am totally unable to express, for your obliging letter with enclosed notes for £50, which came to hand two days ago. After having with the utmost attention perused your letter, my feelings are better conceived than described, for it evidently appears, it is scarcely possible it can be misconception on my part, that you have construed the cause of my being embarrassed in a far different light than I expected. Forgive me when I say, in your letter you seem to conjecture that I have been applying my money to vicious as well as foolish and extravagant purposes. I can scarcely think it possible that for a moment you could harbour such an idea. I thought you had known your brother Henry too well to distrust his word. If

---

2. Presumably Charles had sent advice on what Henry needed to take with him on campaign.
3. His older brother.
4. Charles was with the 1st Battalion of the 52nd in Sicily.

you will allow me to possess a sense of humour, which surely you do, I declare upon my honour to no one purpose whatever and the least tending to vice or any one thing contrary to virtue and uprightness have I applied my money, though with grief I say contrary to all rules of prudence and discretion. I trust I have ever acted virtuously though not discreetly and from want of prudence and foresight alone have my difficulties arisen. For 'God's sake' do not suppose your brother has become a dissipated character. I am not fond of wine, I detest it, but at the same time suffer from a mistaken notion of keeping up one's respectabilities. I have taken wine at the mess where there certainly was no absolute reason for it. Therefore, at least do me the justice to say I still possess a chaste and virtuous mind. If from this dear bought experience you do not see an entire change in my conduct with respect to economy. Errors I may have fallen into, tax me with ingratitude and in short everything foreign to a good disposition and consider me as no longer worthy of your esteem.

However, Henry now upped the stakes, seeking no less than £950 in the hope of getting a captaincy.

Hythe Barracks April 1808

My dear Thomas,

As you have in all instances, ever obliged and acted most liberally towards me, I am again induced in the present case, to beg your attention to the subject upon which I now address you. To be brief, in the event of such opportunity, can I by any means, raise £950 for the purchase of a company? You will observe by the Army List that a Lieutenant Haverfield[5] has got a company by purchase over 21 lieutenants. Strange to say, not one being able to raise the money. We still have every prospect of rapid promotion and at the utmost there are only three above who can purchase, Price, Capel and Brown.[6] As to the former, I know he is negotiating for a company, the latter I and my friends are of opinion

---

5. William Haverfield had gained his captaincy in the 43rd Foot on 31 March 1808.
6. Lieutenant Barrington Price, 43rd Foot, became a captain by moving to the 102nd Foot on 3 October 1811, Lieutenant Thomas Capel, 43rd Foot, remained with the regiment and did not get a captaincy until 1 July 1813. Lieutenant George Brown gained his captaincy by moving to the 3rd Garrison Battalion on 20 June 1811.

will obtain a company without purchase, his friends having very great interest with the commander in chief; Capel is possessed of comfortable fortune, but as a man of the world, is squandering it away in town, so that it is more than probable and indeed, I think there is every chance of my having the option of purchasing in one or two years at farthest. Our captains of the 1st Battalion are of long standing and most of great interest and have every claim for promotion. This will be a most unprecedented instance of promotion, to get upwards of twenty steps, which will be the case with me, should I be so fortunate as to be able to purchase. You are perhaps not aware that from a lieutenancy to a captaincy is the greatest and most important step in the army. Once a captain I am an independent man, the pay and allowance of such situation being with a little economy amply sufficient to support it.

Henry considered transferring to the 95th Rifles as he felt this might get him sent abroad on service and that he then might actually see some action.

Hythe Barracks 13 June 1808

My dear Thomas,
    I wrote to you some time ago requesting you would inform me, whether in the event of such occurrence, I could raise the money requisite for the purchase of a company, to which I would still have awaited your reply, well aware how your time must be unusually taken up, in the removal of my sisters to Brush House;[7] but you will, I am sure, excuse my troubling you again on the subject, when the urgency of the case actually requires it. To be brief, Colonel Wade Rifle Regiment[8] in the handsomest manner, has offered to obtain for me a transfer into his regiment, which of all things would be most desirable, provided I really have not the means of purchasing a company, without being in any degree burdensome to the family, which of all my ideas I assure you is far the most distant and I confess an apprehension on that score has not a little hastened my applying to you this second time.[9] Now I will

---

7. Brush House was the family pile.
8. Lieutenant Colonel Hamlet Wade, 95th Foot.
9. His wording is a bit convoluted and confused, but he means that if the family cannot provide him with the funds for his captaincy then Lt Colonel Wade had offered to transfer him into the 95th where there was, in his view, more likelihood of serving abroad and possibly gaining his captaincy by seniority without purchase.

suppose I have not the means, which I fear is most probable, then I will state impartially, the nature of the service of the two corps, 43rd and 95th and leave it to your judgement whether that of the light infantry is to be placed in competition with that of the rifles and which is most eligible for a young subaltern fond of his profession. In the first place the light infantry are certainly extended in front of a line or column, but in rear of the rifles, ready to act should the riflemen be driven back by superior force. Then the light infantry commence a fire in order to cover and conceal the movements of the column in its rear and every officer can act merely as an individual in the ranks. Now the rifles are not only extended in front of the light infantry but also detached in small parties under command of a subaltern, who is then independent and has an opportunity of exerting his professional ability, if he has any and distinguishing himself either by cutting off parties of the enemy or repelling superior numbers. Thus, he gains some honour and credit for his exertions and is noticed; whilst a light infantry officer, however clever he may be, but by not being detained scarce once in twenty times, has not that opportunity of distinguishing himself and gaining the credit given to the rifleman. So much for the nature of the service. The advantages a rifle corps as over other corps are numerous and considerable. There is never an expedition leaves England in which some company do not form a part. I am heartily sick and tired of the inactive life I have led since my joining the army. I have been an officer very near two years and a half and never once seen a shot fired.

However, Henry was finally able to write that his battalion had received orders to proceed on campaign, but that meant Henry needed money again!

Sunday 3 July 1808

Thomas,

I have at last the most heartfelt satisfaction in informing you that our 2nd Battalion this morning received orders of readiness for immediate embarkation. Spain is our destination beyond doubt.

On such occasion I am sure you will excuse me making long apologies and excuses, for so great is the hurry and bustle here, that I really have not time. I therefore will be candid, and at once request you will, if in your power, oblige me by remitting a second allowance in advance from the 1 July to 1 October and if the £5 I mentioned to you in my last is due to me to send that also making altogether £30.

31

Since writing the above, the company I have hitherto had the honour to command[10] now devolves to a senior officer, but in compensation for which the commanding officer has appointed me to do the duty of Adjutant from this day, which by the bye on service is no joke.

Henry wrote after the Battle of Vimeiro.

August 1808

The 95th behaved remarkably well in the action and the 2nd 52nd performed also what was to be expected from the light infantry.

Our service is rather hard, which of course must be the case. We all sleep upon the bare ground until 3 o'clock in the morning in small huts made of a few branches of trees. The dews are very heavy, eh bien! The more duty the more honour and glory, no life like that of a soldier, always new scenes to engage his attention, no luxuries, all hard labour and fatigue, no idleness, always moving, we have only to hope for a campaign that will make soldiers of us, for we are not quite so yet, John Bull is but too much accustomed to prosperity. The French prisoners we took were all very intelligent sharp eyed fellows, all life, their wits about them, everyone had with him a letter from friends or relations, most sensibly and sentimentally written, they are all well clothed, several of their officers were taken who appeared very intelligent and gentlemanly men, but cruel to a degree, the French very seldom give quarter.

Henry's next letter to his sister shows a war weariness following a severe illness.

To Miss Booth, Brush House, near Sheffield Yorkshire[11]

Campo Maior 24 November 1809

Dear Margaret,[12]

I received your very affectionate letter of the 6th October which has afforded me much reason to believe to believe you are in good health

---

10. He was still a lieutenant, therefore he means that his captain had been absent for some time.
11. In the Parish of Ecclesfield.
12. Margaret was the oldest sibling.

and happy in your retirement at Brush House,[13] happy I know you are in the pleasing reflection of a firm and affectionate conduct, which has never ceased to show itself and at no time more conspicuously than on a *recent occasion;* such a line of conduct he assumed, cannot fail to create the admiration and respect of every member who has the interest and respectability of the family really at heart & by no means in the least degree that of your brothers here. I am glad to hear so good an account of our brother Thomas,[14] I sincerely hope and pray his spirits will not forsake him & that his farm will turn out to good advantage. I picture to myself the estate far different from what it was in former days during the *interregnum;* I hope the fruits of his labour will abundantly repay him.

Charles[15] has received Thomas's letter, I also received one from my brother, he speaks very little of Sarah's marriage.[16] I am glad to hear William came off so well, in the unfortunate expedition to Walcheren. I am not much surprised at his talking of paying a visit to the New Building[17] as long as Santillana[18] has a tolerable nag & a bottle *of good old port.* He is inconsistent and ever will be to the end of the chapter. I hope he will remain in the 95th which is his only stay. He is now pretty high in the list of lieutenants. George I guess is at Cambridge & I hope comfortable settled.[19] I sincerely hope his health will allow him to pursue his studies, he must be an astonishing clever fellow. I have no doubt his superior spirit will some day or other meet with its just reward. I wrote to him some time ago & daily expect to hear from him. If we have the good luck to reach Old England once more, Charles intends paying him a visit. As to myself you must not be astonished if you hear of my coming to Brush House, it is certainly my intention if by [good luck] I can obtain a month's leave of absence. I find it will be necessary for the

---

13. The Booths ancestral home Brush House near Sheffield.
14. The oldest brother Thomas, followed his father into the family business.
15. Lieutenant Charles Booth of the 52nd Foot. He was killed at the storming of Badajoz in 1812.
16. Another sister.
17. This probably refers to Cliffe House at Ecclesfield where their mother, Sarah (née Kay) resided from 1807, Brush House having been willed to Thomas, her eldest son. The relationship between the children and their mother declined dramatically after the death of their father in 1800 and the children rarely visited, referring to it as 'Spite House' or 'Spitfire Hall'.
18. A nickname for William?
19. George was the academic of the family and he became a reverend.

complete re-establishment of my health, which (though I have never once been seriously ill) has not been the best, since the commencement of the campaign, I have not been so strong as formerly. I am now on the list of convalescents from an attack of the ague, which came daily for 8 or 9 days, but I have now I hope completely got the better of it. I take a great deal of exercise, the weather at present being very fine and wholesome. I am also plying myself with bark which is the only remedy for the ague. I wonder how long these ministers of England intend keeping us here, we are in a perfect state of inactivity. The army is wasting away from sickness, there are thousands of reports on the wing, some say we are to advance again into Spain, that we only await the arrival of reinforcements from England. I hope at all events this is not true, for it must be clear to everyone of common sense that we can do no good in Spain. In the first place, the Spaniards are not to be depended on & secondly Buonaparte (if peace is signed with Austria) has only to march an immense reinforcement for the complete subjugation of the whole peninsula; but the stupid boobies are determined to risk everything & when half the English army is destroyed, they gape & stare & wonder & debate how it happened, but it is to be hoped before that happens the people of England will see the serious necessity of recalling the army. But alas! They are too much engaged with the jubilee, which affords a mighty plausible excuse for *stuffing & swilling with ox flesh & ale*, it would open their eyes & their hearts too, to witness the state of our hospitals here. But enough of this, if I continue such dismal strains you will be inclined to think I have lost all zeal for the service & dub me the *soldier tired* &c. Charles & myself are quartered in the same house, we are as *thiefs* [original page is torn here, looks like it reads 'under cover & are likely to continue'] so, he is *bringing me about* famously. Remember me affectionately to Ann;[20] though she will rattle the keys & have her own way. A certain policy is requisite, one thing, constant exercise will keep her in health. Assure Thomas of my sincere regards & affection & believe me my dear Margaret ever your affectionate brother, Henry.

The following letter was written after the near disaster at the Côa River and it is clear who Henry blamed for it.

Camp at Celorico, 30 July 1810

---

20. Another sister.

My dear Thomas,

We are both[21] as well as possible, quite clear out of all the scrapes, thank God! But to the point. Our gallant, I wish I could say wise. General Craufurd, after having been driven from his position near Gallegos, about three leagues in front of Almeida, posted his division a little to the right of that fortress, amongst rocks, walls and vineyards, on the slope of the hill which descends to the river Coa; a worse position, everyone allows, could not have been chosen. However, after a dreadful stormy night, with incessant rain, thunder, and lightning until daybreak, our men and officers thoroughly drenched, I may say half drowned and firelocks nearly unserviceable, we waited patiently the attack of the French on the morning of the 24th.[22] Our pickets were soon driven in and the French fired on our line with musketry, shot, and shells; we returned the fire, and were ordered to retire in line, very wisely and properly ordered! But unfortunately, from the vast quantity of high walls, six feet high generally, the number of rocks, vineyards and broken ground which continued down to the water's edge, our line was very soon broken, past all chance of being formed again, till we had crossed the bridge. In this manner the whole division retired down this tremendous hill. This was fine fun for the French skirmishers, who were following us closely from rock to rock, pelting us pretty handsomely down to the river! However, in all this confusion, our fellows behaved nobly and retired fighting inch by inch, which in the end proved our misfortune; for had we made the best of our way over the bridge and occupied the hills on the other side as soon as possible, we should have suffered less and precisely the same position would have been gained.

But why did our general wait for the attack in so infamous a position? It was impossible for us to keep our ground, nor was it intended that we should. We remained, as it were to be fired upon without the means of defending ourselves till we could cross the bridge. Would it not have answered the purpose if General Craufurd had at first occupied the hills on the other side of the bridge, advancing his pickets some distance in front, which could have retired on the approach of the French, covered by the fire of our line on the hills and then defend the bridge, as we might have done against a much superior force? Everyone asks the same question. The general is universally blamed and Lord Wellington is said to have expressed to him his disapprobation. In proof he has given

---

21. Alluding to his brother Charles, who was with him.
22. This would appear to suggest that the attack by the French was anticipated.

Sir Brent Spencer the command of the Light Division, which has caused no little satisfaction amongst us.[23] To continue my tedious and I am afraid, confused account, we defended the bridge against three attempts of the French to force it, in all of which they failed, suffering heavy loss. At last the firing mutually ceased, on account of the torrents of rain that fell, after five hours' hard peppering at each other. Towards night we retired and have been gradually falling back on this place. The main body of the army is still more in rear and we have only a few cavalry in our front. We must retire when the French advance. Where the army will halt and fight, of course we are ignorant. It depends entirely on the force they bring against us. We have had a good share of fag and shall be glad to have a reprieve. Things are now, I assure you, coming to a crisis. All depends on the force of the French. It is the general opinion that the enemy will bring on such numbers as to leave little doubt of the issue of a battle. Happen what may, we have lads who will do their duty. The people of England, I dare say, are looking to us. Well they may. Now, my dear Tom, with much sorrow, I lay before you a long list of killed and wounded of the 43rd. Killed – Colonel Hull,[24] who had joined us to take command [only] the preceding day; Captain Ewen Cameron; and Lieutenant Nason,[25] a fine young lad of seventeen. Wounded – Captains Lloyd,[26] J W Hull,[27] W Napier,[28] Shaw,[29] Deshon,[30] the four first severely;

---

23. This rumour was incorrect. Major General Sir Brent Spencer, was actually second in command to Lord Wellington, but it is very revealing that the supposed removal of Craufurd brought satisfaction to many of the officers of the Light Division at this time.
24. Lieutenant Colonel Edward Hull, 43rd Foot.
25. Lieutenant John Nason, 43rd Foot.
26. Captain Thomas Lloyd, 43rd Foot, was recorded as slightly wounded in the *Gazette*.
27. Captain James Watson Hull, 43rd Foot, was severely wounded.
28. Captain William Napier 43rd Foot, was severely wounded.
29. Lieutenant James Shaw 43rd Foot, was severely wounded. He was acting as an aide de camp to General Craufurd and his correspondence will be published in the third volume of this series.
30. Captain Peter Deshon, 43rd Foot, was slightly wounded.

Lieutenant McDearmid,[31] Harvest,[32] Johnston,[33] Stevenson,[34] Frederick,[35] Hopkins.[36] Poor Frederick, a fine young boy, has since lost his leg; it was amputated yesterday. Hopkins commanded the company I am attached to and was wounded in the first fire. The command afterwards fell to me. I was not so unfortunate; I came clear off. Sergeants, drummers and privates killed, wounded and missing 130. The 95th has suffered almost as severely as ourselves in officers and men. The loss of the 52nd, I am happy to say, is comparatively trifling. Two officers wounded, and a few men killed.

They were not so much exposed as ours and the 95th. We regret the loss of Colonel Hull; in short, of all who fell. Major Macleod, who has succeeded Colonel Hull in the command, distinguished himself. Is not this a pretty loss for one regiment, owing entirely to the blunders of [Craufurd] I hope we shall be better managed for the future. We only wish for a fair chance; there is then no fear of our lads gaining distinction. Is it not a pity such fine fellows should always be obliged to fight retiring. Yet this must be the game now for a while. The French force in our front, in the neighbourhood of Almeida and Rodrigo, is stated to be about 20,000. It is said they are also advancing in other directions. This is a camp letter; pray excuse faults.

At the end of 1810 Henry was sent to Lisbon sick, where his brother Charles arrived to care for him. Henry eventually returned to England in February 1811, where he attended Harrogate Spa as part of his recovery. He wrote for financial help.

Crown Inn, Low Harrogate,[37] 25 April 1811

To Thomas
   My dear brother,
   I am nervous and much relaxed, cannot bear much walking exercise; the keep of a horse here is 1/6d per day for hay, whatever corn you

---

31. Lieutenant John McDeamid was severely wounded.
32. Lieutenant Horatio Harvest, 43rd Foot, was not recorded as being wounded.
33. Lieutenant George Johnston, 43rd Foot, was slightly wounded.
34. Lieutenant John Stephenson, 43rd Foot, was slightly wounded.
35. Ensign Roger Frederick, 43rd Foot, was severely wounded and had his leg amputated.
36. Lieutenant John Hopkins, 43rd Foot, was severely wounded.
37. Now the superb Crown Hotel at Harrogate.

order you pay for. The servants living, all things included, is about one guinea and a half per week, my own is 7s per day. You are perfectly acquainted with my resources and if you could so manage the means that I could bear the expense of a horse and servant for a week or ten days, it is needless to say, of what service it would be towards promoting my perfect health. For, honestly and soberly, I cannot bear as much walking exercise as my system requires; but in this matter I do earnestly entreat your opinion and advice. If you think it advisable that I should not incur this additional expense of a horse and servant, or that my means will not admit of it, I shall be most satisfied and grateful for your opinion.

Henry received a positive response from Thomas and he wrote back again.

I will, at all risks, venture to accept of the very handsome offer you made me of the use of your horse and servant. I find it will be of real and essential service to me, for the water here is so relaxing in its nature, that walking exercise fatigues me, makes violent perspiration the forerunner of cold. Most happy as I should feel in the pleasure of your company here, yet I cannot help expressing my fears that the place, at present, would be somewhat dull to you, especially as the H's leave so soon; many fresh arrivals are expected daily, as well as a pleasant party of ladies, when this takes place you shall hear from me; at present the only good fellows here, or rather correct and gentlemanly men are three; viz Captain P. Mr S and Mr T. The rest are unworthy of your notice.

I rise early, generally at half past six o'clock, take a glass of the water, walk about 8 or ten minutes, then take a second, walk again and afterwards a third, which generally has the desired effect. Sometimes I am obliged to take a fourth. When this is all pretty well over, I breakfast on a cup of coffee and a basin of milk, read and walk till the hour of dinner, 4 o'clock. I invariably dine on one plain dish, eating plenty of vegetables, taking little or no wine, what little I do drink is merely pro forma mixed with water. I walk always after dinner, return to the drawing room, chat with the women till 9 o'clock, the hour of supper, when I take a basin of milk. I have seen this morning's paper, every breath of wind I see brings fresh accounts of the gallant conduct of the light troops; have not the 43rd immortalised themselves?

Henry now got into trouble as he was reported in the 1st Battalion Orders as 'absent without leave' but his colonel soon wrote to alleviate any fears, with options for the future.

Colonel Macleod to Henry [September?] 1811

I am quite distressed that you should have had a moments' thought upon the subject of your having been returned 'absent without leave', it was not until I had it dinned into my ears by adjutants, clerks &c &c that it was the only alternative that I had, that it was a mere matter of form and would make no difference to you, that I did sign the Return. But fearing that it might cause some awkwardness to you with respect to your pay, I have been on the point of writing to you several times since, to beg that you would let me know if it had had that effect, in order that I might remove it by an explanation, but we have been moving so continually that I have been prevented from doing so. As you were returned since 'absent with leave', I conclude however, that all embarrassment on the subject has ceased. I shall not return you 'absent without leave' again, at all events, as we now have some little allowance on consideration of the length of time it requires to communicate with officers in England. I shall continue to return you, until your leave is expired, for some time as 'absent with leave' and after this, as transferred and ordered to the 2nd Battalion. I have been told that this latter step will be disagreeable to you. But I am sure it will be good for you and you must, therefore, swallow it as you do other things without making faces. I should be most happy to have you with us always, but I am quite convinced that your health cannot be sufficiently re-established for service for a very considerable time and your leave will be more easily managed by reporting to the 2nd Battalion. If I was acquainted with your friends or relatives I should write to them upon the subject, to beg that they would not allow you to come out until you were quite well and until you had been so for some time.

The records show that it was not until late March 1812 before Henry returned to the peninsula, but on his arrival at Lisbon he learnt of the successful storming of the Fortress of Badajoz, but also the horrendous number of casualties suffered. He was devastated to hear of the death of his brother Charles of the 52nd Foot, who had volunteered for the storming party. The detail he included in his letter might well indicate that he wrote it having returned to the regiment and having obtained a great deal more information from his fellow officers.

[April?] 1812

He has fallen like a good and brave soldier. His virtues and most noble character were known alike to all; but to me, who from my situation while on service with him have more particularly experienced his affectionate care and attention under much suffering, this is indeed a painful trial.

He received a musket ball through the head after he had entered the ditch and was making his way towards the breach. His sufferings (if so they may be termed) were but instantaneous. Poor Charles was observed to be in more than usual good spirits before the assault. He had heard a report of my arrival in Lisbon and desired all his things might be kept for me in case any accident should befall him. He also left a full and clear statement of his company's accounts (of which he had the command and payment) with the Adjutant of the 52nd; also some memorandums of a few private accounts with his servant and others, all so clear and distinct that they can be easily settled. All his effects were sold, from the impossibility of their being taken charge of on the march from Badajoz to the north; his gun, however and two pointers and spyglass were preserved for me. His sword, poor fellow, was lost in the ditch when he fell and his body was with difficulty recognised amongst heaps of slain. I need not say how deeply he is regretted by all who knew him both as an excellent soldier and a good and worthy man. Few indeed are to be met with like him. All deplore his loss, both officers and men. His life was without blemish.

Major Napier,[38] who now commands this battalion showed me a letter which he had received from his mother, being an exact copy of one which came to her from Colonel Napier,[39] whose most intimate friend Charles had been for a number of years and also in the same company with him when captain. He speaks of poor Charles in such feeling terms of friendship and respect for his memory, that one could not help being affected by it.

Henry's next letter was written the day before the Battle of Vitoria, which he seems to have no idea was about to take place. He does give detail, however, of the action at San Millan.

Camp at Anucita, a small village in the mountains near Vitoria 20 June [1813]

My dear Margaret,
    My letter to Thomas which I wrote a few days ago in a *hurried manner*, from near Burgos, would prepare you to hear from me very soon; and I now snatch an opportunity of acknowledging the receipt of your affectionate letter of April, the date of which I cannot at present recollect

---

38. Major William Napier, 43rd Foot.
39. George Napier, 52nd Foot.

as I left it with William[40] and as we have been at a distance from each other for a few days, he has had no opportunity of returning it. If you examine our situation on the map, you will find we are at no great distance from the Pyrenees. We passed the Ebro without opposition by a most masterly manoeuvre of the Marquis W[ellington] and the French are still in retreat before us on the high road to France. Whether they intend to pull up before they reach the Pyrenees or to continue their route into France, we are of course perfectly ignorant; but the general opinion is, they will adopt the latter plan. But even if a general action should take place, the chance of victory appears to be greatly in our favour, unless they are reinforced by fresh troops from France; and in this case only, it is presumed, they will be disposed to risk a battle. At all events, a short time I hope will determine our fate in this country and God grant we may soon have the happiness and satisfaction of returning to our friends in Old England in triumph over our enemies.

In so long and rapid a march as we have had since the army broke up from its cantonments, it may naturally be supposed we have had our share of fatigue and privations; but we feel it the less under the prospect we now have of driving the French out of the country. My health I can assure you has not suffered in the least degree since we commenced the campaign and I am happy to say I enjoy the best of it. William too the last time I saw him, was looking remarkably well. You will also derive the greatest satisfaction of hearing that he bears the character of a most active useful officer. I hear him spoken of in these terms from people who are very capable of judging his merits. Bardolph[41] is in famous condition and of the greatest use to William. He appears to take every care of him & seldom works him except when in sight of the enemy. How clearly is Thomas's superior judgement proved, since he always advised William by no means to part with Bardolph and Will now finds his account in having kept him. The strong grey mare which he bought on his march to Portsmouth, has also proved a good & useful charger, the young grey mare, better known by the name of 'Sisey Filly' is exchanged for a strong useful Irish horse, which Will denominates his *third* charger, Sisey was too slight for him. You had better not tell Sarah this, for I find in a letter she has wrote to William, she enquires particularly about the grey mare & begs William never to part with her, as she was a particular favourite of Mr Miller's. But we all know, in matters of this sort, Will

---

40. His brother, William, was now a captain in the 15th Light Dragoons, having transferred from the 95th Rifles in December 1809.
41. William's horse.

has few delicate scruples of conscience, he passes over them really coolly. The country we have been marching through on this side the Ebro, is mountainous but covered with wood and abounding in the most beautiful & richest vallies [sic] one can imagine. But the villages & their inhabitants are wretched in the extreme from the oppression of the French. In time of peace they must have been the happiest people in the world. The scenery is very grand & sublime & reminds one of the descriptions we have had of Switzerland. How I regret my inability to take a sketch of some of this scenery. If ever I return to England I shall certainly put myself under your tuition, every officer ought to be able to take sketches of country.

In winding through these vallies [sic], and just as the head of our division began to debouche into a more open space, we found we had been marching parallel to a French division commanded by General Maucune,[42] but this circumstance had been concealed from us by the high hills which divided our line of march between them. The French were also coming out of the mountains into the same open space through which was also their line of march; but as the head of their column was more advanced on the line of march than ours, part of this division made its escape from us. We succeeded however in cutting off one brigade which dispersed itself into the mountains on their right. The 52nd and the 95th with some Portuguese light troops forming the 2nd Brigade of our division pursued them, took about 300 prisoners, besides killing a great number by their fire, captured all their baggage, and a few only of *this* unfortunate brigade made their escape by taking refuge in the mountains. Our loss was very trifling, nothing to speak of. We have since been close up with the French and some part of the army has been skirmishing with them every day. We often hear the roar of cannon, with musquetry, on our line of march in the mountains, the echo of which is *tremendous* and *sublime* and at the same time quite ignorant what division is engaged, or what is going on, so entirely are we separated by the mountains from each other. Although every division of the army is marching *parallel*, & *close to* each other. With your letter I also received one from George on the subject of an inscription for poor Charles' marble. I am sorry I have not time to write to him at present, if you are soon about to write to him, pray mention that he shall hear from me the very first opportunity. He should have heard from me today, but William has got his letter in his possession and it is necessary to have it before me to reply to it. I wrote to my brother a few weeks ago about

---

42. General Antoine Maucune.

this inscription. I partly approved of one which among two others he submitted for my perusal, but with a trifling alteration which I proposed. But on considering these inscriptions further, I am very much inclined to think they are all too long for all we would wish to say of our dear departed brothers' character cannot be expressed in a *little compass* and it therefore strikes me, it would perhaps be better to have it as short and plain as possible to serve merely the purpose of a memorial of him in Ecclesfield Church. His real worth and excellence can *only* be *faithfully* imprinted *on our hearts.* I will therefore submit to you & Thomas the following, which is George's own, a part being omitted, for the purpose of rendering it as brief as possible and the only alteration I have made in it, which George himself hinted might be omitted if I thought the original too long, 'This marble commemorates the fate of Lieutenant Charles Booth, 52nd Regiment &c &c, of his honourable duties in the career of his profession the best movement is the testimony of his fellow soldiers; of his private worth & rectitude, the remembrance of his afflicted brothers who jointly erect this tribute to his character, which survives, his remains as a pattern for imitation & source of humble confidence in his happy transition to life eternal'. Adieu my dear Margaret, with most affectionate regards to Thomas. Pray remember me also to Sarah. I had not time to write to both of you to obey; but you can tell her how we are going on and she shall hear from me the very first opportunity, all her letters have reached safe. William has received her letter of April 30 and no doubt will write immediately. Your affectionate brother Henry.

Obituary of Henry Booth, *United Services Journal*, June 1841

May 6th, at Northallerton aged fifty one, while on leave of absence for the recovery of his health Lieutenant Colonel H Booth KH 43rd Light Infantry.

In affording a place in your pages for a brief tribute of respect to the memory of the late Lieutenant Colonel Henry Booth of the 43rd, you kindly meet the wishes of several officers, who having enjoyed the happiness of serving under his command, feel acutely his loss, and are desirous that a few words of more familiar detail than is usually found in your obituary notices may be offered to the character of that excellent soldier and man.

The well fought fields of Vimiera [Vimeiro] and Corunna, the Coa, Busaco, Salamanca, Vitoria, and Vera, lend their laurels to his name and to the regiment in whose ranks he began, continued and concluded his long period of service. Colonel Booth's several commissions bear the following dates, Ensign 6 March 1806, Lieutenant 11 June 1807, Captain 25 June 1812, Major 29 August 1822, Lieutenant Colonel 29 June 1830, all in the 43rd Regiment, a constancy to one corps, which together with many brilliant, sterling and amiable qualities gained for him, during the later years of his life, the well merited title of the 'Father of the Regiment'.

His excellent system of command, derived originally from the gallant leader of the Light Division, General Craufurd, pervaded the battalion throughout. His spirit was infused into its smallest details. The 43rd Light Infantry and Colonel Booth, seemed part and parcel of each other. Just, generous, humane and warm hearted, his rule was at once vigorous and lenient; and none knew better than himself the occasion, as well as the manner of applying the stimulus of praise, encouragement and reward to the deserving. That much enduring and rarely commiserated being, the soldier's wife, never pleaded in vain to his charity; and it was common to see the child of the soldier, with that insight into character peculiar to infancy, hurry into the path of the colonel, certain of receiving some little gift, caress, or kindly notice at his hands.

In his demeanour towards his officers, the dignity of the commandant and the suavity of the friend were happily blended; and that delicate line of demarcation between the 'official' and 'familiar' was traced with rare tact and refinement. His messmates had continually before them, in Colonel Booth, a perfect model of the gentleman and the man of honour.

The skill, rapidity and spirit of Colonel Booth's field movements were famed throughout the army. When engaged in the science in which he delighted, the men seemed to share in his enthusiasm. His evolutions invariably displayed a portion of the earnestness of actual service; but few of those officers and soldiers lately instructed by him but will remember the energetic manner in which he threw his skirmishers into cover. 'Dash in like foxhounds!' was the favourite exclamation of the old soldier and sportsman. It is not too much to say that the most ignorant spectator of a field-day of the 43rd would at a glance discover whether or not the battalion were wielded by the skilful and peculiar hand of the late lieutenant colonel.

Colonel Booth was eminently qualified by nature for the profession of which he was an ornament. With a figure of unusual stature and power, and a countenance handsome and expressive, he possessed an eye of wonderful quickness, a voice loud and cheering as a trumpet and an eloquence and aptitude in addressing soldiers rarely equalled.

A severe illness, contracted in leading the arduous advance of the 43rd from New Brunswick to Lower Canada in the winter of 1837, inflicted upon his naturally vigorous constitution a shock from which he never wholly rallied. As an officer of first-rate ability, the loss of Lieutenant Colonel Booth will be generally and severely felt in the British army; and as staunch and true friend and delightful companion, he will be deeply lamented by those who enjoyed his more intimate acquaintance.

Chapter 6

Captain John Paul Hopkins

Description of the action at Sabugal

John Hopkins had become a lieutenant in the 1st Battalion, 43rd Foot, on 19 June 1805 and served at the Côa (where he was severely wounded), Busaco, Foz de Arrouce and Fuentes de Oñoro. He was promoted to captain in the 43rd on 29 August 1811 and served with the regiment at Ciudad Rodrigo, Badajoz, Salamanca, San Millan, Vitoria and the Pyrenees. He became a major in the regiment in 1824 and died on 17 March 1875 at Windsor. He was buried in St George's Chapel.

Early on the morning of the 3rd of April, during heavy rains, the 43rd Regiment was formed in column of companies at their alarm post, close to the miserable Portuguese village in which they had passed the night. They were kept a considerable time under arms, awaiting orders for crossing the river Coa. At last, an officer of the Staff rode up, and in a hasty, petulant manner asked Colonel Beckwith,[1] who commanded the brigade, why he had not marched to the ford. The Colonel replied that he had not received any instructions from the general, Sir William Erskine,[2] for that movement.

On this, however, the colonel marched us rapidly towards the ford. We advanced right in front; four companies of the 95th led. We all crossed the Coa, which from incessant rains had become so swollen as to render the passage difficult and dangerous. The bank on the further side of the river was steep in ascent, covered with thick underwood.

---

1. Lieutenant colonel Thomas Sidney Beckwith commanded 1st Brigade of the Light Division until August 1811, when he returned home due to ill health.
2. Major General Sir William Erskine temporarily commanded the Light Division in March and April 1811 during the absence of Craufurd in England.

We soon gained its summit, halting in front of the brow of the hill to avoid the torrents of rain, fast pouring down, with the wind at our backs. The officers sat themselves with their backs against a low stone wall. The enemy in position at Sabugal discovered us and fired several shot. Colonel Beckwith laughingly said, 'Gentlemen, you have an extraordinary taste, to prefer shot to rain.' He ordered the 95th to advance to the town, which was some distance to our left front. They advanced in skirmishing order, under a sharp fire from the enemy, many of the shot reaching us. The atmosphere was greatly darkened by the bad weather. The firing on the Rifles became incessant, but they gained their ground up to the French position. Colonel Beckwith sent the 43rd forward in support of the Rifles; they descended towards the river, into a sort of plain, interspersed with trees and under wood. As we approached, the heavy fire of the French marked their line of battle and the riflemen retired upon us in good order. Colonel Beckwith having gone some distance towards the left, in order to reconnoitre the position of the enemy, Colonel Patrickson[3] was left in the entire command, and close upon the enemy. He gave orders for an instant advance and charge against the line in our front, which was on an eminence.

At this moment a slight clearance from the rain enabled me, who was in command of the company on the extreme right of our line, to perceive that at some distance, towards our right rear, a strong detachment of the French from Rovena [Ruvina] were directing their march to the ford. I saw all the danger of our being so turned and immediately requested Captain Duffy,[4] commanding the next company, to allow me to take mine to oppose the attempt of the enemy, who were gaining fast upon our rear. He replied that he could not take upon himself such a responsibility as allowing the separation of my company from the regiment. I said no time should be lost, and that I would take the responsibility at such a moment on myself; and instantly I marched off the company, by bringing up their left shoulders, advancing rapidly to the right towards an eminence at some distance, on which I placed the company in position, fronting the enemy, who were marching round the right flank. I was now quite separated from the regiment, which was fiercely engaged with the French. I had above 100 men in the company, as several of Duffy's men had followed. The two subalterns with the company were William Freer and Henry Oglander,

---

3. Major Christopher Patrickson did not become a brevet lieutenant colonel until 30 May 1811.
4. Captain John Duffy, 43rd Foot.

both most excellent officers. The body of French, who were marching towards the Coa, halted on seeing us and despatched a body of infantry against us. I reserved my fire until they neared the summit of the hill, when I opened upon them, causing them to retire in some disorder to the plain. They again formed and advanced as before, but were checked, retreating to a greater distance.

At this time Colonel Beckwith rode up; I reported all that had occurred and that the French had brought up two guns in rear. I requested his instructions. He spoke most handsomely to me, approving and thanking me for what I had done and said that he should give me no orders, but leave me to act entirely on my own judgment, in which he had perfect confidence; that he would not forget me and that he would bring me to the notice of Lord Wellington. On his leaving, Sir John Elly,[5] who commanded the cavalry came up, when I begged that some dragoons might reinforce me. He made no reply but rode off, shaking his head as if unable to comply. During this time the enemy were forming in greater strength, they advanced with the drummer beating the pas de charge; the officer in command, some paces to the front, leading his people to the hill. William Freer[6] asked permission to go forward and personally engage him; this I of course refused, as his presence with the company was more important.

The French bravely stood our fire, and their two guns were brought to bear upon us. I ordered a charge, which was done with great spirit, driving the enemy to some distance. Whilst these attacks were made, the regiment was constantly engaged at Sabugal. The firing was severe and continuous, never receding nor slackening, thus affording me the utmost confidence; for had not the French left been so severely attacked, they would have been able to detach a body against my rear or on my left flank, which would have compelled me to retreat upon the troops now advancing to our support.

It was at this time the captured howitzer was left under command of the fire of the 43rd and Rifles, as every attempt of the French to carry it off was ineffectual, causing severe loss both in cavalry and infantry. The enemy were still at some distance and appeared to be reinforced and intending another attack; and I perceived the 2nd Battalion of the

---

5. Lieutenant Colonel John Elley was actually Assistant Adjutant General of the cavalry.
6. Lieutenant William Freer, 43rd Foot.

52nd advancing rapidly. I went to the commanding officer,[7] pointing out the enemy near and we agreed it would be best for him to form his regiment on the right of my company and make an immediate advance upon the French, which we did. As we advanced, they retired, forming themselves into the line perpendicular to our left and in continuation of their line to Sabugal, where their chief body was posted. I therefore brought up my right shoulders to front them, extending all my men as skirmishers; the 52nd doing the same to my right, we all commenced skirmishing amid the trees in unabated rain.

The French showed fight, in their new line, mingling several dragoons with their skirmishers; their sudden debouch from behind the trees at first shook ours and severely wounded several. One man, close to me, was cut in the face, but he would not leave the field. A marksman, of the name of Cassan, was taking his aim at a dragoon riding towards him, when another horseman appearing suddenly on his right, he turned his firelock and shot him dead, the other dragoon instantly galloping away. Colonel Mellish, of the Staff,[8] rode along the line; he was to be seen in every post of danger, loudly and gallantly cheering the men. Colonel Beckwith, also with the blood streaming down his face, encouraged the men to stand fast against the enemy. Our whole line preserved their ground for some time, until a few of the horsemen getting amongst the skirmishers on the right, a sudden cry, 'The cavalry! The cavalry is in the midst of us!' caused the 52nd to retreat in confusion.

I was with the skirmishers on the left and did not retire my men, seeing that the horsemen who had got into the line were so few. Some men of the 52nd remained on the left with my company. It was fortunate that we remained skirmishing, as it prevented one of the colours of the 52nd falling into the hands of the French,[9] owing to the firmness of the men. The officer bearing the colour came up to thank me, at the same time highly praising the gallantry of my men.

The enemy, perceiving strong reinforcements marching up, commenced a hurried retreat. Seeing that the 52nd were now in line, with an opening between the wings, we forming in the centre, I directed William Freer to wheel the company into sections, as I

---

7. Lieutenant Colonel the Honourable Hugh Arbuthnot commanded 2/52nd from April to July 1811.
8. Captain Henry Francis Mellish of the 87th Foot was Deputy Assistant Adjutant General of the Light Division from June 1810 to August 1811.
9. A rare admission of the near loss of a colour.

intended to rejoin the regiment. He was struck down by a shot in his face, but persevered in marching.

The French, though fast retreating, were not pursued by the divisions of the army which had joined us; instead of which, the Staff officers employed their time in complimenting the regiment for their conduct in the combat and the pursuit was given up.

I marched to my regiment along the line leading straight to Sabugal, on which we had last engaged, and came upon the howitzer, at the point where it had been posted by the enemy and where it had been compelled to remain.

The combat of Sabugal never having been faithfully rendered, justice has therefore been long withheld from the troops, who so greatly distinguished themselves in that action. Every writer on the subject, with the exception of Sir William Napier, only notices the affair of that day as but little more than a sharp and successful skirmish. Napier's account, however, is too diffuse and rather inexact in some parts.

Brialmont, the Belgian writer of the 'Life of the Duke of Wellington,'[10] in his statement of Sabugal, is evidently led astray by the partial reports of the French generals. As he remarks – 'The French passed the Coa and established themselves at Sabugal. It was here that on the 3 April Wellington fought the action,' of which he says, with some touch of exaggeration, 'This was one of the most glorious British troops were ever engaged in.' We only know that if glorious to one party it was equally glorious to the other, for Regnier's troops showed themselves by no means inferior to those of the enemy. Regnier, commanding in a chosen position at Sabugal, did not display high generalship, for having at that point, a force of 12,000 infantry, supported by cavalry and artillery, he failed in defeating the attack of 1,200 British infantry, who nobly proved themselves the decided superiors of the French.

Napier was mistaken in ascribing to General Beckwith the merit of the attack, as Beckwith was then away on the left, which was threatened by a strong force of the enemy. The charge was entirely ordered by Colonel Patrickson of the 43rd. I was close to him when he gave the order and also when he led the men to the charge, and it was during that advance that I found it requisite to move my company to the right, on the appearance of the French troops threatening that flank.

---

10. Henry Brialmont, a captain in the Belgian army, published a four-volume history of the Duke of Wellington in French, which was translated into English and edited by George Gleig in 1858.

It was well known that the Duke of Wellington was the most truthful of men, totally incapable of exaggeration; and it has ever been admitted that he never bestowed praise but where justly due. His report of Sabugal, therefore, that 'This was one of the most glorious actions that British troops were ever engaged in,' ought to be cherished and registered in history, as a lasting tribute to the honour of the British soldier.

Chapter 7

Captain James Fergusson 43rd Foot Memorial

James Fergusson was born on 17 March 1787, a descendant of the Scottish family, the Fergussons of Craigdarroch.
Memorial of a soldier's services during an active War and latterly during peace, Museum of the Oxfordshire Soldier.

[I] Joined the 18th Foot[1] the winter of 1803, my commission dated August 1801. The regiment was stationed at Newry in the north of Ireland, from whence we soon removed to Edinburgh Castle, from thence to Haddington & Dunbar, each place occupied by a battalion of the regiment.

On the 9 February 1804 [I] was appointed to a lieutenancy in the regiment. In the summer we left Scotland and in July of the same year we formed part of the corps under Sir David Dundas encamped at Barham Down near Canterbury.

Was removed in August 1804 to the 43rd Light Infantry encamped at Shorncliffe under Sir John Moore. During that period we occupied in the winter months the barracks either at Salford [Stanford] above the Hythe or those at Shorncliffe & upon one occasion Brabourne Lees & summer months pitched our tents again at Shorncliffe. It was then the Light Brigade was brought to that high state of discipline by Sir John Moore. It consisted of the 43rd, 52nd, & 95th Rifles.

From our encampment at Shorncliffe in clear weather we had a good view of the French Coast & could with our glasses trace the line occupied by the French troops intended by Bonaparte for the invasion of England & called 'The Army of England'. We repeatedly distinguished contests

---

1. The Royal Irish Regiment.

between our gun boats & the enemy's. We continued to be employed on the coast of Kent until the summer of 1808.

First Portuguese Campaign

Was appointed to a company by purchase in the 2nd Battalion 43rd Regiment in December 1806. Embarked on the 16 July 1808 at Ramsgate with a corps under Major General Anstruther[2] consisting of the 2nd Battalions, of the 43rd & 52nd & the 95th Regiments to reinforce Sir A Wellesley who had previously sailed for Portugal.

We disembarked on the evening of the 19 August in the Bay of Maceira near the Berlings.[3] We suffered from the high surf but were not opposed by the enemy. Sir A Wellesley had taken up a position at Vimeiro near the coast and had sent a detachment to cover the march of our brigade. We joined the army in its position the next day and were engaged in the Battle of Vimeiro on the 21 August 1808. Our young battalion took a conspicuous part in this action and distinguished itself. We occupied the church and were hotly engaged in the vineyards in its neighbourhood. We took several prisoners but suffered considerably from our exposed situation. The part of our army engaged lost about 730 killed & wounded. [I] was slightly wounded upon this occasion. Had our gallant chief not been superseded in his command by the arrival of Sir Harry Burrard after the action, we should most probably have been in possession of Lisbon the next day, have made Junot's army prisoners, or at least have dispersed them & we should not have heard of 'The Convention of Cintra', that convention put an end to our first short but glorious campaign.

We enjoyed ourselves during about six weeks in the beautiful villas/ quintas that surrounded us & luxuriated in the rich gardens & vineyards at that season stocked with fruits. After the departure of the French we paid occasional visits to Lisbon & partook of its amusements.

Lisbon is not the cleanest city in Europe, but it had its agrèmens [pleasures], beautifully situated on the bank of the Tagus, a river abounding with the finest scenery. Dysentery prevailed to a great degree in the army & when we were selected as one of the battalions for the corps assembled under Sir John Moore intended for Spain, we were obliged on our departure in October to leave several officers & men in hospital at Lisbon; probably the light wines, the abundance of fruit, & the

---

2. Robert Anstruther, 3rd Foot Guards, was actually a brevet colonel in 1809.
3. Actually the Berlangas is an archipelago of small islands off the coast near Peniche.

exposure to the night dews was the cause of it, as we latterly had not had severe service to account for it.

The Corunna Campaign

Sir John Moore's corps of all arms amounted to about 20,000 men & commenced their march for Spain early in October 1808. Our brigade consisted of the 2nd Battalions of the 43rd & 52nd & the 9th & 77th Regiments under Major General Beresford; our route was through Coimbra, Viseu, Almeida to Salamanca. The roads bad in the extreme, often we had to scramble up goat tracks & descend into ravines almost inaccessible; we experienced heavy rains & suffered a good deal of fatigue during the march, but we were in a great degree repaid for it by the great kindness and hospitality that was shewn to us at the end of each day's march.

The troops at this period everywhere through Portugal were received with the greatest enthusiasm. The inhabitants vied with each other in their hospitality & kindness, which it is to be regretted was so ill repaid by the followers & skulkers of the army, not by the troops assembled with their colours. The chief irregularities with an army are to be attributed to its followers.

We entered Salamanca on the 13 November 1808, a splendid town with its hundred public buildings, churches, monasteries, colleges & we were the first British troops that arrived at Salamanca with the exception of some companies of Rottenburg's Rifles.[4]

When we crossed the frontier between Portugal & Spain at Fort Conception near Ciudad Rodrigo, we mounted the red cockade and entered Spain with the full expectation of meeting a still more cordial reception than we had experienced from our Portuguese allies, but we were woefully disappointed. The Spaniards received us unkindly and regarded us more as enemies than friends; we however found better roads, neater villages & more comfort in other respects.

We expected to have found the Spanish troops strongly posted on the line of the Ebro in our front, but we had scarcely arrived at Salamanca when we heard they were dispersed & nothing remained between us & the enemy; our situation therefore became rather precarious, as it required time to assemble our force. A division of infantry with one artillery & cavalry [corps] moved from Lisbon by the circuitous route

---

4. Colonel Baron de Rottenburg commanded the 5th Battalion, 60th Foot, which was armed with rifles.

of Talavera & our force in consequence was not assembled before the 11 December. During this time however the enemy did not intercept us & we remained at Salamanca. The streets crowded with numbers of great athletic powerful looking monks idling about, that might ought to have been in arms in defence of their country. Disaster after disaster overtook the Spaniards, the French defeating their corps in detail and getting possession at last of Madrid, obliged Sir J[ohn] Moore to move. We had expected to retire upon Portugal but to our great joy we made a forward movement & formed a junction with the troops under Sir David Baird lately arrived at Corunna from England.

At this time our army could get no information from the Spaniards, we were perfectly in the dark as to what was going on and by accident at last heard of the state of affairs. We were assembled in the neighbourhood of Mayorga on the 20 December, [who] had experienced severe weather & some long marches, but our men were strong and in excellent order. We felt much the want of fuel & were obliged to cook with chopped straw, the country was deep with snow. We had in the field including Sir David Baird's corps about 24,000 of all arms.

On the 21 December 1808 Lord Paget[5] moved with the cavalry upon Sahagun consisting of the 15th & 10th Hussars and nearly surprised the enemy. He made a dashing charge with about 400 men of the 15th Hussars upon a very superior body of the enemy's cavalry, killed & took prisoners about 15 officers & nearly 200 men, it was a brilliant affair.[6]

Headquarters were established at Sahagun & on the 23 December we assembled on the road to Carrion during as severe a night of cold as we had ever experienced with the intention of making an attack on the enemy post at Saldanha, but owing to some information received from the Spanish General Romana we broke up & returned to our different posts where we had scarcely arrived when we were again put in motion & the next morning the 24 December commenced our retreat.[7] We were attached to General Hope's force who fell back with two divisions on the road to Mayorga. The remainder of the army continued at Sahagun during the day & on the 25 December retired.

Two squadrons of the 10th Hussars made a dashing & successful charge on a body of the enemy's cavalry near Mayorga,[8] defeated them with a

---

5. Lieutenant General Lord Henry Paget commanded the cavalry.

6. This refers to the Battle of Sahagun.

7. News had reached Sir John Moore that Napoleon had sent his far more numerous army in his direction, forcing him to order a retreat.

8. This again refers to the Action at Sahagun.

less of killed & prisoners amounting to about 120 men. Our cavalry at this period were always successful & upon all occasions rode the enemy's cavalry out of the field; they had already taken upwards of 500 prisoners.

Our rear guard crossed the bridge of Castro Gonzales & destroyed its passage on the night of the 28 December & fell back upon Benavente, a gallant cavalry affair took place here. The pickets, part of the 3rd German Hussars & the 10th Hussar's & under Major General C[harles] Stewart defeated a larger force of the Imperial Guard taking Lefebvre[9] their general prisoner & about 200 men all cavalry.

Lord Paget withdrew with the British cavalry during the night to La Beneza. It was said Bonaparte was present at Benavente & we had hoped he had seen the defeat of his Imperial Guard.

The French were in possession of Astorga on the 1 January 1809 with a force more than double our strength. Our brigade made two marches on the road to Vigo by mistake,[10] caused by a drunken dragoon not delivering his dispatches. We therefore had to return by a forced march to Lugo in continued rain. We arrived at night much fatigued.

On the 3 January part of our rear guard had an affair with the French cavalry at Cacabelos in which affair General Colbert[11] & some dragoons were killed by our riflemen. The next day the rear guard finding themselves so hard pressed were obliged to abandon the money boxes, filled with dollars to the amount of £25,000.[12] They were thrown into a deep ravine & it is to be hoped the Spanish peasantry recovered more of it than the enemy.

On the 7th the army were assembled in position at Lugo. Great irregularities had taken place on our retreat to this place, all attributable to drink, the bane of the British soldier. The road we retired by was the grand mountain road of Galicia leading from Astorga to Corunna and passing through as magnificent scenery as is to be found in Europe. The weather was severe & the ways deep from continued snow, sleet & rain; these drawbacks in addition to the irregularities of the troops caused us many stragglers. Sir J Moore issued strong and severe orders on the want of discipline shewn by the troops & which had a good effect, on this day the enemy attacked our picquets & threatened our left, but he was defeated with a loss of between three & four hundred men.

---

9. General de Division Charles Lefebvre-Desnouettes.

10. This is an interesting claim but one I have been unable to substantiate.

11. General Auguste Colbert-Chabanais was killed by a long-range shot fired by Thomas Plunket of the 95th Rifles.

12. About £1.5 million today.

Although we experienced some loss in our retreat to Lugo we had still under arms from 18 to 19,000 men. With this inferior force our general was anxious to bring the French to action but in vain, they cautiously avoided it.

We had some days suffering from want of food, no provisions in the camp, continued bad weather & the enemy's forces daily increasing induced our general to resume the retreat to Corunna. At about ten o'clock at night on the 8 January, our fires were kept burning & we commenced silently & regularly our march from Lugo; hungry but not spiritless, until the severity of our march, want of food, above all want of sleep overpowered us. A continued storm of snow & sleet pelted us unmercifully from the moment we left our position. Our shoes began to fail & numbers fell out of the ranks with lacerated feet & increased the stragglers considerably. Our sufferings now became severe, but the want of sleep overpowered every other feeling; its torture was dreadful, so much so that the want of food was almost forgotten. Scenes of misery & distress presented themselves on all sides, poor wretches with their feet bleeding falling from exhaustion into the ditches & there dying. The strongest continuing their weary march asleep, occasionally stumbling against a stone & for a moment rose to a sense of the scene about them & again relapsing into the same state of drowsiness, dreaming that they were surrounded with every luxury & comfort but not permitted to partake of it & again awaking to their real situation. Thus, we continued our retreat to the bridges of Betanzos where we arrived the night of the 9 January, broken & miserable & but the remnant of battalions; it took some time before we could march, even the few able to keep the road. Although at this time our battalions were reduced in number but composed of our hardiest & best soldiers, still from exhausted nature the scene described occurred to that part of the troops not wanting in discipline & possessing the best spirit.

The rear guard formed under Major General E[dward] Paget never lost sight of the enemy & being occasionally halted to cover the retreat were not so exhausted & the excitement caused by the enemy being constantly in view, enabled them to make their march with less suffering & greater regularity.

Our brigade arrived on the morning of the 10 January at Corunna & occupied the suburbs of St Lucie until the battle fought on the 16 January.

During the intermediate period some of our stragglers arrived with their feet lacerated & bleeding to such a degree that some absolutely crawled upon their hands & feet to join our ranks.

Sergeant Newman of our battalion,[13] who had fallen out on the march & seeing the enemy's cavalry sabring our stragglers & cutting them off, halted on the road & appealed to the scattered soldiers to assemble under his orders & he would check the French cavalry & save them. Many obeyed his directions until he assembled a considerable body. He then formed them up, ordering those unable to keep the ranks to continue their march & with great resolution awaited the enemy's cavalry, checked them & by his bold conduct eventually saved between four & five hundred men to the British Army. The sergeant received a commission for his gallant conduct.

On the 11 January 1809 the army was assembled about Corunna. Our brigade made the march from Lugo one continued struggle, a distance that would otherwise have been considered 4 day's march. On the 13 January two large magazines of powder were destroyed to prevent its falling into the enemy's hands, the explosions were terrific, one of three thousand & the other of four thousand barrels. The troops not being prepared for it, were at first considerably alarmed and flew to their arms. The moment the column of smoke was observed in the air, the panic ceased. It was three miles distant from us.

On the 14th the transports for the army arrived from Vigo & entered the harbour of Corunna. The artillery with the exception of one brigade, the dismounted cavalry which were numerous, the sick & all the encumbrances of the army were ordered to be immediately embarked, so that the army at any moment could retire to their ships without inconvenience. We had previously been ordered to shoot our horses, which we obeyed with regret.

On the 13th Colonel Mackenzie, 5th Foot[14] was killed in an attempt with some of his men to seize a temporary battery that annoyed our picquets.

In the afternoon of the 16 January the enemy attacked our position in three strong columns covered with numerous skirmishers & a powerful artillery, an arm in which we were deficient. Our picquets were driven in and the village of Elvina gained by the enemy. It was however soon retaken by our troops & the French were defeated in all their attacks & driven from the entire of our position & which we stood in advance of as victors after the battle, our brigade was posted on the extreme right of

---

13. Sergeant William Newman, 43rd Foot. He was rewarded with an ensigncy in the 1st West India Regiment for his actions.
14. Lieutenant Colonel John Mackenzie, 5th Foot, was wounded on 14 January and died of his wounds the following day.

the army and covered the retreat of our troops during the night to their shipping, which took place with great regularity. We had to deplore the loss of our able and gallant commander who was struck by a cannon shot at the moment our troops were carrying the village of Elvina. Both Sir J Moore and D Baird second in command were carried wounded from the field and the command devolved upon Lieutenant General Hope an able and distinguished officer.

Sir John Moore died & was buried by us on the ramparts at night, and never were the remains of a more gallant spirit consigned to the earth. Our brigade (Beresford's) retired within the works of Corunna before daybreak and held them during the 17 January.

The enemy during the morning opened a masked battery upon our transports in the harbour that were slow in getting under weigh & made them hasten their departure. Many cut their cables and ran for it. In the confusion two transports took the shore & were afterwards burnt by us, but the remainder were soon at sea.

Our brigade retired in small detachments from the works during the night of the 17th lighted to the men of war's boats by the brilliant blaze of the burning transports, leaving Corunna to be defended by the Spaniards until we were clear off, which they honourably performed.

We were taken on board the first line of battleships in the offing & the next day divided between the other ships and sailed for England. The weather was so stormy that we experienced some loss in our cavalry transports.

We had scarcely 15,000 men in the Battle of Corunna. The French could not have been less than 20,000, with an increasing force, strong batteries of artillery & cavalry in both of which arms we were deficient & with the additional disadvantage of being a retiring army. Under all these circumstances the Battle of Corunna must be considered glorious for the British Army, and the previous irregularities & want of discipline shewn on the retreat ought to be forgotten. When troops so worn, so dispirited, and broken down, should rally as they did, face their enemy & so successfully to defeat him, it showed a firmness & determination in the British soldier unequalled.

We landed at Plymouth in a miserable state having had the same clothes on for several days, our baggage having for some time been separated from us. We however cleansed ourselves by the aid of baths and a supply of linen which the tradesmen had purchased for us on our arrival, we were soon able to make an appearance.

The good people of Plymouth showed the greatest kindness to the soldiers, their wives & children and supplied them with clothes

& other comforts. We assembled at Colchester and both battalions of the 43rd Regiment quickly repaired the losses we sustained for our deficiencies were increased by several deaths of officers and men from putrid fever caused by the sudden change of living when the blood was so impoverished.

Walcheren Campaign

The 1st Battalions 43rd, 52nd & 95th Rifles under Major General Robert Crawford [Craufurd] again embarked early in the summer of 1809 and arrived to the succour of Sir Arthur Wellesley on the field of Talavera & took the outposts after a most arduous march of twenty six hours. They were too late for the battle, but it was so far fortunate that they were reserved to cover the retreat of the army from Talavera. Our battalions (the 2nd battalions 43rd, 52nd & 95th Rifles) embarked at Deal on the 17 July 1809 on that ill-fated expedition to Walcheren. One brigade landed without opposition at South Beveland on the 10 August. The troops were chiefly embarked in ships of war and it was altogether the largest armament that had left the British shores. It was said we could have landed of all arms 70,000 men. This of course included marines & strong companies of sailors trained under lieutenants of the Navy in the musket.

The troops experienced some little opposition in landing on the Island of Walcheren but it was soon overpowered and the troops were immediately employed to reduce Flushing [Vlissingen]. Fort Batz in the island of South Beveland was taken possession of and our brigade continued inactive in that island until the end of the month when that pestilential climate soon rendered our battalions useless. Sickness increased to that degree & with such rapidity that our ranks were soon thinned & they were obliged quickly to re-embark the troops without having effected any serious service for their country, but on the contrary having experienced a severe loss in the lives of many brave soldiers who were sacrificed ingloriously in that unhealthy climate and at a moment when their services would have been invaluable in Spain.

The islands in the Scheldt notwithstanding their insalubrity are beautiful to the eye, cultivated to the highest pitch, planted & improved in every way and made luxurious as the art & industry of man could render them. We disembarked at Harwich having consigned many poor fellows to the deep on our passage and once more assembled at Colchester where the Walcheren fever continued its ravages killing or rendering unserviceable many valuable soldiers.

Return to Portugal 1810

We continued at Colchester repairing our losses until the summer of 1810 and in June of that year [I] became effective in the 1st Battalion 43rd Regiment caused by severe losses of officers & men from fever and ague in the neighbourhood of Campo Mayor where the 1st Battalion were serving, Crawford's Brigade being cantoned in that part of Portugal after the retreat from Talavera. After a long & tedious journey joined my new company in the 1st Battalion 43rd Regiment encamped in front of Almeida. The French were besieging Ciudad Rodrigo held by the Spaniards under the gallant old governor Herastes. At this time the Light Brigade were formed into a division[15] by incorporating into it two Portuguese Cacadore regiments.[16] Elder's corps [3rd Cacadores] with half of the 95th rifle companies & the 43rd Regiment, the right brigade; Aldjoe's corps [Actually Avilez' 1st Cacadores], the remainder of the rifle companies & the 52nd Regiment, the left brigade.

This division was in the highest state of discipline and although close to a numerous and formidable enemy kept its ground & avoided all surprises. A few minutes during day or night was sufficient to get it under arms and assembled at its alarm posts. The baggage sent to the rear. No wheel carriage of any description accompanied us. Mules & horses were alone employed & could travel with expedition in the worst of roads.

The French at this time gave us plenty of practice in getting rapidly under arms to our great annoyance and always chose the time of meals for putting it in practice. They watched our cooking & at the moment our kettles were prepared they advanced, which obliged us to empty the contents of them, pack up & be off. When they accomplished this object they retired, but we in general had fresh rations out & in the end accomplished our object & satisfied our empty stomachs.

On the 4 July the French appeared in force having a strong body of cavalry. They drove in our picquets, and we retired to the high ground overlooking the road to Almeida and the low marshy bottom, which was immediately occupied by their cavalry. It appeared only passable at the bridge on the road for which place the French made a push. A small stream winded through the bottom & crossed the road at this

---

15. This is slightly incorrect. The Light Division was formed on 22 February 1810 with one large brigade only. But on 4 August Portuguese *caçadores* were added and the division was formed into two brigades.
16. The 1st and 3rd Caçadores.

place. Captain Krauchenberg[17] a gallant and experienced officer with a squadron of Arentschild's Hussars charged the enemy in gallant style, slew some of their leading officers & men & drove them back. The bridge retained his name for some time after. An English officer commanding a squadron of the 16th Dragoons refused to aid the Germans in this affair or perhaps Krauchenberg would have made it more serious for the enemy.[18]

On the 11 July Major General Crawford [Craufurd] failed in an ill executed attempt to surprise some advanced picquets of the French. He had succeeded in taking 2 Officers & 29 dragoons of the cavalry picquet & in place of moving with artillery & infantry upon their infantry picquet, he pushed rapidly on with his dragoons with the idea of riding down the foot. But the French officer, an experienced soldier with 200 men, formed up and gave Crawford [Craufurd] so warm a reception that he killed & wounded of his cavalry 1 Lieutenant Colonel[19] & 32 men in their different charges, repulsing them upon each occasion and at last retiring over an open country triumphant & unhurt, and gained the pass of Barba del Puerco whence he was perfectly out of danger. Good infantry are not to be defeated by cavalry & Crawford [Craufurd] ought to have known better. There was no occasion for his rashness having both artillery & infantry with him. This affair took place at the crossroads of Barquillo.

On this day Ciudad Rodrigo surrendered to the French and on the 21 July we retired to a position with our left resting on the fortress of Almeida, a rocky ravine in our rear through which the River Coa runs & the bridge across the river a good mile from our position. A dreadful storm of rain fell on the night of the 23rd which flooded the river to that degree that the fords were rendered impassable & the only passage was the bridge in our rear.

The enemy before daybreak on the 24 July were in motion and soon drove in our picquets and advanced with such rapidity that we had but time to cover the retreat of our guns and cavalry when the enemy's skirmishers rushed through the vineyards and were only checked by the determination of our men, who slowly and regularly retired before them and eventually crossed the river under a heavy fire when all parts of the division were safe over. Five of our companies covered this

17. Captain Georg Kraunchenberg, 1st Hussars KGL.
18. This refers to the action at a bridge near Gallegos in which Krauchenberg was distinguished, but the claim that a squadron of the 16th Light Dragoons refused to aid them is not borne out by the available evidence.
19. Lieutenant Colonel Neil Talbot of the 14th Light Dragoons was killed in this badly organised and confused action.

retreat, the superior discipline of our men was conspicuous on this trying occasion.

As the Light Division crossed the bridge, they occupied the rocky banks of the river commanding the bridge and defeated many gallant attacks made by the French to cross it. It was soon covered with their dead. Our fire so perfectly commanded it, we held it notwithstanding the great superiority of numbers & the repeated determined attacks of the enemy; and at night we retired behind the Pinhel River.

The Light Division made a gallant defence of the bridge. Our force may be estimated at 5,000 men and the French under Ney at about 30,000.[20] We lost about 300 killed & wounded, the French at least 1,000. Many brave soldiers fell at the bridge. A subaltern's picquet of the Rifle corps were taken prisoners defending some rocks commanding the road. It was our advanced picquet & was early in the enemy's possession. The 52nd picquet under Dawson was stationed on the left when he found he could not rejoin the division, he followed the course of the river & like a good soldier escaped the enemy, crossed the river at Pinhel & rejoined us the next day. Our picquet 43rd more in the centre fell back with ease and joined the division in ample time. We formed one of the companies that covered the retreat.

We remained quiet until the 27 August, occupying Celerico and the 4th Division Guarda, when Almeida suddenly surrendered. The magazine from accident blew up & destroyed all the defences of the place, so as to render it no longer tenable, & it was given over to the enemy. We retired to Mortagua & from thence to the Sierra de Busaco. We had some skirmishing during this retreat. The position we took up at Busaco was exceedingly strong in front and the direct approach to it almost inaccessible. Notwithstanding before daybreak on the 27 September the enemy's columns appeared in the woods below & rapidly advanced to the attack. Loison's Division headed by Simon's Brigade led the front attack against us. They soon drove in our skirmishers & scrambled up the rocks undismayed and actually crowned our position; the artillerymen obliged to fall back from their guns and the summit of the position was for a few moments occupied by them, when Crawford [Craufurd] our general who keenly & anxiously watched their proceedings, had our division in line a few yards retired & out of view from the crest of the hill waiting for his signal which was at this moment given, waving his hat

---

20. Because of the restricted frontage, Marshal Ney only utilised about 10,000 of his troops in the attack.

& with a British cheer the Light Division charged the enemy, overthrew their columns taking a vast number of prisoners and strewing the face of the hill with their dead & wounded. The 52nd Regiment took Simon prisoner.[21]

The enemy's attack to our right upon the 3rd Division was at first more successful. Reynier's Corps was employed there, Ney's against the Light Division. In the attack on the 3rd Division, some of the Portuguese were overthrown and the right of the division was turned & the French in possession of the summit of it for a short time, when the 45th & 88th Regiments charged and Colonel Cameron[22] at the same time attacking with the 9th Regiment soon drove the enemy with great slaughter from their positions and swept their columns from the hills when the Battle of Busaco was finished.

At night the scene was grand beyond description. The position of the hostile armies was divided by a deep ravine, they occupying opposite ridges of lofty mountains, lighted up with innumerable bivouac fires. It was one of the most grand & exciting scenes imaginable and to add to its grandeur the night was exceedingly dark and a stillness & quiet reigned although occupied by such a multitude. On one occasion during a flag of truce our soldiers intermixed with the French upon the most friendly terms. A few hours before they were opposed to each other in a deadly strife, but now they were ready to show mutual kindness. A German general de brigade officer of our legion asked a French officer who he observed belonged to a regiment in the enemy's army in which he had a brother serving, respecting him. The French officer replied with the greatest 'sang froid' you will find him lying dead at the corner of that house; pointing to a village just below us, having been struck by a cannon shot in the attack.

Massena finding that our position was not to be carried by a direct attack, turned it by the Caramulo to Boyalva [Borralha] & we retired toward Coimbra on the 29 September.

The Light Division formed the rear guard through the mountainous country to Fornos when the cavalry took the front. Our division & the cavalry remained on the right bank, the remainder of the army crossed & moved to Condeixa & Pombal.

On the 1 October we had to file rapidly across the bridge at Coimbra. The enemy pressed us so fast that many of our dragoons were sabred

---

21. General de Brigade Edouard Simon was wounded and captured.
22. Lieutenant Colonel John Cameron commanding the 9th Foot.

in the river when crossing the ford. It was a distressing sight to see the inhabitants of that large town obliged to abandon their homes & property and fly for their lives, many of the better classes accustomed to every luxury obliged to travel on foot night and day suffering every description of misery until they arrived at Lisbon. Many died from want and fatigue. The miseries of war never struck us as forcibly. We felt for the poor creatures. But it was not in our power to relieve them. We were hard pressed by the crowd & with difficulty made our way through them to Condeixa and escaped the enemy.

We occupied a position in rear of Condeixa for the night and the cavalry picquets the front, was employed during the night at Condeixa in destroying our extensive magazines of cavalry appointments, supplies for hospitals, tea, brandy, wine, & tents, shirts, shoes, trowsers [sic] & tobacco and after a most disagreeable service without rest had to resume the march at daybreak. We continued to fall back by Pombal, Boa Vista, Batalha, Rio Mayor [Rio Maior], Alcoentre, by Sobral [de Monte Agraco] to Alenquer. At this place, we were nearly surprised by the enemy, through neglect in not posting picquets as they ought to have done. Our men were accoutred & in readiness to move in a moment & no bad consequences occurred with the exception of some officers losing their baggage & several their dinners which were left cooking at the fires, for the French upon their arrival to regale themselves with, particularly our General Crawford [Craufurd] who ought to have had a better look out. Our party were just on the eve of setting down to table, when we saw the French dragoons filing along the ridge of hills looking down upon us within almost musket shot. We had in consequence to make a flank movement during the night by Sobral & we entered Arruda [dos Vinhos], the small town below our station in the lines & the picquet post of our division. This was the first knowledge we had of those famous lines of Torres Vedras. This pretty little town of Arruda was beautifully situated and was a retreat for the rich merchants from Lisbon, their quintas splendidly furnished and made as luxurious as possible. It was altogether a little paradise, but how soon the scene was changed. It was plundered, burnt & utterly destroyed, all the valuable furniture of the houses thrown in the picquet fires to the disgrace of our army for unfortunately, we did not permit the enemy to get possession of it even for a moment to have borne part of the stigma. We took up our position in the lines on the 10 October where we continued until the 14 November. There was an affair above Sobral during the period in which we were as usual successful. During the night the enemy retired & on the 15 November. We followed him cautiously through Alenquer,

Azambuja, Cartaxo to Valle [de Santarém] on the Rio Mayor, where we found him strongly posted at Santarem with a considerable swamp below them & only to be crossed by a long & narrow causeway leading direct upon the centre of the enemy's position. We occupied our side of the causeway with a strong picquet and the French on their side with a strong abatis in their front, the Rio Mayor running between us.

On the 19 November we made a demonstration on the left of their position but after a little firing we withdrew. Probably the enemy was found too strongly posted and if an attack had been intended it was abandoned.

The 1811 Campaign

Massena held this position until the 5 March [1811]. We lost during our sejour at Valle several deserters, chiefly foreigners. We amused ourselves rabbit hunting with small dogs upon one occasion running into our game and giving our English death halloo, we observed the French cavalry picquet getting under arms & galloping down to the bank of the river in our direction evidently alarmed. We held up the rabbit & the officer seeing the cause of alarm, endeavoured to make it appear that he turned out to patrole along the bank of river, to our great amusement. We were often in the habit of receiving flags of truce and upon all such occasions civilities passed between us.

The enemy suddenly broke up from Santarem on the night of the 5 March and retired, leaving a straw figure to represent their advanced sentinel on the causeway. This deception was not discovered until orders were sent from headquarters to advance, stating that the French had abandoned their position. The intelligence was given by a peasant who crossed the river & reported it to Lord Wellington. It shows how vigilant an officer on advance picquet ought to be. Had more attention been paid in this instance the picquet would have discovered the enemy's retreat before intelligence could have arrived at headquarters.

We followed the enemy before daybreak to Piernes [Pernes] where we found the bridge destroyed & which took some time to repair. We then followed them to Pombal where they were strongly posted in front of the town. Upon exchanging some shots they retired in rear of their position occupying the old castle & town from whence they were driven with little loss. They next occupied a position at Redinha which they held on the 12 March. We had a sharp affair with them before they were driven from their ground. Our troops made a splendid display in this attack. In front of Redinha there was an open plain surrounded with wood.

The enemy occupied the village at the extreme end of this plain with a river in their front & a wooded country in the rear through which the road led they were to retire by. The heads of our columns showed themselves at different openings from the wood debouching into the plain & upon a signal given, they rapidly deployed into line and advanced in beautiful order supported by strong columns in reserve with large masses of cavalry ready for a charge, but they did not wait the onset but immediately retired firing the village whence some of their wounded perished, being burnt in the houses and retired upon Condeixa [-a-Nova] where they were strongly posted. The enemy intended to retire by Coimbra but finding that town occupied by Trant[23] with some Portuguese Ordinenza who had possession of the bridge & not being aware of his force which was unequal, to hold it, they suddenly took the mountain by the Puente da Murcella where we had a hard day's work to dislodge them. We commenced at daybreak on the 14 March & skirmished with them across those mountains until 3 pm. It was a difficult country to cross but our men were excellent light troops & we experienced little loss compared to the enemy. It was the best day's lesson in skirmishing we had had during the war. This affair took place at Cassel Nuova near the defiles of Miranda do Corvo.

The enemy abandoned some of their guns and burnt a large quantity of their baggage. On the 15 March we again overtook them late in the afternoon posted at the Foz d'Arouce immediately attacked them & pressed them so hard that many were driven into the river and perished. The passage of the bridge was so crowded that numbers were killed upon it & many forced into the stream & were drowned. It was supposed that independent of the sword about three hundred perished in the water. An eagle was discovered in the bed of the river the next morning.[24] It was dark during the latter part of the attack in the village & their expulsion was so sudden and unexpected that they were obliged to abandon their provisions and leave their kettles with the savoury contents boiling on their fires & well supplied with biscuit. This was indeed a prize to us for we had outstepped our commissariat and had not received bread for the last four days. We partook of the repast without ceremony and remained in the village during the night.

---

23. Brevet Colonel Nicholas Trant, a British officer in the Portuguese service.
24. The Eagle of the 39e Ligne Regiment was captured.

The scenes of cruelty, murder and rapine that everywhere presented themselves on this retreat are too horrible to describe. It was disgraceful to the French troops & left a stigma on the character of that brave & gallant soldier Ney whose [troops] then covered the retreat until relieved by Reynier's[25] at Sabugal.

After this affair we halted, finding the [River] Ceira swollen & also to give our commissariat time to overtake us as the troops were much in want of bread. The French withdrew from the Ceira on the evening of the 16 March and our division forded the river the next morning with great difficulty & danger & found the enemy in position on the Sierra de Moita, having destroyed the Puente de Murcella [Ponte da Mucela] and the bridge near Poimbien [Pombeiro da Beira].

Our columns were again put in motion to attack when the French recommenced their retreat and so rapidly that they destroyed a quantity of baggage & ammunition & even sacrificed some distant forage parties to the amount of some hundreds of men.

On the 21 March the French were at Celorico and in communication with Almeida, Reynier's Corps at Guarda. Some skirmishing took place in the neighbourhood of Celorico. The Light Division with the cavalry crossed on the 28 March the Mondego at Celorico & drove the enemy out of Freixedas.

On the 29th different columns of attack were directed upon the strong position of Guarda, when it was abandoned by the enemy. Had our cavalry pushed forward with more vigour the enemy must have suffered severely. General Slade[26] who commanded them was always late during this retreat.

On the 1 April our army reached the Coa & we found the right bank of that river occupied by the enemy. The Light Division suffered very much for want of bread during the last days of operations.

The commissariat found great difficulty in transporting their supplies to our advanced columns through the mountain country, our only means of transport being mules.

On the 3 April we had an affair with Reynier's corps at Sabugal on the Coa in which our regiment the 43rd displayed great gallantry & discipline. The morning was foggy with rain. The advanced cavalry and Light Division were under Sir William Erskine[27] and owing to want of

---

25. Marshal Jean Louis Reynier.

26. Major General John Slade commanded a cavalry brigade.

27. Major General Sir William Erskine temporarily commanded the Light Division in March and April 1811 during General Craufurd's absence in England

correct orders, the columns of attack were not properly directed. The cavalry & Elder's Portuguese corps [3rd Caçadores] were separated from us. The companies of the 95th Rifles attached to our brigade crossed the ford and were soon in action with the enemy's picquets. The 43rd Regiment took the same direction & crossed the ford about half a league to the right of Sabugal and as each company gained the opposite bank of the river it moved rapidly forward in support of the riflemen, each company getting into line as it arrived. We had scarcely formed when the riflemen were driven in and passed silently through our line, when immediately two strong columns of the enemy appeared in view. We were aware (by the peculiar noise of musquetry when near) that they were approaching but the weather was so thick we could see but a few yards before us. The 43rd Regiment stood alone to defend the ground, our 2nd Brigade not having yet passed the river, the whole of Reynier's Corps in our immediate front, but the fog prevented our relative situation from being seen. We immediately with a British cheer charged the columns routed them & threw them back in confusion upon their main body.

We had gained the low ground in our charge and discovered the enemy's main body strongly posted above us. We cautiously retired to our original ground and had scarcely gained it when three fresh columns of greater strength again advanced against us, the fog at this time in a degree clearing away, we discovered a wall in our front lined with one of the enemy's battalions with a howitzer in rear which had been dealing destruction in our ranks. We remained firm and steady under a heavy fire of grape & musquetry until the enemy's columns neared us, when we again charged them, routed them, drove the enemy from the wall and took the howitzer that had so much annoyed us. Our soldiers were so much excited and advanced with such rapidity that our front was rather scattered. Their cavalry took advantage of it and imperceptibly gained our flank and charged along our front. The greater part of the battalion took shelter behind the small wall & formed up, others behind some trees that offered a certain protection & we drove them from the field, preserving the howitzer from being retaken.

About this time the 2nd Brigade arrived; the 2nd Battalion 52nd formed on our right and the remainder a second line when we again charged & drove the enemy before us. Another division of the army showed themselves on the left and the enemy retired in columns. Colonel

on leave.

Sidney Beckwith[28] commanded our brigade & showed during this action great coolness & firmness.

Colonel Patrickson[29] commanded the 43rd in this gallant & distinguished action as brilliant as any during the war. Our loss in the 43rd was only between 70 & 80 men killed & wounded. The enemy suffered considerably, our musquetry fire much more destructive than the French's.

[On] 4 April the Light Division moved on Valdespina [Vale do Espinho] in search of the enemy. They continued their retreat with great regularity and on the 5th crossed the frontier into Spain.

On the 7 April a French brigade was driven across the Pass of Barba del Puerco with severe loss, the last of the French Army in Portugal. It was said that Massena (Prince of Essling) entered Portugal with 65,000 men & had received reinforcements of about 10,000 when at Santarem, but re-crossed into Spain with a reduced force of between 40 & 50,000 men.

The French withdrew to Salamanca and our division occupied Gallegos [de Arganan], Alemida [La Alameda de Gardon] & Espeja and the rest of the troops the line of the Coa. Headquarters at Villa Formosa [Vilar Formoso].

We had an affair of picquets at the bridge of Marialva [Marialba] on the 23 April. The 52nd Regiment was engaged in that affair & another on the Azava [River Azaba] on the 27 April. The enemy's sudden retreat from Sabugal left Almeida exposed, which was then but badly provisioned and we immediately blockaded it.

On the 2 May the French threw a large convoy into Ciudad Rodrigo. We fell back from Gallegos [de Arganan] towards the plains of Fuentes d'Onoro & on the 3 May our division filed through the village of Fuentes and took post on the high ground behind [La] Alameda [de Gardon]. Our troops were now concentrated behind the Dos Casas River. We all experienced the greatest regret to see the village of Fuentes plundered and destroyed and the poor inhabitants driven destitute from their homes. Our regiment had occupied it during the last year & the people were well known to us. It was a beautiful & retired village, its inhabitants perfectly primitive, good, kind & hospitable, appeared to enjoy all the happiness of a quiet, simple & retired life, until that dreadful scourge

---

28. Lieutenant Colonel Thomas Sidney Beckwith 95th Rifles commanded the 1st Brigade of the Light Division between August 1810 and July 1811.
29. Major Christopher Patrickson, 43rd Foot, who became a lieutenant colonel on 30 May 1811.

war suddenly drove them from their homes & property to poverty & misery. Poor Camillo's family we greatly pitied; a good Spaniard who possessed large flocks and great property as a farmer, his daughter Josepha beautiful & lovely with some fine young men [as] sons, were all driven from the shelter of their homes. We collected a subscription for the poor inhabitants. The left of our army rested near Fort Conception [Concepción] and our right at Fuentes [de Oñoro] with the river in our front.

On the 3 May the enemy attacked with great vigour and drove our people from the village of Fuentes [de Oñoro]. It was soon regained by a determined charge made by the brigade composed of the 24th, 71st & 79th Regiments[30] and they drove the enemy across the Dos Casas. In these contests we suffered as well as the enemy severe loss; our troops continued to occupy the village during the night & next day the 4 May, some changes of position took place in both armies.

On the 5 May, the enemy were observed moving troops to their left & in consequence our division & the cavalry were sent to support our right, where the French had already commenced their attack, some changes having been already made by their cavalry on our arrival on the right. We were thrown into square being threatened by their dragoons, the ground being particularly favourable for cavalry. They had already charged & been repulsed by the Chasseurs Britanniques[31] who were formed in line under Colonel Eustace,[32] Norman Ramsay's[33] guns (a troop of Horse Artillery) were for a moment cut off by the rapid advance of the French cavalry. They however in a most dashing manner reformed, drove through the enemy & regained our troops in full view of our square. Our right drew back being outflanked by the enemy. Indeed, our position was too extended on that flank to protect it & we retired in squares, every moment threatened by their cavalry & under a heavy cannonade, but having soon concentrated in a closed & more secure position, the enemy abandoned the idea of forcing our right.

During this day's contest there was some hard fighting in the village of Fuentes [de Oñoro]. The lower part was taken & retaken several times.

---

30. The Second Brigade of the First Division consisted of the 2/24th, 1/79th and the 2/42nd. The 1/71st was part of a different brigade of the same division.
31. A regiment of French émigrés that was incorporated into the British army.
32. Lieutenant Colonel William Eustace, Chasseurs Britanniques.
33. Second Captain William Norman Ramsay.

Both armies suffered severely. Colonel Cameron 79th[34] a gallant young officer was killed with many other valuable officers & men. Our troops retained the upper part of the town to where the river divides it.

In the evening our brigade occupied the village & other troops were withdrawn. Our officers & men were well accustomed to the outpost duty & we quietly occupied all the advanced posts directing our men not to fire excepting under great emergency and by this well-timed precaution, quiet was soon established in the village where a continued roar of musquetry had been hitherto kept up.

We exchanged the dead & wounded that were lying along our advanced posts & continued in occupation of it to the 10th having strongly entrenched ourselves.

On the 10 May the enemy retired across the Agueda and thus ended the Battle of Fuentes d'Oñoro. Our force was estimated at about 35,000 and the French at about 50,000 men. During this night General Brenier[35] with great skill and ability blew up the works of Almeida & retired with its garrison through the British lines and finally made his escape by the pass of Barba del Puerco with some loss. This could not have been done had the blockading force been attentive to their duty, Lord Wellington issued severe orders in consequence of it.

The French troops withdrew to Salamanca. Our division formed part of the force left with Sir Brent Spencer on the Azava [Azaba] while Lord Wellington with two divisions moved to the south to the relief of [Marshal] Beresford & for the purpose of attacking Badajoz. It was invested on the 5 May and on the 12th the siege was raised; on the 16th the Battle of Albuera was fought & won by British valour but with a dreadful loss of brave men. It was as hard a contested battle as any fought during the war.

The Light Division again occupied its old station & we took possession of Gallegos [de Argañán], [La] Alameda [de Gardón] and Espeja where we continued until the 6 June. On the 29 May they broke ground before Badajoz. The attack was made on Fort San Christoval. Our troops failed in two assaults and suffered a severe loss.

On the 10 June, the stores & guns were removed & the attack turned into a blockade, Marmont having introduced a convoy into Ciudad Rodrigo, moved out of that fortress on the 6 June, directing his march on Gallegos [de Argañá] & Espeja, the villages occupied by us.

---

34. Lieutenant Colonel Philips Cameron, 79th Foot, was severely wounded at Fuentes de Oñoro and died of his wounds on 13 May 1811.
35. General Antoine Brenier de Montmorand, commanding at Almeida, escaped with over a thousand men.

We retired across the plain upon Alfaiates and General Spencer who now commanded our force in the north withdrew the troops behind the Coa. Finding the French moving by the pass of Baños we directed our route by Soito, Penamacor and crossed the pontoon bridge at Villa Velha [Vila Velha de Rodao] by Niza [Nisa] and arrived at Arronches on the 22 June & took up our ground at Monte Reguingo [Reguengo] on the banks of the Ceira [Caia], ready to move into the position behind Campo Maior when necessary. During our sejour on the Ceira [Caia] a squadron of the 11th Dragoons were cut off by the enemy & a portion of the 2nd German Hussars escaped with severe loss. On the 20 July Marmont retraced his steps to Salamanca and our division to the banks of the Agueda. We returned by Portalegre, Castelo de Vide, Niza [Nisa], Castelo Branco & occupied our old cantonments. We had possession of Fuente de Guinaldo [Fuenteguinaldo]. We arrived there on the 9 August and continued quiet until the 23 September when the French advanced with a strong convoy for the relief of Ciudad Rodrigo. We retired by Soito & Rendo near to Castelo Branco.

During these operations we had two affairs with the enemy in which our troops displayed their usual gallantry, the most serious at El Bodon & the other at Aldeia da Ponte. When Marmont had accomplished his object of succouring Ciudad Rodrigo he returned to Salamanca & we again to the same cantonments where we continued until the end of the year.

Don Julian Sanchez the famous guerrilla chief on the 15 October carried off & from under the guns of [Ciudad] Rodrigo their governor General Renaud[36] & about two hundred head of cattle.

General Hill in a most able manner on the 28 October surprised the French General Girard at Arroyo Molinos [Arroyomolinos] and out of a force of 3,000 men, a few hundred only escaped. We only lost in this dashing exploit about 60 or 70 killed & wounded.

During the month of December Tarifa made a noble defence & the chief credit of that defence is to be given to Colonel Charles Smith Royal Engineers[37] & Captain Mitchell Royal Artillery.[38] The enemy having made an extensive breach in the walls assaulted the place on the night of the 30 December but were repulsed with great loss.

The French during a period of heavy rain in November managed to get a convoy with a new governor into Ciudad Rodrigo & withdrew before the river had fallen. Thus ended the campaign of 1811.

---

36. General Antoine Francois Renauld.
37. Second Captain Charles Felix Smith, Royal Engineers.
38. Second Captain Edward Michell, Royal Artillery.

The 1812 Campaign

The campaign of 1812 commenced early. On the 8 January our division assembled from its cantonments and invested Ciudad Rodrigo. During the night six companies of volunteers, mine of the number, under Colonel Colbourne [Colborne] 52nd Regiment carried in a most masterly way by escalade the outwork of San Francisco, our loss trifling & we took with the exception of one man its entire garrison and immediately commenced our first parallel on the spot. We broke ground under a heavy fire from the town but soon established a good cover.

The duties of the trenches were taken alternately by the Light, 1st, 3rd, & 4th Divisions of the army & we relieved each other every 24 hours returning to our cantonments, a distance of 4 leagues when relieved. The weather was severe with sharp frosts which rendered it too harassing to keep the troops longer in the field. We had to force the Agueda on going & returning. It was cold work for the foot men breaking through the ice with their naked legs. We always made our men strip on such occasions if not near an enemy or not in great force to feel the consequence of the delay caused by it.[39] During the siege the enemy kept up a heavy & incessant fire, threw many 13-inch shells and from the nature of the ground we suffered a good deal from them.

It was stormed and carried on the 19th January. Two breaches having been pronounced practicable.

Having commanded the storming party of the 43rd Regiment composed of 100 volunteers with a proportion of subaltern officers viz Lieutenants Brumwell, Steele & O'Connell, and finding night attacks are in some degree confused, have entered into the following detail as an eyewitness of what is related, & being the officer in command of that portion of the Light Division storming party ordered to clear the ramparts to the great breach. The little breach being the one intended to be attacked by the Light Division.

On 19 January 1812 at about 8 pm the storming party of the Light Division was formed behind the convent of San Francisco and consisted of 100 volunteers with officers from each British regiment in the division. The 43rd party commanded by Captain James Fergusson,[40] the 52nd by

---

39. Proving the falsity of the claims that the Light infantry marched through the rivulets fully dressed, a sure guarantee of mass disease.
40. The author.

Captain Jones[41] & the 95th Rifles by Captain Mitchell,[42] the whole under Major George Napier 52nd, a forlorn hope[43] of 25 rank & file under Lieutenant Gurwood 52nd.[44]

Major Napier gave orders that when the breach was carried, the 43rd party was to clear the ramparts to the right towards the great breach and the 52nd party to the left. The riflemen followed in general the latter direction but forgot what their orders were.

The forlorn hope led and immediately after the storming party. We hurried to the attack hearing the fire from the 3rd Division who were ordered to attack at the same time the great breach. An engineer officer was with us. The 43rd were in front & we advanced rapidly across the glacis & descended into the ditch near the ravelin under a heavy fire. We found the forlorn hope placing ladders against the face of the work and to which spot our party turned when the engineer officer called out 'You are wrong this is the way to the breach in the fausse braie which leads to the breach you are to attack', immediately calling the men to come on we ascended the breach in the fausse braie and soon reached the breach in the body of the place without the use of ladders. We remained for a few moments on the breach until we had collected about twenty or thirty officers & men when we cheered & rushed in carrying the breach. A gun stretched across the entrance, near which some of the enemy were bayonetted and among the number some deserters from the Light Division in arms defending it against their countrymen. A soldier of the name of Jonathan Wild 43rd Regiment was the first man that mounted the breach in the fausse braie, but no individual could claim being the first that entered the breach in the body of the place. It was a simultaneous rush of from twenty to thirty of us, some men of the 3rd Battalion Rifles among the number who had been ordered to line the crest of the glacis. Major Napier commanding the party must have fallen wounded about this time, as we did not see him after we carried the breach.

The forlorn hope were not the first to enter the breach. They were thrown in some degree behind in having mistaken the point of attack and being engaged in placing ladders against the face of the work instead of

---

41. Captain William Jones, 52nd Foot.
42. Captain Samuel Mitchell, 2nd Battalion, 95th Foot.
43. An advanced party of volunteers would lead the assault, to draw the initial fire of the defenders before the assault column arrived. Officers volunteering to lead the 'forlorn hope' could expect a field promotion if they survived, for their bravery.
44. Lieutenant John Gurwood, 52nd Foot.

moving to the breach in the fausse braie. Lieutenant Alexander Steele 43rd Regiment was with the officer commanding the forlorn hope & well remembered those circumstances. Upon carrying the little breach, the 43rd party cleared the ramparts to the right and drove the enemy from the different traverses they attempted to defend until they arrived near the great breach at a spot where the enemy's defences of that breach were overlooked; at this time the great breach had not been carried and was powerfully defended by the enemy. It appeared to us that the houses bearing upon it were loop-holed and a deep trench lined with musquetry also. The flanks of the breach were cut off and the descent into the town from the top of it appeared considerable, so as to render it in our opinion exceedingly difficult if not impossible to force it while defended as above stated. The moment the Light Division storming party arrived at the spot described, they made a determined attack upon the defences of the enemy having taken them in flank and at the same moment the 3rd Division storming party entered the breach and Ciudad Rodrigo was instantly carried, little resistance having been made after the breaches were taken. [I] was wounded in the body at this time and carried back by one of the men a little way on the rampart when an explosion took place which blew up several of our party on the spot we had just quitted.

[I] was immediately supported along the rampart and as we were descending the breach, we met the head of the 43rd Regiment. Captain Duffy's[45] company in front entering the breach, this proves that the storming party's carried the place before the division entered and it also proves that the great breach was not carried until the 2nd Division party turned its defences. It appeared to us to be next to impossible to force the great breach by a front attack only, as long as the enemy held their defences, but the moment our storming party had turned those defences, the breach was carried.

The Light Division was ordered to advance to the breach in double column of sections, the 43rd to the right and the 52nd to the left on entering, but night attacks admit of great irregularities and many officers and men left their division and followed the storming party. The town became the usual scene of sack & plunder. Our General Crawford [Craufurd] was killed on the glacis or in the ditch during the assault (and died of his wounds the next morning).

---

45. Captain John Duffy, 43rd Foot.

We returned to our cantonments where we remained about six weeks. During this period [I] was confined from the wound received in the assault, a musquet ball having lodged under the backbone. [I] was however sufficiently recovered to accompany the regiment about the end of February on their march to Badajoz.

On the 7 March we were in the neighbourhood of Castelo de Vide and arrived at Elvas on the 16 March from whence we moved on the 17th to Badajoz and in conjunction with the 3rd & 4th Divisions invested the fortress. We broke ground during the night in a storm of wind & rain and established a good cover before daybreak when we were discovered by the enemy, the storm and darkness of the night having concealed us during a dangerous service.

Our duties in the siege were harassing, [I] was wounded in the side by the splinter of a shell when on covering party on the 25 March. During that night Fort Picurina was carried by escalade by the parties in the trenches under Major General Kempt,[46] but our loss was severe.

[I] was recovered sufficiently to take the command of the volunteers for the storming party on the 6th April, the night of the assault. The three British regiments viz 43rd, 52nd & 95th Rifles furnished each 100 volunteers with officers as at Ciudad Rodrigo under the command of Major O'Hare 95th Rifles (killed). Captain Jones commanding 52nd party (killed), Captain Crampton 95th party, killed (died of his wounds) & Lieutenant Harvest 43rd Regiment forlorn hope (killed). This turned out the most desperate service we had yet been employed upon. Our storming party were descending from the covert way into the ditch in profound silence when in a moment (the enemy having been well prepared for us) let loose every implement of destruction. The scene was beyond description terrific. It was one blaze of fire, from various explosions & a continued roar of musquetry which soon levelled our party, very few having escaped. [I] was amongst that fortunate number having received only a slight wound in the head. I had at this time three wounds open, I received a medal as the senior surviving officer of the Light Division storming party.

The breaches were not practicable & it was impossible to carry them. The French had strongly retrenched the breaches and had cut them off from the bastion St Maria to the bastion Trinidad. On the top of the breach a chevaux de frise of sword blades immovable and on the sloping part of the breach were planks attached above that could be let down

---

46. Major General James Kempt, commanding 1st Brigade of the 3rd Division.

or pulled up by the enemy at pleasure. These were moreover covered with spikes & when let down threw the assailants over, rolling down on those behind. Various attempts were made both by the Light and Fourth Divisions but in vain and we at last owed our success to the escalade of the 3rd Division at the castle & the 5th Division the escalade of the bastion San Vincente.

Our three fine British regiments as gallant and as well-disciplined soldiers as ever stood under arms suffered a dreadful loss in this assault. We commenced with 2,400 men, lost 1,200 killed & wounded, the latter chiefly bad, owing to the very destructive fire. Our gallant young chief Lieutenant Colonel Macleod 43rd Regiment fell on the breach. Four officers only of the regiment were able to attend his funeral and follow his remains to the grave. He was an honourable, fine & gallant spirit. We had, 43rd Regiment, 25 officers killed & wounded & 40 rank & file.

On the 11 April we returned to our old cantonments in the neighbourhood of Ciudad Rodrigo. [I] was confined from the wound in my back some time at Castelo Branco, but having the ball at last extracted immediately relieved me & [I] was soon able to rejoin the regiment in their cantonments at Fuente de Guinaldo [Fuenteguinaldo] where we continued until the middle of June 1812. At this time the Light Division made a movement upon Salamanca. The French previous to abandoning this place left garrisons in three forts they had constructed in the town by the sacrifice of some of its finest buildings & which perfectly commanded it. In due time but with some loss we got possession of these forts & their garrisons.

On the 26 June we took post at Aldea de Lingua [Aldealengua] in consequence of a movement made by the enemy, the French having crossed the Tormes and taking up the line of Toro & Tordesillas behind the Douro.

On the 16 July during the night we were put in motion and took up a position near Castrejon on the Trabancos [Castreón de Trabancos]. While in this position a disgraceful cavalry affair took place within our view. [I] was detached a little in advance with 5 companies 43rd Regiment in consequence of some movements of the enemy on our left. At no very considerable distance on a small height were posted two guns of Ross's troop & two squadrons of British cavalry to keep a look out while Lord Wellington was making a reconnaissance. Two squadrons of French cavalry, to all appearance not stronger than our own, advanced at rather a rapid rate and as they had some distance to pass over, they were visible to us for some time before they arrived at the height occupied by the British squadrons. We saw our dragoons move up the hill to meet the enemy and even saw the left squadron exchange sabre cuts, when suddenly the right squadron gave way & the left followed, and the French dragoons shouting at their heels fairly rode them into our camp. The French were led by a dashing officer, who we were delighted to see at last escape. Lord Wellington & Beresford with their orderlies rallied the runaways and drove back the enemy. Some of the most advanced [of] the officers in the number, passed close under our musquetry. Not a soldier fired. Our men were hurt at the retreat of their cavalry (British) and were anxious that these few gallant fellows should escape. A brave soldier always admires dashing & bold conduct in his opponent. The French officer was closely pursued and received some several sabre cuts. Notwithstanding he regained his own troops & we heard of his recovery afterward although badly wounded.

During the day & from the 18th to the 21 July, the movements of both armies over that fine country more resembled the order of review than battle. We moved in parallel lines ready to take advantage of each other, should a fault be committed. We moved under cannonade & our columns of division often marching at attention & with the greatest exactness.

On the 21st we crossed the Tormes above Salamanca. This movement was made after dark in one of the severest storms of thunder & lightning we had ever experienced. The lightning was so vivid that many of us were blinded for some moments. We heard several of our cavalry horses galloping about having broken from their pickets. Some of them fell into the enemy's hands. We halted on the banks of the river for the remainder of the night and on the morning of the 22 July the Battle of Salamanca was fought.

During the movements of the French army on the 22nd, Lord Wellington was anxiously waiting for Marmont to commit some mistake or to make some false movement. He patiently watched him until the afternoon when Marmont attempted to cut in upon our communication on our right. This was the signal for attack & without loss of time the British columns were put in motion. A column on our extreme right under Sir Edward Pakenham[47] commenced the battle which only ended in the dark glorious for the British Army. The Light Division towards the end of the day moved in line for a considerable distance towards the Tormes in the direction of the ford of Huerta in as good order as at a review and to the admiration of Lord Wellington, but owing to

---

47. Major General the Honourable Edward Pakenham commanded the Third Division.

Don Carlos d'España having abandoned Alba de Tormes the French escaped by that bridge in place of crossing the ford at Huerta which they otherwise would have been obliged to do. We bivouacked on the banks of the river for the night. Major General Le Marchant[48] was killed in a brilliant charge of cavalry made by the British on the enemy's left.

On the 23 July we overtook the rear guard of the French troops, consisting of a brigade of infantry with cavalry & artillery posted on the heights above Lerna [La Lurda], when Bock's Brigade of Heavy German cavalry made one of the most memorable charges during the war, having actually rode down the enemy's infantry and capturing the rear guard, but the Germans suffered considerably.[49] We arrived on the ground immediately after and saw many of these splendid men and horses dead, close to the enemy's column. It was a most daring and dashing service and reflected great credit upon the Germans. They were invaluable to our army and possessed much more information and experience than the English dragoons.

We passed Penaranda [Peñaranda de Bracamonte], Olmedo and on the 26 July arrived on the banks of the Douro near Valladolid where we halted for a couple of days, which gave up the opportunity of visiting the town, the French having abandoned it. It brought to our recollection Gil Blas & Doctor Sangrado.[50] A division of infantry and cavalry were detached to watch the enemy's motions and we moved upon Madrid.

On the 7 August we were at Segovia a fine old romantic town beautifully situated. There is a fine old Roman aqueduct built without cement. The tower in which Le Sage confines his hero Gil Blas is well described by him. Segovia in some degree resembles Edinburgh. Passed near the palace (hunting lodge) of El Rio Frio[51] on the 8 August and next day crossed the Guadarama mountains and bivouacked in the park of the Escurial. It is a fine situation, a heavy mass of building, you may fancy a resemblance to the gridiron when looking down upon it from the mountains. The mausoleum is handsome, its form an octagon. In the different recesses of its sides lay the remains of the Spanish monarchs. It is built of variegated marble, with a beautiful winding stair of the same material. It is lighted by a large lamp which is always burning.

---

48. Major General John Gaspard Le Marchant commanding the Heavy Cavalry Brigade.
49. The Action at Garcihernandez.
50. The hero of the novel *L'Histoire de Gil Blas de Santilanne*, by Alain-Rene Lesage. Doctor Sangrado was another character in the novel.
51. Palacio Real de Riofrio.

On the 13 August we entered Madrid in the midst of rejoicing, greeted by the Spaniards with the greatest enthusiasm. It was a most exciting scene. Madrid is a walled town with fine approaches and handsome gates at the different entrances, the streets regular & the houses in general magnificent. We remained some time in this luxurious capital where we fared well, the women lovely & graceful. The palace[52] not surpassed by any in Europe, several fine pictures. The enemy left a garrison in the Fort La China in the El Retiro which soon surrendered.[53] The walks of the El Retiro form the public promenade, is beautiful and admirably adapted for it. In the evening all the beauty of Madrid exhibit on the promenade, and a brilliant display it is.

On the 23 October, we moved in the direction of Alcala [de Henares], in consequence of Lord Wellington's want of success against Burgos and some movements in the French army. Their troops under Soult, Jourdan, & King Joseph in person were in motion upon Aranjuez.

The Light Division having made some marches in the neighbourhood of Alcala [de Henares] fell back on Madrid on the 30 October, bivouacked outside the gates during the day, joined by another division during the afternoon and at night with reluctance bid farewell to Madrid & commenced our retreat to Salamanca; (called the retreat from Burgos). We retired by the Escorial and the pass of the Guadarama, and on the 7 November were at Alba de Tormes where we formed a junction with Lord Wellington from Burgos, our division having been under Lord Hill in his retreat from Madrid.

The French crossed the Tormes in force on the 14 November and we assembled on our old battlefield. On the 15 November there was some cannonading and we retired in the afternoon in most unfavourable weather, with continued heavy rain. The enemy followed us close & from the nature of the country we suffered some loss. We retired through woods sufficiently open to move without inconvenience, but our view was too much interrupted & in consequence irregularities took place.

On the 17th the French dragoons showed themselves in our bivouac before we had commenced our march and closely pursued us during the day. Lieutenant General E[dward] Paget was taken prisoner between our divisions, and we also lost some baggage, the wooded nature of the country concealing the enemy from our view enabled them to take these

---

52. The Royal Palace of Madrid.
53. The Retiro was a fort constructed around the old royal porcelain factory. Being short of water and aware of the real danger of the fort exploding if fired upon, it surrendered. A mass of stores were captured and two eagles.

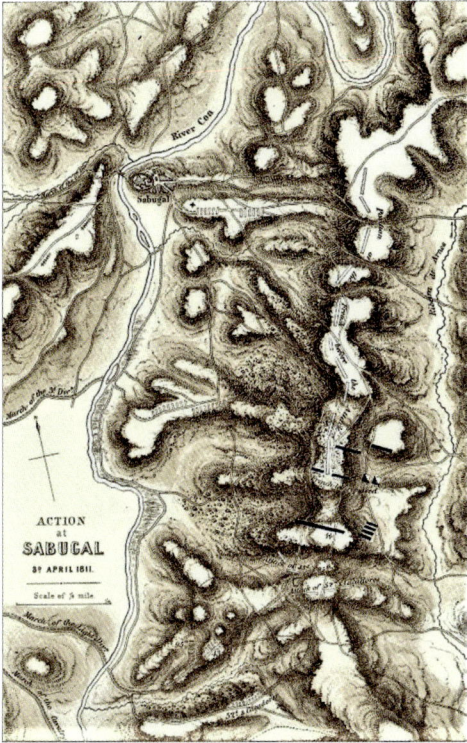

The Action at Sabugal, 3 April 1811, by Col. James.

The Storming of Ciudad Rodrigo, 19 January 1812, by Col. James.

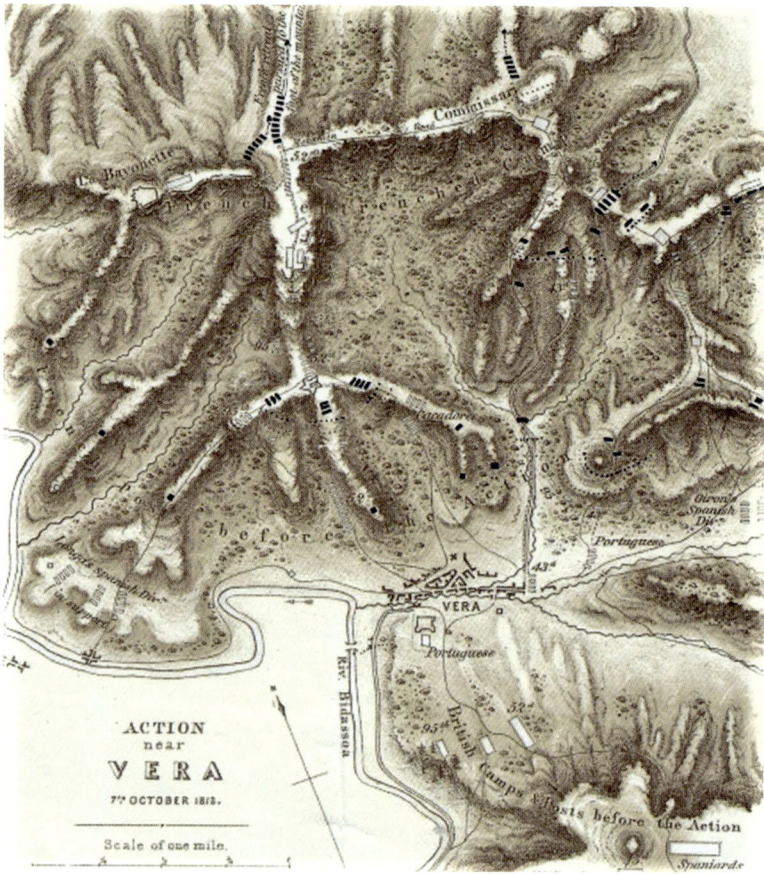

The Action at Vera, 7 October 1813, by Col. James.

The Letters of Lieutenant John Meyricke.

The 43rd capture a cannon at Sabugal, by Richard Simpkin.

The retreat of the 43rd over the bridge at the Coa, by Richard Simpkin.

Lieutenant George Brown
(as General Sir George Brown).

Lieutenant Richard Brunton
(as a major in 13 Light
Dragoons).

advantages. The enemy's cavalry hovered so close to us at times that we were obliged to form squares and as we approached San Munoz their infantry columns made their appearance and we were obliged to cover our retreat across the rivulet with skirmishers which in some degree protected the columns that had to ford. We were exposed to a heavy cannonade passing the rivulet in addition to the musquetry & experienced some loss. We continued exposed to fire for some time after crossing and at last withdrew and bivouacked in the low swampy ground in heavy rain for the night & which continued during the next day when we retired upon Ciudad Rodrigo and occupied the environs of that fortress. The enemy did not follow us this day but withdrew. Thus ended the retreat from Burgos.

Our troops went into cantonments and the campaign of 1812 closed. It commenced in January & ended late in November. We laid the remains of poor George Ridout[54] of the 43rd under the little breach of Ciudad Rodrigo, a worthy man and excellent soldier, he died from the effects of a wound received on the 17 November at San Munoz.

The 1813 Campaign

James Fergusson left the 43rd Foot and was initially appointed as a major in the 79th Foot on 3 December 1812, but he was then appointed to join the 85th Foot on 25 January 1813. However, as the remainder of his memoir of his part in the Napoleonic wars is quite short, I have included it here in full.

[I] was appointed to a majority by purchase in the 79th Regiment by the recommendation of Lord Wellington in December 1812 and in the following month, January 1813, was removed to the 85th Regiment and was obliged to return to England to join them at Hythe in Kent, where we continued for a few months and again in August 1813 joined Lord Wellington's army. We were appointed to Lord Aylmer's Brigade[55] attached to the 1st Division & were stationed in the neighbourhood of San Sebastian during the siege. We covered the great road between Irun and Oyarzun [Oiartzun] in communication with a Spanish corps on the heights of San Marcial, when Sir Thomas Graham returned home for the purpose of commanding a separate corps in the neighbourhood

---

54. Lieutenant George Ridout, 43rd Foot, died of his wounds received at San Munoz on 23 November 1812.
55. Major General Lord Matthew Aylmer.

of Bergen-op-Zoom and General Sir John Hope[56] took the command of the left column. We continued quiet until San Sebastian fell and on the 7 October the different columns of the British army were formed at daybreak. The passage of the Bidasoa was carried in a most gallant manner and the enemy driven from every point he attempted to defend. Our troops gained a position commanding a fine view of the plains of La Belle France, a cheering sight to a British army to look down upon that country hitherto considered invulnerable & whose armies had been overrunning all Europe. We crossed at fords above the 5th Division & in view of Fuenterrabia,[57] that division met with great resistance which they gallantly overcame and gained the enemy's position. The French now retreated and intrenched themselves strongly in front of San Jean de Luz. We remained in our present positions until the fall of Pamplona.

On the 10 November 1813 our columns of attack were again formed to force the enemy's intrenchments along the line of the Nivelle. Our regiment carried Urogne [Urrugne] with little loss and the different columns along our line were successful in their attacks and at nightfall we were obliged to desist, but were established considerably in advance particularly on their right which obliged them during the night to retire, leaving all the guns in their intrenched works & about 1,500 prisoners. We lost in this day's operations about 2,000 men, the enemy considerably more. They destroyed all the bridges on their route.

On the 11 November late in the day after the bridges had been repaired, we crossed the river at San Jean de Luz and the enemy retired to the neighbourhood of Bidart on the road to Bayonne. We had heavy & continued rains during these movements. From the state of the weather, it was found advisable to put us in cantonments on the main Bayonne road. Headquarters were established at San Jean de Luz. The enemy withdrew into his intrenched camp in front of Bayonne,

We had a line of outposts established to cover our cantonments from surprise. Our right & centre guarded the left bank of the Nive at Cambo [les Bains], Ustaritz & in front of Arcangues & our left wing continued it to the sea between Bidart & Biarritz crossing the great Bayonne road at the house of Bacouillett the Mayor of Biarritz.

---

56. Lieutenant General Sir John Hope.
57. Now Hondarribia.

We continued in our cantonments to the 9 December 1813 when the weather improving we made a forward movement and were engaged along one entire line. The weather again becoming unfavourable we returned to our cantonments during the night.

On the morning of the 10 December the French attacked the 5th Division, in the neighbourhood of the mayor's house and the Light Division at Arcangues but were eventually repulsed.

On the 11 December the 5th Division drove in the enemy's picquet & re-established the original line of advanced sentries withdrawn in consequence of the attack on the 10th. In the afternoon the French rather unexpectedly, when our men were employed in cutting wood for their fires, made a sudden attack on the 5th Division and at first caused some confusion advancing rapidly until nearly in possession of the mayor's house when our brigade was brought up fresh to support the 5th Division, when they were immediately driven back with some loss. These attacks continued to the 13 December when the enemy finding he could not anywhere penetrate our position but was defeated in all his attempts, he at night withdrew within the intrenched camp between the Nive & the Adour.

All these affairs occupied five successive days from the 9th to the 13 December 1813 on the banks of the Nive. We lost during these operations nearly 5,000 men British & Portuguese. We again returned to our cantonments.

The 1814 Campaign

On the 14 January 1814 we moved up and took the outposts in turn with the other brigades of the 1st Division & occupied the ground in front of the mayor's house.

On the night of the 22 February the 1st Division moved and under our escort, a brigade of 18 pounders were conveyed to the banks of the Adour towards its mouth. We moved through the Bois de Bayonne and the next day the guns were placed in battery on the extreme left opposite to the right flank of the enemy's intrenched camp.

On the 23 February our brigade and the 1st Division kept up a smart fire during the day against the intrenched camp, to occupy the enemy's attention while a small detachment of the Guards were endeavouring to get across the Adour in a small ferry boat they had got possession of. When they had accomplished this with 500 men, the enemy discovered it and immediately detached a superior force to oppose them, in which they were unsuccessful & our gallant little party aided by some excellent rockets & the guns on our side of the Adour drove the enemy back upon Bayonne & our force was rapidly increasing during the night in the event of another attempt by the enemy to dislodge them.

On the 24 February the 1st Division continued ferrying over the river and they bivouacked upon the sandhills during the night. Captain O'Reilly[58] after a dangerous & difficult service succeeding in getting his flotilla across the bar and into the mouth of the river but with a severe loss he sailed up with his different vessels and by the evening of the 26 February, established a most excellent bridge across the Adour.

The bridge consisted of 26 chasse-marées firmly anchored at the bows & stern, to resist the current both at ebb & flow tide; they were also lashed together at the bows & stern to render the whole as little liable as possible to disconnection. Five strong cables were stretched by capstans across the middle of the vessels, and upon these strong planks were placed, & strongly lashed to the outer cables, making a strong platform, sufficiently pliable to adapt itself to the rise & fall of the vessel with the tide. Major Todd of the Staff Corps[59] was in charge of the bridge. Bayonne was now completely blockaded by us.

On the 27 February we heard the cannonade at Orthez. That afternoon we more closely invested Bayonne and this movement was ably conducted by our General Sir J[ohn] Hope and we commenced our preparations for the siege. Our picquets were stationed so near that we were obliged to be very cautious and keep under cover. We continued this harassing service until 14 April, when the enemy made a sudden sortie, drove in all our out picquets & gained possession of all the buildings of the village of St Etienne taking several prisoners and were only repulsed when the brigades of the Guards & the Germans were able to make a combined charge by signal which drove the enemy before them & they hastily fled for their fortress leaving the field covered with their dead.

Our loss was severe but the enemy in killed & wounded lost considerably more. It was to be regretted that the French should have made this ill-advised attack sacrificing the lives of so many brave soldiers at a time when peace reigned for Bonaparte was known to have abdicated the throne.

On the 28 April at midday the white flag was hoisted at Bayonne and thus terminated the contest. Lord Wellington appointed me to a lieutenant

---

58. Commander Dowell O'Reilly, Royal Navy, became a full captain on 29 August 1815.
59. Brevet Major Alexander Todd, Royal Staff Corps.

colonelcy in the Buffs[60] by purchase and was directed by General Order to take command of the regiment until His Royal Highness the Prince Regent's pleasure was known. Returned from Bayonne to England and took command of the 2nd Battalion at Brighton where we made a most agreeable séjour of about a year. [I] was presented to the Prince Regent and attended all the pavilion parties during that period. In the summer of 1815 marched to Hythe in Kent where in the month of December our 2nd Battalion was reduced and we [were] placed upon half pay.

[I] was at the Military College for some months in 1816. In the spring of 1817 paid a visit to my old regiment the 43rd stationed at Valenciennes in France, being part of the force of the Army of Occupation. Left London on the 11 March 1817 & from Calais travelled to Valenciennes, visited all the places in the neighbourhood, saw our troops and the Russians at Mauberge [sic] reviewed by H[is] R[oyal] Highness the Duke of Kent accompanied by the duchess. Visited the different places occupied by the various contingents of the allied powers viz English, Russians, Prussians, Austrians, Hanoverians, Saxons & Danes. Travelled through the Low Countries & Holland, down the Rhine from Strasbourg visiting all the strong places on this route and returned to Cambrai to see the grand & last review of the Allied troops in presence of the Emperor Alexander, the King of Prussia, the Prince of Orange and their suites. This review took place previous to the army breaking up and returning to their different countries. It was a grand military display. The troops of each nation in different columns having a supposed enemy in their front, moved between Cambrai & Valenciennes threw their pontoons over the river & crossed under a heavy cannonade. A large force of artillery & cavalry in the field, several good charges made by the latter. Upon arriving at the open ground overlooking Valenciennes, the troops passed the Allied sovereigns in review order, and the next morning they were all in motion for their different countries. Some of the Cossacques [Cossacks] had to return to the walls of China. There was a grand ball given by the Duke of Wellington at the theatre of Valenciennes to the sovereigns in the evening.

Left Valenciennes for Paris the next day where we remained for the winter and returned to England by Calais in March 1818. Visited Scotland during the shooting season and returned to London early 1819.

Battles, Sieges & Actions engaged in during the War in the

---

60. 3rd Foot.

Peninsular

Vimeira (Portugal)		21 August 1808
Corunna (Spain)		16 June 1809
Coa (near Almeida) Light Division		24 July 1810
Busaco (Portugal)		27 September 1810
Pombal (Portugal)	Massena's retreat	11 March 1811
Redinha	" "	12 March 1811
Casal Novo	" "	14 March 1811
Foz de Arouce	" "	17 March 1811
Sabugal on the Coa	" "	3 April 1811
Fuentes de Oñoro (Spain)	" "	3 & 5 May 1811
The Great Teson – or Fort Renaud San Francisco (escalade) out work of Ciudad Rodrigo		8 January 1812
Ciudad Rodrigo (storm) the siege was from 8 January to 19 January		19 January 1812
Badajoz (storm) the siege was from the 17 March to 6 April (*Commanding the storming parties at both places*)		6 April 1812
Castrejon on the Trebancos (Spain)		18 July 1812
Salamanca		22 July 1812
San Munoz near Ciudad Rodrigo		18 November 1812
Bidassoa (River)		7 October 1813
Nivelle (River) Urugne		10 November 1813
Nive (actions on the banks of that		December 1813
River) 9th, 10th, & 13thUrugne (Pyrenees)		10 November 1813
Investment & Blockade of Bayonne		28 February 1814

Date of Commissions

Ensign 18th Regiment (Foot)	20 August 1801
Lieutenant 18th Regiment (Foot)	9 February 1804
Lieutenant 43rd Regiment,	7 August 1804
Captain 43rd Regiment (Purchase) (Foot)	December 1806
Major 79th Regiment (Purchase) Highland	3 December 1812
Major 85th Regiment	25 January 1813
Lieutenant Colonel 3rd Regiment (Purchase) (Foot)	16 May 1814
Lieutenant Colonel 3rd Regiment (Half Pay)	25 February 1816
Lieutenant Colonel 88th Regiment	2 August 1819
Lieutenant Colonel 52nd Regiment	2 June 1825

Colonel & King's Aide-de-Camp	22 July 1830
Companion of the Bath	26 September 1831
Medal for the Storming Party at Badajoz as Captain in the 43rd Regiment	9 October 1813
Retired to half pay without difference (having commanded regiments for 25 years)	10 May 1839
Major General (Brevet)	23 November 1841
Placed on the Pension List for distinguished services as Major General £200 per annum	25 August 1843
Placed on the list of Major Generals at 24/- per diem	4 July 1845
Received medal & 8 clasps for battles & sieges in the Peninsula granted by her Majesty vide General Order 1 January 1849. One to be added for the (Nivelle) 10 November 1813	7 February 1849
Appointed Colonel of the 62nd Foot vice Fitzgerald	9 March 1850
Removed to the 43rd Light Infantry vice Sir Hercules Pakenham	26 March 1850
Promoted to the rank of Lieutenant General (Brevet)	10 November 1851
Appointed to the command of the troops at Malta	1 June 1852
43rd Regiment placed on the East India Establishment	25 July 1853
Knight Commander of the Bath by Gazette	5 July 1855
Appointed Governor of Gibraltar by H[er] Majesty	6 July 1855
Appointed General	12 February 1860

General James Fergusson died on 4 September 1865 at Bath.

Chapter 8

Lieutenant George Brown–Letters

R eference NARS861/4/6, from a copy held by the Museum of the Oxfordshire Soldier.

Born on 12 August 1790 at Linkwood, near Elgin, George Brown became an Ensign in the 43rd Foot on 23 January 1806; he became a lieutenant on 18 Sept 1806. He later became a captain in the 3rd Garrison battalion on 20 June 1811; and was then appointed to 85th Regiment on 1 July 1812; he became a major on 26 May 1814 & brevet lieutenant colonel on 29 September 1814. He went on half pay on 17 July 1823; exchanged to the Rifle Brigade, becoming a lieutenant general in 1851.

Having joined the 43rd aged only 15, he served at the Battle of Copenhagen in 1807 and then in the Peninsula from 1808–11; serving at the Battle of Vimeiro; the Battle of Oporto; then with the 1st Battalion of Detachments at the Battle of Talavera where he was severely wounded; the action on the Coa; Battle of Busaco; action at Sabugal and the Battle of Fuentes d'Onoro.

Appointed to the 85th Light Infantry on 2 July 1812; he saw further action at the siege of San Sebastian; the Battle of the Nivelle; Battle of the Nive and investment of Bayonne. He also served with the 85th in the War of 1812; serving at the Battle of Bladensburg and the capture of Washington where he was severely wounded.

Promoted to colonel of the Rifle Brigade in 1824, he commanded the Light Division in the Crimean War, and became Commander of the forces in Ireland in 1860. He died on 27 August 1865, at Linkwood, near Elgin.

Only his letters while serving in the 43rd Foot are reproduced in this book, however his entire correspondence will be published in due course by Ken Trotman Books.

From Lieutenant George Brown at Oporto, to his uncle Colonel John Brown[1] at Hythe.

Oporto, 13 May 1809

My dear Uncle,

I have just time before the mail goes off to tell you that we have been engaged with the enemy for three days, in all of which my detachment has not been idle. Marshal Soult has gone off with all his plunder and I suppose we shall follow him tomorrow. I was struck with a spent ball in the throat on the 11th but it never gave me the least inconvenience. Remember me to all my friends, while I remain, yours truly G Brown

From Colonel John Brown, at Hyde, to his elder brother George Brown (senior) at the family home at Linkwood, near Elgin.

Hythe, 28 May 1809

Dear George,

I am very happy in sending you the enclosed letter from George, who is in high luck in having the command of a detachment who have been thanked in public orders, as well as in having escaped the danger he mentions and I trust he will always remain as fortunate. I am using my interest to get him a company but I am not very sanguine upon that subject. With the most affectionate regards to all at Linkwood. Believe me with the truest regard, yours while (I remain), J Brown

Arruda [dos Vinhos], 20 October 1810

My dear father,

I received your letter yesterday by which I am glad to find you are all well. I generally desire my uncle to forward my letters when there is anything particular to you, as it is 'killing two birds with one stone', I hope he has sent you my letter from Leiria after the Battle of Busaco.[2] We did our business there in high style and with very little loss, as we always shall when things are well managed, you are perfectly right in disapproving of opinions upon the conduct of superiors being put to

---

1. Lieutenant Colonel John Brown, Assistant Quarter Master General in the Royal Staff Corps.
2. Unfortunately not extant.

paper. We are now within 24 miles of Lisbon and our position which is very strong but extensive, being I should think not less than 16 to 20 miles in length, extending from the Tagus at Villa Franca [de Xira] on the right to the sea near Torres Vedras on the left; there are redoubts on all the heights with heavy cannon besides, I should suppose from 80 to 100 pieces of field artillery although we are this far back we look upon the campaign in a more favourably [sic] light than ever.

Lord Wellington finding that they would not fight him generally at Busaco retreated to this place where his flanks are safe from being turned & has drawn Massena with the whole of his force after him, while 20,000 Portuguese Militia have cut into his rear and taken 4,500 prisoners at Coimbra besides completing cutting off his communications with Spain and all his magazines, so I think they are rather in a bad way, for as sure as they attack us here they will be beaten and that most shamefully. They are deserting in great numbers being driven to desperation for want of bread. We have received large reinforcements since we came here from England & have in the country 48 battalions of infantry and 7 regiments of cavalry besides artillery and Romana[3] has joined us with 12,000 Spaniards. The enemy have as yet been very quiet, if they remain so long I dare say we shall move out some morning and begin the business. The country of course has suffered most dreadfully from two such armies moving through it, but that is unavoidable. We are well provisioned & quartered but the people have left their houses & we are able to eat biscuits.

I am sorry that James[4] is still going on in that thoughtless state, a captain of military ought to live well on his pay and not be a tax on an indulgent father who makes his money by his own hard labour. I am astonished that you should honour his bills any longer, it is doing an injustice to his sisters. I am glad to find that Peter is doing so well although I disapprove of the intended expedition to England, not being able to see what good it can do him; unless he is accompanied by some steady person he may get into bad company & really what I have seen of English farming I think you know more about it at home. I think upon the whole that it would only put ridiculous notions in his head and perhaps spoil him for ever.

---

3. Lieutenant General Pedro Caro, 3rd Marquis de la Romana, led a Spanish force that had been transported back to Spain from Denmark in British ships in 1808.
4. Possibly Captain James Brown, 82nd Foot, who was on Half Pay.

Being constantly on the out[post] duties of the army I have not been able to see Major McGregor[5] yet, I called for him once but he was not at home, and he called for me in return and I was also out of the way, his friends Maxwell & McDonald of the 92nd[6] have come out the other day but I have not seen them yet. Tell old Fraiser that his son[7] is very well and esteemed by every officer and man in the corps, he will send him some assistance soon again. We have a fine young man joined us lately from the north of the Manse of Bailie, I dare say you know something of him.

Remember me kindly to my sisters, Mr Ross, Peter and all friends (not forgetting Drumbain), while I remain your must dutiful son, G Brown

Vale [de Santarém] 3 miles from Santarem on the Lisbon road, 14 December 1810

My dear Uncle,

I had your letter of the 20th enclosed to Colonel Ross[8] about five days since. You seem perfectly right in your opinion with regard to the enemy surrendering, although from all accounts from England you were almost singular, Massena began to draw off his troops in the rear about the 12th of last month keeping up appearance to the front until the morning of the 16th when we could see nothing of them, and the whole of our army marched in pursuit of them in the course of the day, but they only retired into winter quarters in the very strong position of Santarem where no doubt they will remain for reinforcements and the establishment of magazines.

When they arrived at Santarem they sent some troops to the rear of the road to Abrantes, it is supposed to make Lord W[ellington] believe that only their rear guard was at Santarem and induce him to attack them in their positions, and it is even said that the attack was determined on by his lordship. If so, it is very lucky that he changed his mind as I do think on that ground he might have lost all his former glory. The position of Santarem extends only about 3 or 4 miles having its left close on the Tagus & extending nearly at right angles to that river. The ridge is

5. Either Major Robert McGregor, 88th Foot, or Major William McGregor, 11th Foot.
6. Captains Donald Macdonald and Samuel Maxwell of the 92nd Foot.
7. Quartermaster David Fraser of the 43rd Foot, who had become Paymaster on 11 October 1810.
8. Lieutenant Colonel John Ross, 52nd Foot.

naturally very commanding & inaccessible but is rendered more so by *abatis* formed by cut down olive trees with which it is covered. There is also another great strength in it, which is the small river Rio Major along its front in a broad marsh, at present flooded and impassable except by the causeways on the high roads. It is not to be turned without going by the road leading through the town of Rio Maior, these lying to our left & General Hill being on the opposite side of the water, I doubt whether we could afford to make this movement without leaving the road to Lisbon open to Lisbon, which would not be *altogether* convenient.

We are kept upon the alert owing to our peculiar situation for if the enemy came into Rio Maior in force we must fall back as they will then be as near to Carregado where that road meets this. As we are, our pickets are at one end of the causeway and theirs on the other about 500 yards asunder and the sentries are within speaking distance. The headquarters are at Cartaxo about 4 miles from this on the Lisbon road. It is said that the admiral has reported officially to Lord Wellington that the shipping cannot lay in their anchorage on the river in case the enemy bring guns on the other side. This I always thought and everyone knows that ships cannot lay in Cascais Bay with westerly winds: I am also told that in consequence his lordship is fortifying a neck of land on the other side opposite Lisbon.[9] I do not think that Massena can force our lines if his army was much stronger; but with a strong corps on the opposite side I do not know what might be the consequences. When we were in the lines I went down for a day to Lisbon, they are under no apprehension there for the French, but the town is very crowded, every house having two or three families in it. God knows what is to become of the unfortunate inhabitants if the business is protracted much longer, they are already in a most wretched condition, bread that formerly cost 3d now costs 1/- here.

We have not heard anything of the militia since we have been here but they are round the enemy in every direction, in fact no one can account for them having subsisted so long. You mention in your letter that you could not find the town of Arruda on the map, nothing is a greater proof of the incorrectness of the maps of this country, it lies under the guns of the redoubts Nos 9 & 10 from the right, that is a little better than half way between Alhandra and Sobral [de Monte Agraço], it is at the bottom of the heights and has room enough for our division (5,000),

---

9. This refers to the fourth line of defences at Almada, which formed part of the lines in front of Lisbon.

we were kept there in rainy weather but engaged in constructing *abattis*, building stone walls, scarping the sides of the hills etc, as much for the amusement of our brigadier as anything else during the good weather. Lord Wellington allowed the enemy to occupy Sobral although it is also under the guns of the largest redoubt. The redoubts are works thrown up on the most commanding points with 9 to 24 pounders on them, they are built of sods or fascines according to the nature of the ground with a parapet of 6 to 7 feet thick, a ditch and strong palisades, and occupied by Portuguese troops and a few English artillery in each. I have no idea of the number of these works but it is immense.

Colonel Ross has shown me every attention, he is a great favourite in his regiment he desires to be remembered to you. I wish I could have seen James before he went off, I had a letter from him on the 9th, he seems to go out with good spirits. I also had a letter from home of the 11th they are all well. While we were in the line there was a grand fete given at Mafra in honour of the instalment of Marshal Beresford as Knight of the Bath, I went there, a distance of about 25 miles, but was very disappointed, the thing was very ill conducted. His Lordship met the officers of this brigade to go coursing in the fine plains along the river a few days since, with some very fine greyhounds that we have got, we had most excellent sport having killed 7 hares. The Marquis Romana, Marshal Beresford and about all the general officers of the army were present, his lordship was much pleased and is going across the water to course today. I begin to wish this business over, it is now nearly a twelvemonth since I have slept without my clothes [on], but never was in better health. Let me know from you as often as you have time. While I remain yours truly G Brown

To his sister May Innes, in Edinburgh.

Vale [de Santarém], 3 miles from Santarem 14 December 1810

My dear May,

I have not had the pleasure of hearing from you since your happy marriage, but I have no doubt that such a correct correspondent as you will have a letter on its way to me at this moment. I had letters from Anne, James and Uncle by the last packet. The latter is in London but says not a word of my promotion. I do not really know what to think of him, if I did not know him, I should begin to think him insincere with me, as it is now 12 months since he might have had a company for me in a Ceylon regiment & which he certainly would not have refused had he not better prospects. That 12 months however, have made my claim stronger for I suppose no part of the British army ever continued so long at so hard work as our division has done. You will hardly believe me when I tell you that we have never slept with our clothes off since we went up to Pinhel last January.

Massena finding that he could make nothing of our lines began to withdraw his army from before ours about the 12th of last month but kept up appearances so that we did not know of it until the 16th in the morning when we could see nobody in front of our outposts. Our army was instantly put in motion but we found it was only a retreat into the strong position of Santarem 12 leagues from Lisbon, where they have remained perfectly quiet ever since having our outposts within 100 yards of each other. This is certainly the best position they could have taken up to wait for reinforcements and magazines. It extends only about 3 miles so that very few men can defend it, at the same time that the ground is nothing very strong, besides what they have done to strengthen it by cutting down trees making abattis & 30,000 men will be able to defend it in the front against any force while the rest of their army opens their communications with Spain and the neighbouring country. Santarem besides will afford them excellent quarters for their army during the rains, this position is besides very much strengthened by the small river (Rio Maior) that runs along the front of it in a flat marsh, at present impassable, so that there is no access to it but by the causeways or by the high roads.

You will ask why not turn by going round them? This cannot be done without going by the town of Rio Maior about 3 leagues to the left, but by which movement the Lisbon road would be left open and they would be nearer it than us. General Hill's Division being already on the other side of the water, we cannot afford to divide our force. When they first came here they made show of sending troops off towards Abrantes, wishing to make Lord W[ellington] attack them in this position and it is said that he was on the point of doing it, but he wisely moved up our division as if to attack them on the river side which made them beat to arms and show their whole force.

I am extremely sorry that I had not an opportunity of seeing James before he left England. He himself goes out in good spirits and I have no doubt will soon get promotion and come home.

You would hear before this of the grand fete given at Mafra on the occasion of Marshal Beresford's instalment as Knight of the Bath. I rode 25 miles there and was dreadfully disappointed, all the officers of the army were invited, leaving a certain proportion with the regiments. The consequence was that the building though the largest I ever saw in this or any other country, was crowded & the place being in the lines and 25 miles from Lisbon very few ladies (16 only) had the courage to come, for you must know that the Portuguese ladies have not the spirit of our lasses at home. So you must believe that there was little or no dancing; 300 sat down to supper and three times that number went without. In short it was the worst conducted business that ever was.

There is a very fine plain along the side of the river here and we have three very fine greyhounds with which we do great execution. Lord Wellington agreed to meet the officers of our brigade on the flat a few days since, to have a day's sport. He met us with the Marquis Romana, Marshal Beresford and almost all the general officers in the army. We had a most excellent day's sport with those three dogs, having killed 7 hares. There were no less than 120 horses on the plain and the French on the heights looking at us. I have seen Maxwell, Macdonald and Captain Campbell.[10] They are quartered about 3 miles from this and are all very well. Colonel Ross has joined the 52nd Regiment, he is a most excellent fellow and a great favourite of Uncle, very much liked in the 52nd.

Let me know how you like Edinburgh, it will be new to you but I have no doubt you will soon get reconciled to it. Anne says she is coming up in the summer. You will be tired of this long insipid letter some time before you get [to] this length, but it is ten to one if you ever get one so long from me again, as I am sure you nor anyone else got one so long before. Compliments to Mr Innes, while I remain yours truly, G Brown

Camp near Miranda do Corvo, 16 March 1811

My dear Uncle,

The enemy retreated from Santarem on the night of the 5th. We of course followed them at daylight and marched to Pernes, where we found the bridge blown up. On the 7th we came to Lamaroso, on the 8th to Caxarias, on 9th to within 2 leagues of Pombal, on the 10th we halted to allow some of the army to close up, on the 11th we came up to the enemy at Pombal and had some skirmishing. On the 12th came up to the enemy in force at Redinha and attacked them, on the 13th came up with & turned the enemy at Condeixa [-a-Nova], on the 14th they made a stand in the mountains about a league on, when our division had some

---

10. These officers all appear to be from the 92nd Foot, they were Captain Samuel Maxwell, Lieutenant Donald Macdonald and Captain Dugald Campbell.

sharp work and lost a good many men and our regiment three officers wounded.

On 15th we came up, attacked and drove in their outposts with little loss, we are halted today to refresh the men and get up provisions, not having had bread for three days. The French have burnt the villages and murdered the inhabitants as they passed through them. The weather is very hot and we are lying out, so you must forgive this scrawl. Colonel Ross (52nd Regiment) will write you the 1st opportunity. Most truly yours, G Brown

The French have destroyed a great part of their artillery and the country they have now got into probably will be obliged to destroy all. Their loss in prisoners is not very considerable and ours is almost the only division as yet engaged. G.B.

Espeja, 29 May 1811

My dear Father,

I had your welcome letter of 25th April by the last packet, by which I am glad to find that you are all so well. There has been a most sanguinary battle in Spanish Estremadura (Barossa) between [Marshals] Beresford and Soult, in which although we have suffered a very great loss, yet it has given the country another proof of what its army can do when put to it and has also shown that the Spaniards can and will fight when properly led and in this instance they behaved most nobly from all accounts, the loss on the part of the Portuguese was small, the enemy's immense. They had as usual an immense superiority of cavalry which did great mischief to us. We have not yet heard the particulars, the Lisbon Gazette not having come out, you will see it nearly as soon as us in the English papers.

I had a letter from my uncle about a week, since he says nothing of my promotion although one would suppose he might do almost anything he pleased at Horse Guards now.

I am extremely sorry to find that you imagine yourself getting old, you ought to try and forget those things or you will get old in reality.

We are all perfectly quiet in our old quarters about 9 miles from Ciudad Rodrigo in which the enemy have a small garrison that gives us no trouble whatever. Lord Wellington has now half the army with him in Estremadura, where I suppose they are not idle, we had got a day's move there too on the 26th but were countermanded.

Things begin to look better here than ever, the Spaniard will yet do something, they have taken the strong fort of Tejanos [Figueras] in

Catalonia[11] by surprise & the French are said to have lost 700 men in the attempt to retake it. You would be surprised to see the quantities of all sorts of provisions that we bring into our cantonments to sell, one would scarcely believe there had been a war here these ten days, such are the immense resources of Spain. Lord Wellington has recommended Major Patrickson[12] and Captain Napier of our regiment for brevet rank as a mark of his approbation of the conduct of the corps on the advance on the advance of the army. We expect this will be a busy season and I should not much wonder if we saw Madrid before the end of it. I was very sorry to see by your letter, the death of poor Tom Craig it will be a great loss to Peter.

We are well supplied with provisions of all kinds, but I suppose the Portuguese are starving in the interior. I had a letter from Fraiser [sic] our 2nd Battalion Paymaster, by which I am sorry to find such a bad aspect amongst the militia, he says that the commanding officers will not allow their men to turn out for the regiments of the Light Division. Remember me to all my sisters, Peter, Mrs Ross, Drumbairn etc. While I remain, yours truly, G Brown

George Brown left the 43rd Foot in June 1813, initially to the 3rd Garrison Battalion, before returning to the peninsula with the 85th Foot. His full journal will be published in the author's Napoleonic Archive series.

---

11. The Fortress of Figueras fell to a Spanish attack by stealth while the majority of the garrison were asleep at 1 am on 10 April 1811.
12. Major Christopher Patrickson, 43rd Foot. He would not know it for some time, but the *Gazette* of the very day after this letter appointed Patrickson brevet lieutenant colonel and William Napier became a brevet major.

Chapter 9

Lieutenant Samuel Pollock

Fraction of pocket diary

A fraction of the pocket diary of Samuel Pollock is all that has been found, and the whereabouts of the original is presently unknown. Samuel became a lieutenant in the 43rd Foot on 21 May 1806. He saw action at Corunna, the Côa, Busaco, Foz de Arouce, Sabugal, Fuentes de Oñoro, Ciudad Rodrigo and Badajoz. He was severely wounded at Badajoz and was sent home to recover, never returning to the peninsula. He later became a major in the same regiment. The short section details the details of the famous march of the Light Brigade to Talavera de la Reina.

Left Coria on the 24th [July 1809] for Galesta [Galisteo]; on the 25th to Malpartida [de Plasencia], a distance of four leagues, under soaking rain. Next am 26th, about three leagues, crossed the River Tietar, and after marching two leagues found we had taken the wrong road; obliged therefore to cross the country about two leagues, where we halted, having marched upwards of seven leagues; next morning marched for Naval Moral [Navalmoral de la Mata], four leagues. Next on 28th, the brigade marched at 1 o'clock with the intention of only going four leagues, but before we had got so far we met the Spaniards running away in all directions, with baggage &c, and who reported an engagement; proceeded therefore about six leagues to Oropesa, where we filed off to a wood and stopped until 4 o'clock, when we again continued the march at a very quick pace until 11 o'clock. The brigade then lay down with their arms in their hands, and after remaining in that situation for three hours again marched and reached the ground where the action had been fought the day previous, a harrowing march of 66 miles in thirty hours.

Chapter 10

Lieutenant John Livesey Maclean

Description of the Battle of Nivelle

John Maclean entered the 43rd as an ensign on 2 May 1811. He served in the Peninsula with the First Battalion from August 1812 until the end of the war in April 1814. He was gazetted as a lieutenant on 10 December 1812. He served at San Millan, Vitoria, the Pyrenees, the Bidasoa, Nivelle, Nive, Tarbes and Toulouse.

His letter describes the regiment's actions at the Battle of Nivelle:

12 December [1864?][1]

On the night of the 9th [November] we received orders to hold ourselves ready to march at an early hour the following morning, to assault the position of the enemy on La Petite Rhune.[2] Breakfast was ordered at 2 am, which we managed to eat most heartily; and having some remarkably thick American biscuits,[3] Madden[4] observed that their thickness would turn a bullet aside, at the same time putting one into the breast of his jacket. Never was prediction more completely verified, for early in the day the biscuit was shattered to pieces, turning the direction of the bullet from as gallant and true a heart as ever beat under a British uniform. Another bullet passed through Madden's left arm immediately afterwards.

The regiment having moved off about 3 o'clock, ascended the side of the mountain, halting within a short distance of La Petite Rhune and close

---

1. This is dated 1813 in Levinge's history of the 43rd but he mentions Charles Gore being a general, which did not occur until 1863.
2. A mountain that lies virtually on the French–Spanish border near Zizkuitz.
3. Presumably an American version of a ship's biscuit.
4. Lieutenant Wyndham Madden, 43rd Foot.

to our left we saw and passed the Rifles, lying down in close column, covered by their white blankets, in the faint light resembling a flock of sheep much more than grim warriors prepared for the strife. The most perfect silence had been enjoined, and the 43rd were directed to lie down in close column to await the signal of attack; the firing of a third gun from the right.

We heard the French drums beating to arms and even could distinguish voices, although not in sight of them; for being on the slope of a hill, we had no idea we were so near or about to attack. Sir James Kempt,[5] who commanded the 1st Brigade of the Light Division, ordered that two companies of the regiment should lead in skirmishing order, followed by a support of four in line under Lieutenant Colonel Napier and a reserve of three companies under Lieutenant Colonel Duffy.[6] Major Brock's[7] and Captain Murchison's companies[8] were to lead the advance in extended order.

The sunrise in those regions is most sudden, for darkness is dispelled by a burst of glowing light as the sun clears the head of a high mountain and startles the beholder with its glorious brightness. Such was its appearance as it glanced on the recumbent troops and sparkled from their bayonets along the arms piled by companies that eventful morning. The next moment the sound of a gun followed by others was heard, and every ear was on the alert to count each shot. The men were on their feet in an instant, and the words 'stand to your arms' being given, each soldier seized his Brown Bess. The Rifles folded their blankets and moved off to their left. General Kempt mounted his horse and said, 'Now, 43rd, let me see what you will do this morning' and pointing to an entrenchment on a rising ground in front [&] to the left of the regiment lined with French infantry, gave the order to advance and carry it; and then await the arrival of the support before an attempt was to be made on the stone redoubts on the ridge of rocks on the top of La Petite Rhune. The companies then extending and bringing their right shoulders forward, were at once in fire, and after descending a short distance and crossing a piece of marshy ground, made a rush for the breastwork, which was quickly evacuated by the enemy; but not before they had by their sharp

---

5. Major General James Kempt commanded the 1st Brigade of the Light Division from January 1813 to April 1814.
6. Actually Major John Duffy, 43rd Foot.
7. Actually Captain Saumarez Brock, 43rd Foot.
8. Captain Robert Murchison, 43rd Foot, was severely wounded at the Nivelle and died of his wounds on 11 November.

practice dropped a few of their assailants, who had scarcely returned their fire, so intent were they on rushing at the intrenchment [sic]. On clearing the breastwork, we brought our left shoulders forward to face redoubt No.1 and as we were directed to wait for the four companies, we took such shelter as some scattered rocks afforded at about fifty or sixty yards from the first redoubt. The enemy made our quarters pretty hot, as they when firing were well covered, which our men perceiving were endeavouring to check by aiming at their heads when opportunities offered; but, to avoid exposing themselves, they preferred firing at the support and reserve, although not so close, for thus they had a far better chance of killing and not being hit by our men and consequently could fire coolly. The redoubts were built of rough stones, but had no cannon. Captain Murchison and myself got alongside of a flat piece of rock within about forty yards of the redoubt, and as they could see part of us, they made the rock smoke with their shots. Captain Murchison raised his head to look over and instantly his face assumed a livid appearance as if choking. I inquired what was the matter, when he with difficulty said, he was struck in the neck and must see a doctor! But in the meantime, should the support arrive, he desired me to take on the company. Shortly after the surgeon examined him, and found that the bullet had got entangled in his neckcloth and had run round his neck. A sergeant pointed out better cover about twenty-five yards nearer the redoubt, to which we both went; and I borrowed his fusee and fired several shots at the heads of the French, the sergeant loading for me. While so employed, Colonel Napier and the support came sweeping up behind us, on which I gave the order to advance, and we all dashed forward with a cheer. Napier, boiling with courage and being withal very active, attempted to scale the walls without observing the bayonet points over his head; and being rather short-sighted, would certainly have been very roughly handled had not James Considine[9] and myself laid hold of the skirts of his jacket and pulled him back, for which we received anything but thanks. We of course apologised to Colonel Napier for the liberty we had taken, for he was [the] very wrath at the time. We then pointed out an easier ascent for him, and assisted each other over the wall. To show the danger he was in at the moment, I was even under the necessity of striking a bayonet up with my sword, though they were giving way, as a hint that we were coming over in spite of them. The hint was taken and a free passage left.

---

9. Lieutenant James Considine, 43rd Foot, was severely wounded at the Nivelle.

On getting inside I saw a French officer kneeling with his arm raised begging for quarter and his head and face covered with blood. I told one of the men to take care of him and proceeded through the gate at the rear, following the retiring enemy towards the second redoubt on the ridge of rocks, similarly constructed to the one we had just taken. I then met Cooke[10] and Considine, and we consulted what was best to be done, as we had not a sufficient number of men with us to assault the second redoubt, most of them having joined the regiment below the rocks. We were then about 100 yards from it and exposed to its fire. I proposed to Considine to follow a path leading along the face of the ridge of rock, which I expected would lead to the redoubt, and if I found it practicable would not return. I had judged correctly as to the direction of the path, for it led direct on the redoubt in question; but although the enemy must have seen me distinctly they did not fire in my direction: I suppose from seeing me alone, and being occupied by the others who were gathering for a rush.

I quickly discovered they were about to quit the redoubt by the gate behind, for some were taking that direction, and before I could get close up they were off.

On reaching the top of the ridge again, I found that I was on the flank of a long trench, filled with a regiment of French infantry, but high above it. The entrenchment was cut across a nearly level green, approaching which I perceived a portion of the 43rd advancing in column under General Kempt, and the French having fired a volley, I observed he had been wounded, and his adc Captain Gore[11] (now Honourable General Sir Charles Gore[12]) KCB, binding a handkerchief quickly round his arm. The order to charge was then given, a British cheer followed, a line of levelled steel showed what the enemy might expect. I saw them waver, then spring out of the entrenchment and retire down the hill at a rapid pace.

This had no sooner taken place than I observed on the other side and also below me, a French officer waving his sword and encouraging his men to advance and retake the redoubt, but he could not induce them to follow. One of the 43rd skirmishers rushed at him with his bayonet at

---

10. Lieutenant John Henry Cooke, 43rd Foot.

11. Actually Lieutenant the Honourable Charles Gore, 43rd Foot.

12. Charles Gore became a general in 1863, therefore the letter published in Levinge's History of the 43rd Foot with a date of 1813 must be an error, the letter dating after 1863. Writing so many years later would also explain his many errors as to the ranks of the various officers at the time of the action.

the charge, and in spite of his attempts to defend himself with his sword ran him through, and then returned to the level ground behind the trench the regiment had carried in such gallant style.

Gore then rode up to me with orders from the general to stop the pursuit on which the men were eagerly bent; and it was with considerable difficulty that their ardour was checked and the men halted, for they were rushing after the enemy like greyhounds, so excited were they. The French, finding that they were no longer pressed, retired more tranquilly but still in confusion, our men firing on them as they descended the hill to some huts forming an old bivouac. I observed an officer on the way separate himself from the mob of fugitives, which removed him from our line of fire, and walk quietly along: on which a short stout soldier asked my permission to follow and take him prisoner. I consented, provided no one accompanied him; and although his musket had been discharged, he would not wait to reload, but ran forward. He had not gone above 300 or 400 yards, when he overtook the officer and called on him to surrender. The Frenchman presented a pistol on turning round, which the 43rd man observing, and being then very near, poised his musket over his head, and pitched it with such precision that the bayonet penetrated his thigh and brought him to the ground, where he lay at the mercy of his adversary, who merely took possession of the pistol and, what he considered of greater value, a flask of brandy. On rejoining his company, after offering it to me, he gratified his heated comrades with a sip as far as the supply would go. Both these French officers, who fell under our bayonets, were removed to Vera and I was told were doing well.

I now learned that Considine had his thigh broken by a bullet and that Murchison, shortly after the doctor had examined him, was struck by another musket ball, which carried him off in twenty-four hours.

After about a quarter of an hour's halt, the division moved on, the Rifles and 52nd leading: and some of the former were sent down the hill to drive the French from the bivouac to which they had retired. This was quickly done, but the French being reinforced again advanced; the drummers beating the pas de charge to retake the huts. The Rifles however, were too wily, for perceiving that the wind blew in the enemy's faces, they fired the huts, which with the straw therein blazed and smoked to such a degree that the French were obliged to relinquish their intention. The sight at this moment was truly grand: we looked from our vantage ground over an extent of about twenty miles occupied by two gallant armies, of which the Light Division composed the centre of the British. To the right the pass of Mayar [Maya] and St Jean de Pied de Port, to the left St Jean de Luz and from each extremity could be distinctly traced, by the flashes of fire and rising smoke, the advance of our troops and the gradual retreat of the French, offering an obstinate resistance at every favourable spot. But the British were not to be denied and went in to win; and in short carried everything before them, notwithstanding the gallant resistance they met with.

While looking around, William Freer came up and inquired anxiously for his brother Edward.[13] Seeing that something was amiss, he turned round, saying, 'I see how it is,' and started off to the rear, where his worst fears were too soon confirmed: his brother having been shot through the head. Both brothers were fine courageous fellows, much liked in the regiment; each had been wounded, the elder had lost an arm at Badajoz. The younger frequently told me had a presentiment he would be killed in the attack of La Petite Rhune. He happened also to be in the last company that went into action that day, when his presentiment was fulfilled, to the great sorrow of all his brother officers and the entire regiment.

The division then crossing a narrow valley ascended the nearest hill, driving in the French skirmishers, and at the top came upon a fine star fort of earth, surrounded by a deep ditch containing about 700 men; and although the 52nd attacked it with their accustomed determination, they were repulsed with loss. The commandant was then called upon to surrender, which he at first refused to do; but seeing that he could not defend the work for any length of time, he agreed: provided he was not to be marched to the rear by Spanish or Portuguese troops. This being accepted, the redoubt was given up and the French disarmed. This may be said to have ended the day's fighting.

---

13. Lieutenant Edward Freer, 43rd Foot, was killed at Nivelle.

Chapter 11

Lieutenant Richard Brunton[1]

Services

Completed at Bangalore 27 November 1838

Richard Brunton was gazetted an ensign in the 1st Battalion 43rd Foot on 10 November 1808 and embarked for Portugal with the battalion in May 1809.[2] Brunton served in the advance to Talavera, at the Côa, Battle of Busaco and the retreat to the Lines of Vedras, then to Santarém and the pursuit of the French back into Spain. In March 1811 he transferred into the Portuguese service.

I was appointed to an ensigncy in the 43rd Light Infantry on the 10th of November 1808, embarked with my regiment in May following and the Light Brigade under the command of Brigadier General Robert Crawford [Craufurd] to which it belonged, landed in Portugal on the 4th of July 1809. The arduous services of that brigade during the advance to Talavera, their subsequent retreat, their advance again into Spain and their operations on the Agueda and Coa during the siege of Ciudad Rodrigo by the French, are so well known that I shall not dwell on them, and as it is not my object to write a history of the war, but simply the humble share I had in it.

I shall [therefore] pass over everything which occurred until the first action in which my regiment was generally engaged, viz the 24th of July 1810 on the banks of the Coa near Almeida. On that day the brigade was attacked by an overwhelming force, they were unsupported and had in their rear a rapid river with steep rocky and precipitous sides, and the heavy rain of the preceding night having rendered all the fords impassable,

---

1. National Army Museum Reference 1968-07-461.
2. Lionel Challis' Peninsula Roll Call has Brunton in 2/43rd in Spain from October 1808 to January 1809 and serving at the Battle of Corunna, but this is incorrect.

their only retreat was by a bridge of very few feet in width. I had the honor [sic] of to carry one of the Colours and the care of it when retiring with the regiment broken up nearly into skirmishing order, by the difficult nature of the ground and the necessity for repelling attacks in various directions; was a duty of no small anxiety, difficulty and exertion. On being forced back in some disorder on the narrow and rocky road leading down to the bridge, General Crawford [Craufurd] came up to me and the other ensign and desired us to cross the bridge, take up a conspicuous position on the opposite side as near the bridge as possible, and display the Colours for the regiment to rally on. This was done and we remained standing under a tremendous fire of musquetry from the opposite side which was precipitous and well within range until the regiment had passed the bridge and rallied. I do not now exactly recollect, but I think there were 2 officers and either 3 or 4 serjeants killed and wounded with the Colours on that day. I escaped unhurt and in the evening I handed them over to Ensign [James] Considine (now a major general in Africa[3]) who had joined from England during the action, and being then a lieutenant I was appointed to command a company, the captain of which (Cameron[4]) had been killed. Our loss in officers on that day (which I think was 16 killed and wounded) left me the senior for that duty.

From this time nothing of consequence occurred with the Battle of Busaco; we remained close up to the enemy, occasionally skirmishing with them and kept so constantly on the alert, that for weeks together we had no cover except such as our bivouacs afforded nor opportunities sometimes of changing our clothes. On the 25th of September we formed the rear guard of that part of the army and retired skirmishing and hard pressed into our position on the Sierra of Busaco. On the 27th we were attacked by two heavy French columns. We were lying down in line behind the brow of the hill and allowed the heads of their columns actually to reach within a few yards of us near the summit. We then jumped up and immediately charged them. The result is well known. The French General Simon was taken by a part of the brigade.

On it being perceived that the enemy was attempting to turn our left flank, the army retired on the morning of the 29th and the Light Brigade again formed the rearguard and were again constantly on the alert, but not much annoyed by the enemy until we arrived at Alenquer on the 9th of October, when the day being extremely foggy the enemy appeared

---

3. This clearly confirms that this memoir was written in the late 1830s.
4. Captain Ewen Cameron, 43rd Foot, was killed at the Cóa.

in force on the heights close above the town, we however made good our retreat but were obliged to pass by Sobral to the position assigned to us in the Lines of Torres Vedras, at Arruda, at that place and on the heights above it we remained until the 7th of November, constantly on the alert and having occasionally trifling affairs of picquets. On the 7th it having been ascertained that the enemy was retiring we followed them all night and on the 9th came up with them halted between Cartaxo and Santarem. The brigade was ready formed on the road to attack, but we were prevented by the arrival of Lord Wellington, who knew that a larger force was hidden in the hollow than we were aware of. On the 10th we followed the enemy to the Ponte Sica, a causeway leading to Santarem, but after a reconnaissance and some skirmishing, finding the enemy strongly posted at Santarem we took post at the Ponte Sica and Vallee [Vale de Santarém], having a French picquet close to us on the other side, and thus remained inactive though constantly on the alert till the beginning of March 1811.

It was during this interval of partial repose that having acquired a little knowledge of the Portuguese language my commanding officer Lieutenant Colonel Patrickson[5] thought it would be advantageous to me to enter the Portuguese Service. He accordingly recommended me very strongly to Marshal Beresford and I was appointed to a company in the 6th Cacadores commanded by Lieutenant Colonel Pinto in February 1811. I joined them on the 1st of March near Torres Vedras, and on the 7th we marched in pursuit of the French Army.

The remainder of Brunton's statement concerns his time in the 6th Portuguese Caçadores and then the 13th Light Dragoons and is not continued here.

---

5. Major Christopher Patrickson only became a brevet lieutenant colonel on 30 May 1811.

Chapter 12

Lieutenant John Meyricke

Letters

I must thank Paul Ridgeley for bringing these letters to my attention and to Rory and Richard Constant for permission to publish the same. John Meyricke became an ensign in the 43rd Foot on 4 May 1809 and was promoted to lieutenant in the regiment on 23 August 1810. He appears to have suffered from a malarial disease similar to that prevalent at Walcheren; he possibly caught it from men returned from there. He then served with the 1st Battalion 43rd Foot in the peninsula from August 1812 to April 1814, serving at San Millan, Vitoria, the Pyrenees, the Bidasoa, Nivelle (slightly wounded), Nive, Tarbes and Toulon. He then went with the regiment to America and died of wounds received at the Battle of New Orleans on 17 February 1815.

To Mrs Meyricke, Captain Meyricke's Shropshire Militia,[1] Plymouth.

Colchester, 6 September 1810

My dear mother,

I have been every day this week after I came from drill, to meet the corporal, in the hope of receiving a letter from some person of your party, but I have been disappointed so often, that I have given it up.

I have received a letter from Sophia, she likewise complains of not having heard from you and says that she is afraid you have quite forgotten her.

I would have written to you before but that from being clumsy I ran the bayonet into my finger whilst at drill and like the chapter of accidents

---

1. His father was Captain John Meyricke of the Shropshire Militia.

I strained the same hand. Now then to begin the letter. Major Hearn[2] called of me the other day and said that he was going to send out four additional recruiting parties on account of our battalion being so weak and asked me if I had any objection to command one of them being just lieutenant. I had no excuse as I am not likely to go out with any [foreign] detachment, I told him that I might pick up some men in Shropshire. He said that he could not send me there, but that he wanted me to relieve one of the first battalion that was recruiting at Barnard Castle, but that if I had any objections to going, that he would endeavour to find somebody else. There is an old Captain (Kyplan[3]) of ours in that town who would be a very good friend to me and I would inform of anything relating to the party. Everybody says that it is a very pretty little town and more recruits got there than anywhere, and as the major was so very kind that I could not refuse. I did not choose the place therefore it is not my fault if there are no recruits to be had.

It must be intended for me to marry my little girl or else I should not be sent without applying for it, to reside for not less than six months within forty miles of her residence. I go from here on the 25th and I am to be returned there on the 10th, consequently I shall go straight down from Carlisle per coach. Ensign Steel[4] of ours goes as far as Halifax with me, where he is to be stationed until further orders.

So I wanted good muftys[5] and recollecting the application of Dallas[6] to my father, I ordered a blue coat and a waistcoat which he sent at once, the coat was damn badly made (& as I told him) it would fit a person that was hunch-backed. He wrote a very polite letter back that he was very sorry and would be glad if I would allow him to make me another and likewise if there was anything else in this line. For his politeness he is to make me a great coat as I shall want one next winter.

That uncle of mine sent me back five guineas and an uncivil letter informing me that having lost so much by Sophia and having a great many on his list already, he could not provide for me. I had a great mind to send it back but however considering that he was an old man and knew no better than to affront a nephew I pocketed the affront. I hope that we shall never be the least indebted to them in future, at least I won't and my father shan't if I can help it.

---

2. Major Daniel Hearn, 43rd Foot.
3. Captain Robert Kipling had retired from the service on 1 December 1806.
4. Ensign Alexander Steele, 43rd Foot.
5. Civilian clothes, often referred to then as coloured clothes.
6. A tailor.

I have got on with my drill famously, we have began skirmishing yesterday, I had lots of running, I could not make my rear rank man go fast enough to please me and as I was on the flank I had plenty to do.

Having good eating and drinking and exercise and good health I am getting fat & have got a belly like Mrs Skeldon, perhaps you cannot fancy that meagre carcass of mine grown fat but I look rather different now than when I had the ague. But as they do not spare the skirmishes in the 43rd, I am not likely to grow too fat.

To Captain Meyricke, Shropshire Militia, Plymouth

Colchester, 3 June 1811

My dear father,
I should have written to you before, only I have been so much engaged. I had a very pleasant march and brought the men on very well. One day I proposed to go on about five miles further than the party expected, we had only come ten so as to divide the distance, but some of your Shropshires grumbled. Roberts E, J Jones, Edward Williams I believe were the men. I didn't go on that day but had a regular parade that evening the same as the regiment. I cautioned some of the men to prepare, I fell in the party in sections and although a bad road and a hot day I marched them twenty miles in the same style as I would command a company on the drill ground. I allowed two good men to fall out but the others I marched though only halting for five minutes in an hour. I heard one of the men call out right, left. I told them that if they gave their opinion in the same way in the 43rd as they did in the Salop that they would be tried by a drum-head court martial or perhaps shot.

When I came in, I quartered one bad one with three good ones and I am sure that he led a pretty life of it, they expected that I should be obliged to stop to breakfast but in that they were mistaken. I told Hill that if the men wished it, I would have a field day every day but that I would rather march without, he say'd [sic] that it had done them a great deal of good. Murphy[7] says that it is the finest party of recruits that ever joined the 43rd Regiment. The men so near of a height and so well disciplined, not a man drunk and all so clean, the bugles met the party at Lexden[8] and blew all the way in[to] the barracks 3 miles. They astonished your Light

---

7. Lieutenant and Adjutant Bernard Murphy, 43rd Foot.
8. Now a suburb of Colchester.

Bob's all the old hands came out, when it was dirty [weather], I passed by files and then formed up to their astonishment, the other parties came in one after another.

350 fine fellows marched off this morning for Portugal, most of my lads volunteered to go, I have only six left here. Sergeant Manley is in hospital, he has not taken care of himself. I do not think that the 2nd Battalion will ever go to service, seven lieutenants went but it does not come to my turn yet and I am afraid that the war shall be over before I go out.

I called [on] Sophia when I marched into town, she has delayed going into the north for another week, but I suppose that she is gone by this time.

Only £1-40s-0d of that money belongs to me I would thank you to [send] the remainder to the innkeeper as you are able to get it and when I have some more cash I will send to Harriet 3s & 10d.

We expect to send some parties to Ireland but I hope to remain here, we have plenty of rooms. I wrote to Franton the other day to send the report, it must be signed by the commanding officer, Adjutant & Paymaster (in one loan) the same as a district Paymasters Report. Fidlor[9] has got another month's leave and joins [on the] 24th.

If you could borrow the key that opens my trunk, I wish that you would pack my plain clothes in a bow and send them off as soon as convenient, I sent the bugle back by the coach and will send you some money to pay for the carriage.

I had done as you advised (with respect to that girl) before I received your letter, she belongs to the Westminster parish and I believe that Mr Stevenson is the Adjutant of it. I did not call at the Andrews but dined with Sophia & H[arriet] at lodgings.

I am very much obliged to you with respect to Lewis he is a very fine fellow, I have the major's leave to take Edwards for a servant now that he is a recruit, he says he would not go back into any militia regiment for £20, all the lads seem to like the corps.

Tell Harriet that I have written to the north as she desired me. Pay'd Simmonds the D[ebt?]. I have stopped it. Murphy finds fault with your men standing on their heels, only those that were going out have been drilled, the others walk about like gentlemen.

Give my love to my mother, there is no danger of her son [being killed] yet. I march through some towns where the L M[ilitia][10] were

---

9. Ensign David Fidlor, 43rd Foot.
10. Lancashire, Lincoln or Leicester Militia.

quartered, they were very much afraid of my fellows. They lay three in a bed and one of ours asked what was good for the rich and kept the bed for himself, three G[renadiers?] sons did not like to sleep with him. The man told the story in such a dry way that I could not help laughing, it was a very good plan. A great stout fellow of ours saw the beds full and therefore sat down upon three of the locusts who soon quitted the bed for him.

Remembrances to Captain Betton[11] & Mr Crichton[12] and the doctor & all the rest of them. I wish my mother would make me one of those felt jackets we were talking of with purple edges, thick felt.

I shall write soon to my mother and sisters but not until I am settled, tell them to write to me (soon) on foolscap, I expect to pay you a visit next year and bring Manley, Hill & Edwards, he looks very genteel in plain clothes and will wait well, he expects to remain some years with me. Give my love to them all and believe me dear father, your affectionate son J M

Colchester, 27 July 1811

My dear father,

I received the book &c safely yesterday evening & I take the first opportunity of answering your letter.

I am very glad to hear that Mr Landlord was satisfied, thank you for the trouble that you have taken, I will take very great care that nothing of the kind shall happen again. I have at last found out that I am only to receive 6d per mile for returning & nothing for going down to Plymouth, total £13 13s therefore with the present month's pay I am only 4 & ½ in credit, so much for volunteering.

With regard to your expedition to Ireland I see it in a very different light to what your hero's do. I am inclined to think that the times are altered since Strong Bow, Earl of Pembroke[13] first landed in that country.

I do not like the idea of the family parting, in the first place it will not do for three females to remain at a seaport town or the neighbourhood

---

11. Captain Richard, Betton Shropshire Militia.
12. Surgeon William Crichton, Shropshire Militia.
13. Richard de Clare, 2nd Earl of Pembroke, nicknamed 'Strongbow', sailed to Ireland with a force to reimpose the King of Leinster on his throne in 1170, despite Henry II forbidding it. His invasion was successful and he appeased Henry by handing over much of his conquests in exchange for the return of his ancestral lands.

and it will cost a very large sum to remove them to Shrewsbury. I think it would be for the best plan for them to accompany you, you will be allowed excellent transports & a very pleasant time of the year and if you have favourable winds you will not be long in the passage and it will be in the power of the captain to make the voyage pleasant. And if your battalion is ordered into the field, it is very easy for them to remain at Dublin, where they will be perfectly safe. In some garrisons you will find excellent barracks, it is most likely that your regiment will be quartered in Dublin being one of the *oldest*. I really think that the Old Shropshires will never fire a shot except at a *blanket* during the time they are on service. I would not advise you to take all your baggage. You will not want the flowerpots & variety of furniture for the head may as well be left behind. Mr L had better take plenty of shoes & stockings & some spare leather that he may have them mended in the bogs. You want Captain Jervis who with his pistols &c, they should take plenty of portable soaps etc.

The captains should furnish their men with three spare oil [skins?] previous to embarking. Tuft should be sewed into the caps & the cap tied under the chin, for if you recollect your regiment lost some hats last war when they embarked for the Isle of White, but that was their first campaign. The men should be furnished with oil bottles, to keep in the pouch. The officers should carry packs whilst they are on service. The militia will become fine old soldiers when they return from this expedition, at least, they will tell tuft stories, after this they will forget Blyth camp in Northumberland[14] & the skirmishing on Rushmore Heath.

I hope that the first action will be fought near a place that has an easy name or it will be forgot. If you are employed, I think it likely we shall come over and have a brush as well as your rifles. The Northumberland have received the route and march on Tuesday for Harwich, they will be the first body of [Militia] men that will leave this country.[15]

I believe that lodgings as well as provisions are cheaper than in England, besides if my mother remains in England, it would not do for Robert to remain with them without going to school, and if he does go to one will be very expensive. I do not think you will be moved about so much in Ireland as you have been lately, Fidlor joins on the 24th he was quite surprised to see so much difference in the regiment. He says

---

14. The camp at Blyth had seen a major spectacle on 28 August 1795, when seven thousand troops had been reviewed by the Dukes of York and Gloucester. The camp here was in the vicinity of modern-day Gloucester Lodge Farm and was used regularly as a training ground in summer.
15. ie to serve in Ireland.

that we are strict in everything, the appearance of the drill has frightened him, he had no idea it was possible to be so strict. He says that I quite forgot to tell him anything about the duty I only said about the drill, he thinks that our fellows march like soldiers. I am glad that he likes the appearance of the corps. I have not received the letter you speak of, the date of the last June 15th. I should write oftener only the postage comes very high and I do not think my letters are worth so much. Write again soon, I suppose that I shall pay you a visit in February next. Indeed, I have not anything wonderful to tell you but when I have I will try to draw as long a bow as our friend Charley, but I am afraid he will beat me hollow at a story. Remember me kindly to the doctor and the rest of your friends and believe me dear father, your affectionate son, J Meyricke.

My dear mother,

I am extremely obliged to you for the jacket it fits me very well, all the others are going to have jackets like it, they are very comfortable things to wear in the barracks or on the water. I went on a water party the other day with Bulham and some others, we passed a pleasant time & Edwards was as much pleased as the rest of the party, he likes the regiment very much.

I have received two letters from my little girl since my return, but in the last she desired me not to write again as she does not wish to deceive Mr Rolson. She has never written to Sophia except the time she wrote the letter you saw, the time will soon pass, I shall look forward with hope. I am very much obliged to Louisa for her comical letter, it is the best she ever wrote. Harriet is in love, which makes her letters, like mine worth very little. I hope that you have a good passage to Ireland, this is the best time of year [to sail?], that you are all preparing for [service?].

I have not heard from Sophia lately but I expect to hear from her every day. Fidlor is going to teach me drawing, I think that we should be very good companions, for he is quiet and fond of walking, we went sixteen miles the other day through a delightful country.

Do not see any occasion for the family to part, going with the regiment is only attended with a very little inconvenience, not so much as you experienced during your passage in that little boat and when you arrive you will meet with as good barracks as in England, it will be much better for the party to be together than for you to separate. As Mr Lacy[16] intends only to take a change, perhaps he thinks that he can procure shirts cheaper in Ireland.

---

16. Lieutenant John Lacy, Shropshire Militia.

Perhaps the regiment will remain there until the war is over. I do not suppose the Irish Militia will like coming to England, they will find this country rather more expensive than their own. God bless you my dear mother. J M

To Captain Meyricke, Shropshire Militia, Plymouth.

Brabourne Lees, 7 June 1812

My dear father,

I have tried to get a Bank of England note everywhere, I went yesterday to Hythe and could not get one, but I am promised one today. I have been expecting a letter from you every day. The proud Salopians came in on Wednesday last, there was a devil of a huff in the papers during the volunteering saying the proud Salopians had turned out their quarters, principally to the 5th Regiment and they marched out in high spirits &c. The officers have given me the name of the 'Proud Salopian', I went out beyond Ashford to meet them and got for leave all the men that volunteered last time to go out & six of the best bugles, they came into Ashford in high style, the bugles brought out all the flat foot bucks, they had marched twenty miles that morning and were to have stayed at Ashford but they would go on six miles further which pleased our officers very much, they said they were worthy of their title and fit for the 43rd.

Most of the officers were dressed for the ball, and they went out to see them in silk pantaloons, forage caps, cocked hats &c, not two in the same dress which quite astonished the Shropshire heroes, one fellow told me he had been dreaming of the officers & bugles (for they all came out when they went near the barracks), all night.

Mary has told them already that her first husband was a pay sergeant in the Guards. Jervis is appointed sergeant from the day he was sworn in & Sheny & Boot corporals. Hill is full corporal. They are all to go on furlow [sic] as soon as their clothes are altered, some of them are to go to Dover, they like the regiment very much indeed, a great deal better than I expected they would. The officer of the Cheshires that marched them up, dined with us & had my bed, for he behaved very well to the men.

I am under order for service at last and I am to be in Captain Champs[17] company; Lieutenant Hill[18] not being strong enough to go out, his

---

17. Captain Thomas Champ, 43rd Foot.
18. Ensign John Hill, 43rd Foot.

mother wrote to Captain Proctor,[19] saying that the fatigue would kill him and that she was a widow & he was her only child & so forth. I hoped they would allow him to go home on the recruiting service, he has been upwards of three years in the regiment and never done a day's duty. The major said it would be unjust and that every officer must have his turn & he must go out, without he would sign a paper promising to exchange within a certain time. The major said that he was very sorry that it was not within his power to let me go, the arrangements were already made. Hill's mother has desired him to exchange which he has done, this gives me a step & I go in on my own turn to the 1st Battalion without asking any favour from Colonel Hearn. Captains Hull & Strode[20] have resigned which brings me only two from the first battalion. I have got everything ready to go and I am waiting patiently for the order. They say I am to have between seven and twelve pounds prize money for Flushing first payment, which will help me procure a mule, which I should be obliged to purchase to carry my baggage. Talking of baggage, Mary's box came very safe and only cost 11s/5d. I have written to my uncle to tell him I am going out. I received a letter from Harriet this morning, I wrote to her a few days ago through London on my way to Portsmouth where we expect to embark, we shall have a very pleasant party. Mrs Champs came up to the barracks the other day to take leave of her friends as she was going to Hythe and when she got in to the square & saw our lads all merry she could not help crying, she is so altered since the order came, she cannot bear the thought of his going & all the officers wish him to stop, she will not allow it, she says she would rather lose him than have so great a stain on his honour. He is not likely to return for he has very bad health.[21] They are the best couple I ever saw and two fine children, his going will almost kill her.

I have been troubled with a very bad toothache and our surgeon says it is a pity to take it out but I was obliged to have it drawn, the first pull he broke it to pieces it was so very fast and the next time he gave my jaw such a wrench that it quite astonished the rest of the teeth and has been aching ever since. Jones said it could not have been half the pain to have had a finger taken off, his colour came in his face, I believe he thought the pain was broken, it was not half the pain of the toothache. I thought that he did not like the trouble. I was thanking him when I found it was

---

19. Captain John Proctor, 43rd Foot.
20. Captains James Hull and T[homas?] Strode, 43rd Foot.
21. Thomas Champ served in the peninsula for two years and lived until 1851.

putting me in so much pain that he minded. Fidlor has caught a young pigeon and he is highly amused with it.

We have a young Irish lad who has taken it into his head to be fond of my company, he has got a stylish cloak, value six guineas and wants me to give him an old carpet and some teacups &c, value not equal to two pounds, nearer one pound. I have offered him two pounds also & he won't have money & he wishes me to have a [coat?] down to my heels lined with silk in exchange for my great coat which he intends giving to his servant and he is so obstinate that he will not take money the coat is worth £4 he has got other coats besides & he says he does not want these.

I have just received a very kind letter from my uncle with an enclosure of ten pounds, five from him and five from Aunt Judy; they seem to think that I am going *into very great danger*; Tunstall,[22] the young lad I knew at Ludlow is very ill in Portugal & they are afraid of his dying. We have garrison parades twice a day now, six in the morning and six at night and we expect to be sent out to take drawings of the country and give our opinions of how the different positions are to be defended &c. Advance guards, picquets, &c &c, there are very long orders that we have to copy on the subject.

I shall enclose a two pounds note No 30705 Bank of England. The proud Salopians are to go off on furlough tomorrow.

Give my love to mother and my sisters & Bob,[23] this letter is long enough for the whole party, you may have a bit a piece. God bless you, write soon to your affectionate son, John Meyricke. Remember me kindly to Mr Crighton[24] and all my friends.

To Mrs Andrews, Vintners Hall, Thames Street, London, England.

On board His Majesty's ship *Meteor*,[25] 24 June 1812

My dear Mrs Andrews,[26]

The long promised letter from you has never arrived, if you knew what pleasure an English letter gives to a poor devil in this country I should have had more than one. Not knowing where my father is at present,

---

22. Lieutenant William Tunstall, 36th Foot.
23. His brother Robert became a clergyman.
24. Surgeon William Crighton Shropshire Militia
25. An 18 gun brig originally named HMS Starr but renamed Meteor in 1812 and converted to a bomb vessel.
26. His aunt.

I have directed this letter to you, will you be kind enough to forward this when you get his direction. I have not time to write much as it is late, the letters go out at 4 in the morning. We march tomorrow four leagues nearer to Pamplona which is one of the strongest places in Spain but the garrison has but very little provision. We expect soon to have a little rest after a very severe July.

I did not like to write on the cover as it is so easily read. When you have read this letter, I will thank you to forward it to my father, I think there is sufficient in this letter for you and my father. I am inclined to think that in a short time we shall have no more of those round shots whizzing about our ears. Some of these mornings I shall be walking into your house, begging as usual for a cup of coffee or a glass of the old currant wine. You must excuse the bad writing for it is not as easy to write on the knee as it is on a table. Give my love to Harriet when you see her.

Remember me kindly to Mr Andrews, Edward [Andrews] & to my cousins. I daresay that you are very glad that you have got your dear sons in the neighbourhood of London with a snug house & no want of bread.

I know very well that you do not approve of the life of a soldier, I only wish to have you with us on one bad day, I think you would be more anxious to get home than I was when inside the Winchester Mail. I don't think being drowned with rain one day & boiled the next with heat would agree with your constitution. God bless you, I hope to see you as fat as ever. Believe me your affectionate nephew, John Meyricke.

To Captain Meyricke. Shropshire Militia, Plymouth [undated, July 1812?]

My dear father,

At this moment I cannot recollect whether I have written to you since I marched from Brabourne Lees, I have been so much employed since that evening that I have had but very little time, very long marches and a great deal of trouble. I had an idea that we should have stayed at Hilsea for some time, but instead we marched in on Sunday evening and embarked directly. When we came on board we found that the captain had received orders to sail directly and advised us not to lose time in getting off whatever we wanted as we could not wait. Walking through Portsmouth I met Harriet's friend the Purser with Mr Napier and an officer of the Marine Artillery who was going out in the same ship with us, we all went on board the *Meteor* to dinner where I was kindly received by Mr Luckcraft. I passed a very pleasant day & he sent me on board my own ship in style in a gig with Mr Taylor to take care of me, it gave me some consequence. We got under weigh next day and sailed form St Helens with the wind against us which soon after changed into a favourable breeze, which has continued ever since. Some days we have gone at 11 miles ¾ in the hour. We are now off the Burling Islands about forty miles from Lisbon on board the *Freya* Frigate[27] going at 7 nots [sic] with a pilot boat coming on board, she is one of the fastest vessels in the Navy we have been only six days on our passage, it is impossible to have had a better mess, vessel or passage than we have had. The day we marched out [blank] volunteered to do the duty of Adjutant, but one day he was out of the way and I had the duty to do, & I believe I was more alert but since that time I have been Adjutant to the detachment of the 43rd. to the great surprise of all the strange officers we have on board, so young a lad & the junior lieutenant. With 16 officers it is certainly a very great compliment, I have very little to do while I am on board ship, no watch or orderly duty to do, we have a very pleasant crew and I have passed my time very agreeably since I have been at sea. It is eleven hundred miles from Spithead, a good long voyage it has been pretty foul and she has rolled. We shall have 300 miles to march when we land before we can join the Light Division.

5 July Lisbon. We landed on the 2nd after a very pleasant voyage, the entrance into Lisbon is delightful but the town is as dirty as it had been described and very hot, this is the warmest time of the year and I have been almost melted, I am only afraid it will spoil my complexion. I am already nearly *brown*. I met Charles Mortimer here,[28] the 82nd is doing duty at Lisbon for the present. I have seen Madden[29] who is going to England with some of our wounded officers. I understand we shall have to march 400 miles before we join the regiment and mules are very dear, Fidlor intends joining with me to purchase one to carry our baggage. I have got a very good billet with an old lady, three rooms to myself, there are two young girls upstairs, one is very pretty and the other sings delightfully. I cannot keep that vagabond Fidlor out of my house, he will mess with me and Mr Edwards is our cook & we live very well, almost always upstairs. The people are very kind and seem very partial to the English and from what I have seen from the Portuguese I think I shall do very well. I was never better off in my life, nothing to do, it is almost too warm even to write. Fidlor is asleep and I am more inclined to sleep than anything else. I shall write to Mr Meyricke[30] when I join

---

27. HMS *Freya* of 40 guns.
28. Lieutenant Charles Mortimer, 82nd Foot.
29. Lieutenant Wyndham Madden.
30. His grandfather.

the army, at present I can give him no information, and I shall write to Harriet. I wrote to my uncle before I embarked to thank him.

I was obliged to collect all the money I could raise to buy a mule when I arrived in Lisbon & I find that have hardly enough, I was obliged to leave several bills unpaid, I owe Mr Westmorland the tailor in Colchester £3, Hawkes for a cap[31] and Mr Watkins 17 Cork Street, Burlington Gardens £2 18s, for altering my wings. To cover these debts I wish you to receive my Flushing prize money which will be paid in a few weeks, £11. Fraser said it would be three weeks before he could receive it. In case of my death I wish for you to send for my baggage I left in Brabourne, I wish my mother to have my desk and Robert my watch if it ever comes back to England. I have enclosed Harriet Faulder's letters in a packet for you, I wish them to be sent to her together with the locket I have tied round my neck, Fidlor has promised to bring it to England should he survive, I wish for Sophia to have the red case. I have met a great many old acquaintances in Lisbon. Captain Champ seems very partial to me, he takes care of me on allocations 'come we must not forget the Adjutant.' I think it a very high compliment to me as a soldier to be appointed to do that duty and I am to be quartered with the commandant. On the march therefore I shall be well off. Fidlor has joined with me and we have purchased a mule for 60 dollars, a fine little fellow but like Rodney it likes to kick. I have purchased everything I think I shall want. We march on Friday the 9th. What would be two days march we go in boats, I met Dr Laffan[32] the day before yesterday. He did not know me, he stared at me some time and then said I was as broad as a side of a house, he had not seen me since I had the Walcheren Fever,[33] he was very kind, he says I must get on the staff, he is the principal medical man in Lisbon and it may be in his power to be of service to me if I am unwell.

Fidlor desires to be remembered to the family and his friends in Shropshire, I shall write to Greenhead when I join the Light Brigade. Remember me to Mr Crighton. Give my love to mother, Louisa, Harriet & Robert. God bless you my dear father ever your affectionate son, John Meyricke.

PS Direct to me 43rd Regiment Light Division. I am going up to Captain Champs & I must take this letter with me. I will write again when I have

---

31. Founder of the current Gieves & Hawkes.
32. Physician Sir Joseph Laffan. He is not recorded as having been Principal Medical Officer at Lisbon.
33. Meyricke did not serve at Walcheren, but he believed that he caught it in Britain, possibly from sick soldiers returning from this dreadful expedition.

time, but I expect to be in a bustle for a little time. Madden is going to England wounded in the breast, Little, Green & the rest are pretty well.

To Captain Meyricke, Shropshire Militia, Plymouth or elsewhere, England

Head Quarters, 6th Division, 19 August 1812

My dear father,

I wrote to you last from Lisbon & besides writing to you,[34] I have written to Mrs Andrews & Sophia, and when you consider that I have had a march of 30 days, and some days we have gone five leagues, 4 & ½ miles to a league over a rocky country and only one day's halt between this & Lisbon at Salamanca where we were obliged to halt for want of bread. I have had a detachment of regiments which has given me a great deal of trouble. I marched a party of 2 officers and 47 men, out of that number there is only myself & four men left. I had a reinforcement of 50 men at Abrantes and I have only 11 of them left. We embarked 16 o[fficers] & 200 men and out of that number Captain Champs & Fidlor who I met here says he has only 5 o[fficers] & 18 men. Fidlor & Beckham[35] were both left here sick, Fidlor with the ague, but when he got a little better, he was told off to take command of the Light Division that had to join a regiment of detachments & all officers & men are stopped at this place. I had money in charge, I laught [sic] at all my friends who have been travelling the same road with me, & I may thank my stars that I did not go with Captain Champs as they had hard work to escape [commanding detachments].

Madrid 26 August 1812

I arrived here yesterday but I was so much employed going over my party that I was quite [fatigued?]. I had to account for every man I brought from Lisbon & Abrantes which took me half a day. I dined with O'Connell[36] & in the evening I went to the Prado, a place where our bucks assemble. Bayley[37] was driving tandem with a large bow coat and straw hat & Havelock[38] dressed in a purple silk jacket with red sleeves riding

---

34. Not extant.
35. Ensign Thomas Beckham, 43rd Foot.
36. Ensign Richard O'Connell, who had originally been a Volunteer in the 43rd Foot.
37. Actually Lieutenant Mackay Baillie, 43rd Foot.
38. Lieutenant William Havelock, 43rd Foot,

postillion. They had all sorts of dresses. I breakfasted with Captain Booth[39] this morning and I fancied myself in England after being almost starved on the march. After breakfast I went with Captain Champs (who is getting a little better) to see the king's palace, it is a noble building, it paid us amply for our walk. I never saw so fine a set of paintings, the rooms are elegant, the floors are composed of different sorts of marble. I saw one table in particular, the most beautiful marble it is possible to imagine, the centre several precious stones of an uncommon size.

Out of 16 officers & 200 rank & file, that left England, there are only Captain Murchesion,[40] Anggove[41] & myself & 16 privates that is fit for duty. There is only the 1st Brigade Light Division & part of the 3rd Division in Madrid, the Guards are about three miles from the town. I think it is a compliment bringing in the 43rd, the men are in convents & the officers are in billets, I have a superb one.

Stokes[42] bears the highest character it is possible for an officer to have for bravery, he took a fort very gallantly a few days before the storm [of Badajoz]. I met with a sergeant in my march that was with Stokes taking this fort on the 25th & there was only this sergeant, Stokes & a man on the wall & Stokes killed the officer at the head of the defending party & took his sword from him. At Badajoz he was made quite a target for his thigh was broken & he called out to be removed & they could not get at him & the French hearing a noise fired, some say thirty, some say sixteen balls [went] through him, poor fellow; he died like an English soldier.

Captain Champs has been as good as his word, he has got me into his company & I am the oldest lieutenant. I have the command of the company now that Champs is unwell. Fidlor is very unwell, but he is much better than he was, the men look very well & the battalion is about six hundred strong. I have always heard that Madrid is a dirty place, but it is a cleaner town than any I have been in either Spain or Portugal, the streets are all very wide and the entrance into the town very pretty. As I passed through Salamanca I went to the famous church [cathedral], it was far superior to anything of the kind that I had ever seen before, there is a very handsome church at Segovia, but not equal to the other. I had 47 fine men when I left Lisbon & I only brought two in that were fit for service, Edwardes is very unwell and Corporal Lyol, the strongest man of the party is dead. The 1st Battalion laugh at our detachment,

---

39. Captain Henry Booth, 43rd Foot.
40. Actually Captain Robert Murchison, 43rd Foot.
41. Actually Lieutenant John Angrove, 43rd Foot.
42. First Lieutenant James Stokes, 1/95th Foot, was killed at the storm of Badajoz.

we certainly had a very long march by way of a trial, everyone expected that I should have had the ague but as yet I have disappointed the knowing ones, I have dined with most of them and it surprises me to find such good dinners, when I have been almost starving they contrive to have pudding & pie. I have often wished for one of Louisa's plum puddings nicely baked, it would be a treat & a slice of bread & butter & some coffee in the morning. I would give up all the good things in Spain which are very few. I have just heard that the letters for England are to be sent off at 4 o'clock and as I expect you will be anxious to hear from me, I will send this letter off by this pacquet. We expect to march in a few days, they say towards Toledo, but those things are uncertain. I have to lay in a stock for our mess and not one of the three has any money, sugar is most wanted, brown sugar is two shillings per lb & tea as dear, the salt is as large as English peas but the grapes are beautiful and only two pence for a lb & a ½ in the country. As for wine, their best would make a dog sick, English vinegar is far better, the bread is good & cheap in some places, no butter. I could live in England like a prince for half the money it costs to live like a pauper in this country. Madrid I think is about the size of Norwich, the houses look like prisons. If you knock at a door, they open a little grating and look at you and then withdraw the bolts of the door, the principal apartments are at the top of the house; there are generally two families in one house & the ground floor is the stables and lumber place which gives the town a bad appearance, all the windows have venetian blinds, then glass doors & inside these are large folding doors about three inches thick strangely.

I am very anxious to hear from you, it must be a very long letter, written very close, if you have not time then perhaps Harriet or Louisa will contribute to fill up the paper, I think this a long letter of mine. I will send you a copy of my route that you may trace my road through this country, I am just sent for to Captain Champ but I must finish this letter for if it does not go now, it may be two months before I can send it. I met Charles Mortimer[43] at Cuellar, he was very kind to me. I was rather unwell the day I was with him; he says twenty officers of the 82nd are sick & one dead, I am in hopes that this country will agree very well with me, all of the party have got the ague and I have escaped it, I suppose I had my fair share when I was in England. Remember me to all my friends. Give my love to my mother, my sisters & Robert. God bless you my dear father, write soon to your affectionate son, J Meyricke.

---

43. Lieutenant Charles Mortimer, 82nd Foot.

ROUTE

Lisbon to Sacavem Leagues	2
Vila Franca [de Xira]	4
Azambuja	3
Santarem	4
Golega	4
Punhete[44]	5
Abrantes	
Gaviao	
Nisa	
Sarnardas [Rodao]	
Castelo Blanco	
Lousa	
Pedrogao [de Sao Pedro]	
Meimoa	
Sabugal	
Aldeia da Ponte	
Ituero [de Azaba]	
Ciudad Rodrigo,	

3 days march to Salamanca
Cabeza Veloso [Cabezabellosa de la Calzada]
El Pedroso [de la Armuna]
[El] Carpio
Medina del Campo
Olmedo
Mata [de] Cuellar
Cuellar
Two days to Segovia
[San] Ildefonso

Naivco ceria da Torres Lodones [Torrelodones]
Madrid 25 August, rather a long march

Madrid 9 September 1812

My dear father,
　The sickness this detachment has had has been dreadful, it must be owing to so long a march, I am quite recovered from the little illness I

---

44. Now Constância.

had, but my poor friend Fidlor has fallen a sacrifice, he had been unwell a short time before he went to this town, but he was not seriously ill until about ten days ago when he complained of the ague & was ordered to keep his bed. He was attacked by the same kind of fever as I had whilst I was at Sophia's, which carried him off the day before yesterday,[45] I saw him twice the day he died but he was quite insensible, he was buried yesterday near the fort, near the Retiro, the Spaniards would not allow him to be buried in a churchyard. I miss him very much, we were such intimate friends. Steele, the lieutenant of the camp tries to divert me, he took me to the coffee rooms & the principal places of the city.

I have had the fever and afterwards the ague, I never took my medicine and am now, thank God, as well as ever I was in my life, my constitution must have been stronger than Fidlor's for I was worse than him a short time ago. I wish Major Betton would write to his father to tell him of the death of his son,[46] every attention was paid him by Captain Shaw, the captain of his company. He had medicine at 7 & ½ per bottle and brandy at a very high price at the same time, a dollar was quite a fortune. He had everything necessary the same as if he had been in London. J[ames] Shaw went on purpose to buy things for him.

I must now turn from this melancholy subject to give you an account of the famous Spanish bullfight that we have heard so much about in England. I went to one the other day, I suppose that it was in honour of Lord Wellington, for they very seldom take place. It was in a space enclosed by a circular building about three storeys high with boxes the same as at a theatre, the people sat below on benches like the pit. Between the people and the ring is a space of about four foot for the men who are engaged to save themselves when vigorously pursued by the bull, this divided from the ring by a railing about seven feet high, with a kind of step to assist the people employed to vault over. I saw two bulls leap over this first railing and astonished the sentries posted there. Before the bull comes in there are posted two men on horseback armed with a lance with a small point that it should not kill the bull, besides these there are six men dressed in silks and cloaks of different colours but without arms. These try to play the bull to make him attack the horsemen who only act on the defensive and only one at a time, the other horsemen go to the background. When all is ready the doors are opened & in rushes the bull, he looks about for a short time & then rushes

---

45. The records state that he died on 8 September 1812.
46. Captain James Shaw, 43rd Foot.

on the horseman who endeavours to defend himself with his spear, if he is too hard pressed the men with cloaks endeavour to attract the bulls attention, who generally runs after them. They are so closely pressed that they are obliged to leap over the railing, when the bull has attacked the horseman several times, four men enter without cloaks armed with small arrows which they stick in the beasts sides, when the bull is quite mad, the matador enters armed with a sword with which he kills the bull but runs great danger of being killed himself. When the bull is dead, three beautiful [horses] enter & draw him off. I saw several men thrown & two horsemen killed but no other accident.

11 September. This morning poor Fidlor's kit was sold for auction, the things went so high that everything sold for what it cost, some things for double, things I thought not worth a shilling sold for a dollar, I got his journal as I would not allow it to be sold to strangers, I intend to go on with it, I have not begun drawing yet, I shall soon. Steele has got a billet on the floor under me and as we always dine together, it makes it very pleasant. Major Napier has ordered me to write to Major Betton & he will write and enclose a letter partly finished that they may be sent to his father as we do not know his address, but it will cost the major a great deal for postage & I don't like to write.

13 September. This Madrid is the most unlucky place in the world, a fellow this morning broke into the stable and stole my mule that I gave between 17 & 18 pounds for at Lisbon, there were three horses of Captain Champs in the same stable and they took no notice of them, I cannot tell how my baggage will be carried, I have no animal & no money to buy one, I am not the only officer who has suffered in this case, four other mules have been stolen besides mine, I shall make myself perfectly easy, something or other will turn out to make up for the bad.

We have just received the English newspapers with accounts of the Battle of Salamanca, what a row the people made, it seems to have made some noise in the world. The Spaniards say that one army of the French is returning into Biscay & the other army is found in Valencia or Murcia and here we are doing nothing between the two armies. I wish they would send us against the Murcia heroes, I want to drive them to the other side of the Ebro, they seem to have forgotten that we are stationed here, we have the Light, 3rd & 4th Divisions in this neighbourhood.

It will come very hard upon you as you will be obliged to pay for postage both ways, for there is nothing charged for postage in this country, but if you like, I will not write so often, I have not written either to my uncle or to Mr Meyricke, I shall write when we march from Madrid. I suppose that our division is part of an army of observation to watch Joseph Bonaparte. Lord Wellington is in the north. Will you have the goodness to write to Mr Fraser the Paymaster of the 2nd Battalion to know if my Flushing prize money is payable, if it is I wish him to send you a draft for the amount, I owe money to people in London to the amount of nine pounds, but keep the money until they apply for it. I must try and save a little money to replace my mule, it will not do to mind these sort of disagreeables in this country, I know my mother will begin to find fault with my carelessness & Louisa will bring Mrs Jenkins silver knife on the carpet. How does old Rodney get on, I wish he had walked off and you had my mule, he was such a handsome fellow. I have met with several English books in the house where I am quartered and Captain Murchison has lent me *The Citizen of the World*,[47] which has afforded me great amusement, you can have no idea what a treat an English book is. I have begun to draw but I fear I shall make but a poor hand without Fidlor.

I climbed up one of the highest church steeples in Madrid and had a wonderful view of the country, the town is not quite as large as Norwich but there are trees planted on all roads leading from the city. The entrances to the city are very neat. The walk called the Prada is a fine lounge, there are a great many marble seats and fine fountains & there is a handsome fountain in most of the streets which improves the look of the town. The mutton here is extremely small and sells for one shilling a pound.

People talk of the fruit of Spain, they have nothing fit to eat except grapes and I cannot get any raisins. Everybody seems very sanguine, we expect to drive the enemy across the Ebro this summer, but they have so many strong places the other side so that we expect a few sieges, we do not expect much rest this winter. It has rained for the last three days and the rain in this country is very heavy, the less work the better this wet weather. I went the other day to the military museum where there are models of everything you can mention in the military line, even the method of carrying on the approaches to a siege, the way to form a battery of [cannon], a model of Cadiz & Gibraltar & most of the ports in Spain, it is well worth the attention of every military man. There is another museum in the town but I have not had an opportunity of seeing it yet.

I am almost tired of Madrid, we never know when we are well off, if we stay here much longer our battalion will be very strong, most of the wounded men from Badajoz have joined, the 2nd Battalion men

---

47. *The Citizen of the World, or Letters from a Chinese Philosopher residing in London, to his friends in the East* was written by Oliver Goldsmith and published in 1762.

are dying very fast, we are near 800 strong and they were only 400 a short time since. Do you remember the name of a young lad of the name of Price of the light company who volunteered the first time I came to Plymouth[?] He went out with the 1st Battalion and soon afterward deserted to the enemy. He was taken at Ciudad Rodrigo & shot with some of the 95th & 52nd. There is Salopians for you. I was very sorry for the lad. The 74th that volunteered were promised four guineas extra bounty. I have seen some of the men who came from the Shropshire who say it was a mistake for they never got it, I thought it was a mistake at the time.

Ridgway's friend, Adams is in the same company with me & Shawcross is servant to Mr Baley [Baillie]. I should like to receive as long a letter from your party as I have sent, surely Louisa & Harriet can contrive to give me all the news, I won't ask my mother to write, I know my mother thinks it as much trouble to write as I do to go on a day's march. I am very anxious to hear from you, I have not received a letter from you these three months and I have wrote several times to England. I have heard that Colonel Hearn has landed and coming up country, I fear he will not stay long for he has very bad health, I believe I told you I wrote [to] Mrs Andrews. I should like to have an answer, a little London news would be very acceptable. In this country we have either very hard work or nothing to do & the latter is the case at present. I have read all the English books I have been able to meet with, and cannot draw all day, therefore I naturally think of home and wonder what is passing there. I am trying to procure a Spanish & English vocabulary, learning Spanish will be a good way to pass the time. We have two parades a day, the same as in England, and we have guards at the forts &c, &c.

They only give you about two hours' notice when the post goes off, therefore I am obliged to have the letters written ready to send, we have just heard of the deaths of eleven of the detachment.

Well, I have bought another animal, a little ugly pony, and Steele goes halves with me, we are to pay three dollars down and three dollars some time hence. Steele has his baggage carried by the commissary, a friend of his and I intend to poke some of my baggage along with it, if I can get my baggage carried (that was all the mule was wanted for) if that can be done for three dollars, ergo, I have only lost three dollars. I am going on with my drawing famously tell Miss Betton. I shall bring home sketches of the wildest country in the world.

10 September 1812. The letters must be sent in immediately, give my kindest love to mother & sisters & Robert & remember me to my friends. God bless you my dear father, from your affectionate son, John Meyricke.

Ciudad Rodrigo, 22 November 1812

My dear father,

I received your very affectionate letter this morning, you can form no idea of the pleasure it gave me not having heard from any person since I left England. I will now begin and give you an account of all my marches ever since I last wrote to you. You want to hear how I lodged on the march. I cannot give you a better idea than by desiring you to go to some wet ploughed field in the neighbourhood and fancy you are ordered to remain there the night and all your baggage gone to the rear. On the 21st of October the division marched to a village about 2 leagues [to] the south of Madrid, from there to Alcala [de Henares], a very pretty town that you will find in the map. On the 27th we marched 5 leagues to Arganda [del Rey] a town to the south situated among the mountains about 9 o'clock an order came for us and in consequence of the French having passed the Tagus, we marched back to Alcala [de Henares], and arrived at daybreak, and encamped (that is to say piled arms) outside the town, that was the beginning of the retreat you must hear of before you receive this letter.

30th at 10 am formed on the road leading to Madrid with the rain coming down in torrents, which continued all the march, we passed Madrid and encamped in a ploughed field about a league from it, at daybreak we marched back to Madrid to cover the retreat of the other divisions of the army as the light formed the rear guard. While we halted the 82nd passed and I walked as far as I could with him [Charles Mortimer], he had had but little provisions and I had none to give him, he got an allowance of bread and he then moved off and we followed in the rear. I have seen him frequently on the march and always went to see him whenever we came near the 4th Division.[48] We went on very well marching taking up positions &c every day from morning until after dark until the 11th of the month, when the rain set in, and I will defy any person to walk 2 yards off the road without being over the ankles in wet. I was in most places over my knees in heavy mud on account of our marches being through ploughed fields, besides the mud we had to wade through, rivers and pools of water. On the 18th I do believe we waded through 60 at least.

I must give you some account of an action we had on the 17th [November]. Early in the morning I saw some dragoons about 200 yards

---

48. The 82nd were initially placed in the 4th Division following its arrival from Cadiz.

from our camp and Lieutenants Houlton[49] and Baily [Baillie], went to
see what they were, the fellows allowed them to come close and then
fired but missed them. We formed on a space rather free from trees and
waited an hour or more for the approach of the enemy, the rain coming
down as usual. As they did not come, or I suppose the other divisions
had crossed the river, we retreated and after marching some miles
we were again attacked in a thick wood. We sent out the cacadores 2
regiments, the 52nd, 3 companies of the 43rd and some 95th to skirmish,
the rest formed column at quarter distance, loaded and fixed bayonets,
the whole retreated in this order through the wood down a very steep
hill. The enemy were so strong that they drove our skirmishers beyond
the column, we then crossed a plain through which runs a river that we
had to ford. I jumped in and found it up to [the] middle and the bank
on the other side very steep and slippery. Just before we reached this
river the French opened a battery of 9 pounders with a well directed
fire of shot and shells on the troops crossing the ford. Just above our
heads was a brigade of our guns driving back the F[rench] which I am
afraid killed some of our own men, we then formed on the right and a
few yards in rear of the above mentioned guns, in open column, it was
Captain Macdonald's Troop[50] of H[orse] A[rtillery] Captain Macdonald
was wounded soon after we formed. The enemy then got some guns
on the high hills we'd just left, but on account of the height, most of the
shot went over our heads and fell among some Portuguese in our rear.
The enemy had another battery on our left, we were exposed to the fire
of these guns for 2 hours and if ours had not been the luckiest battalion
in the service we should have lost a couple of hundred men, as it was
we only a few (Lieutenant Ridout,[51] Mr Napier's friend) lost his leg and
is not expected to live, Lieutenants Hobkirk[52] and Baily [Baillie] slightly
wounded, and a few men 43rd might put an end to the affair, and we
took up a position in line on the left of the guns, where we remained
until morning. We marched all the day and encamped after dark in as
wet a place as any in the country. We had been without bread ever since
we left Salamanca and this day I only had a few acorns that got roasted
when we halted, I was extremely cold above my knees in wet but not
withstanding these disagreeables, I laid down in the wet not being able
to keep my eyes open. I slept very well until 3 o'clock next morning at

---

49. Lieutenant George Houlton, 43rd Foot.
50. Second Captain Alexander Macdonald of A Troop Royal Horse Artillery.
51. Lieutenant George Ridout died of his wounds on 23 November 1812.
52. Lieutenant Samuel Hobkirk, 43rd Foot.

which we got under arms, waiting for the other divisions to move off, which was very unpleasant as the rain had changed to a frost and we were on a very exposed place. We heard that we were to be quartered in Ciudad Rodrigo but when we arrived at the suburbs, we heard that the town was so full that we could not enter, but were to be encamped about 2 miles off. You may guess that was rather unpleasant news, instead of getting under a roof to be again exposed to the weather. After halting about 2 hours we marched to the ground whose mentioned (during our stay in the suburb McLane [Maclean][53] procured a 4lb loaf – the knife was soon out, the bread parted into 4 shares, called out, and in the course of a short time devoured, it was the first bread or bisket [sic] I had tasted for 5 days, one day on the march Houlton offered *four dollars* for a loaf but could not get it. The men all say they never suffered so much since they came into the country, the Corunna retreat is not equal to it as they always had plenty to eat and went into villages when they halted. I had not my clothes off before last night (since the regiment marched from Madrid) during which the rain came on, and next morning we crept into an old convent, with a very small proportion of roof. But to balance that we had an great quantity of rubbish and we soon *found on our entrance that we were not the first inhabitants*, we set to work and made a space free from stone and mortar &c &c we remained in this comfortable abode 2 days, we marched to this place and on my arrival found the long looked for letter. We did not want for companions in the convent, we had some hundreds English, Portuguese, Spaniards who on account of the rain seldom troubled themselves to go far from the place they had fixt [sic] upon for quarters, and as every group had a fire you may guess we did not want for smoke which was so great that we could not see the other faces. The morning we left this den Mac[lean] and I were laying as close as 2 pigs under the same blanket when a large piece of tile came down and hit him on the head, which I told you before is *rather* of an *uncommon size* and almost made it as big as two. If any other person had received the blow they would have gone to the other world, some of the fine people in England would think it *misery* to live in the place I have just described but I assure you I never was happier in my life, we were quite comfortable, we had bread and a dry blanket and what could we wish for more.

My mother must think me a poor sickly devil, fancying me always, I never had better health in my life than I have had since I have been in

---

53. Actually Lieutenant John Livesey Maclean, 43rd Foot.

this country and if it had not been for the wet I should not have been incommoded by the retreat. Some parts of your letter are like a sermon against fear, although I told you what I wished, there was no reason for you to suppose it was from fear. I have not been troubled with that complaint since I came into the country, and again you write in very low spirits in consequence of the Russel P business. Just think for one moment of the comforts you enjoy viz, when night comes you have a roof over your head, a good bed and next morning you find bread ready for your breakfast, and a comfortable fire to eat it by. Coming to this country has done me a great deal of good. I shall never be incommoded at not having an excellent dinner, as long as I have bread and potatoes, I shall be satisfied and never think of what is to happen next day, I shall be able to live on a small income. Ladies of rank in this country have been known to dress themselves in ragged clothes and *beg* in the streets, and I have seen very genteel girls and women begging in the streets for the value of a farthing. The woman of the house where Captain Champ was quartered in Madrid, was so poor that she could not buy bread for her children, and asked Steele to take her oldest son for a servant that he may have bread, the lad has received a good education, draws, understands several languages and was brought up in a very good style, the mother had a very handsome house and was very well off before the war, but when the French came to Madrid, she put a bundle on her head and after taking leave of her son set off on foot with her other children for Cadiz, the poor boy, (younger than Bob) not being accustomed to hardship was almost killed by the severity of the retreat, he got over it, and as we are all very kind to him, I think he will do very well.

I am sorry to say that poor Ridout died this morning a mortification took place in the other leg, in consequence of cold and bad treatment, he travelled in the rain all the way to Ciudad, seven leagues before he could get the limb amputated and on the 18th we passed him in a miserable village three leagues from this town.

Poor Beckham never joined in, had a very bad liver complaint which near killed him, he was given over by everybody but I have since heard that he is on his way to England with an intention of resigning, Cundy[54] is with him, I hope he will not resign as Ridout's death will give him a lieutenancy and then he can remain with the 2nd Battalion. We hear worse accounts of the men of that detachment every day, I don't think

---

54. Ensign Nicholas Cundy, 43rd Foot, did become a lieutenant on 24 February 1813.

there are 50 of them alive, Sergeant Mauley and Bowen are both dead. This country agrees with me very well, I am much stouter than when I was in England. If you was aware of the pleasure your letter gave me I am sure you would give me another treat very soon.

I hope it will never be your fate to come to this country, to experience a retreat, to advance is very pleasant, but no person can describe the horrors of a retreat. By sending a militia to the Mediterranean Islands and Gibraltar and those garrisons it will give a great many more troops to the service, at the same time these places will be well defended for I consider the militia excellent troops. Something must be done this next summer or else it will be no use, but God forbid that you should ever set foot on this wretched land, I would sooner lose my life than you should come here. I am no croker I have experienced fatigue and I can stand it, but I hope to God that you may never make the trial. I am in excellent health and as happy as a king, but when I reflect on the numbers dead and dying from fatigue and sickness, on this day's march we passed I believe 9 dead bodies lying on the side of the road and above a hundred dead animals. When poor Fidlor died I said thank God my father is not liable to endure these hardships, I hope neither you nor Robert will ever come nearer to this country than you are at present. I have no wish to go home, I have only myself to think about, and when I get up care little about where I am to lay down. My mother cannot fancy that I am very bad after writing such a very long letter. I made out every word of both your letters the first time of reading them over, therefore cross the writing as you like, if you are able to read it, I shall make it out. Gallegos is the name of the village I am in at present it is [within] 3 leagues of Ciudad Rodrigo, I intend to employ most of my time in drawing, but the weather is rather too cold for sketching, Beckham is gone sick to [blank], Ridout's death will give him a *lieutenancy* which takes him back to the 2nd Battalion, I hope he will go to England as he is not fit for this country having a bad liver complaint, I am afraid he will not live, he did not join the battalion. Mortimer I have not seen since I left Salamanca, I must try and do without prize money, it is quite the fashion to be poor. God Bless you my dear Father. J M

PS

I was advised not to send this letter by Baily [Baillie] as he is a very wild fellow and perhaps would forget to post the letter into the office, therefore I think it is better to send it by the post. What is Sophia doing at Richmond[?] I wish she would write to me. You want a description of this part of the country; Ciudad Rodrigo lies in an open country surrounded by hills or rather mountains, but out of the reach of cannon shot, there is not wood enough in the neighbourhood to build a bird's nest. Every sort of provisions are extremely dear and difficult to be had. I think that I shall save some money notwithstanding as our mess is composed of very poor personnel. We are obliged to go without things we should purchase with eagerness if the army was paid up, and those days we had nothing to eat we had nothing to pay for. This place is a mess, from the shot during the siege and very little to be sold, it is not equal to a village in England. It was formerly one of the best cities in Spain, the houses have no windows, which is very unpleasant in cold weather, as the shutters are obliged to be kept shut. I suppose the people in England will grumble at this retreat, I suppose fate is determined that nothing honourable shall take place when I am with the army, the Flushing business was not very glorious. Surely that would not have been General Thomas' reason, for the 43rd got many men from the Salop the last time.

I am sorry that Horton dislikes the regiment, he has got into a very bad company. How does Jervis and Shery like it, they seemed very well pleased with the corps when I left them, most of the Shropshire Heroes that I got the first time are dead, your old friend young Beadle[55] went home to England. I am so poor at present that I intend parting with my favourite crooked guinea.

Tell Robert I am pleased with him for sending the letter, tell him I have already got a few coins and some Spanish nobleman's seals and I will collect some more before I come home, it has astonished me that 3 of the family should walk off so soon, there is one thing it will save me the trouble of calling in Cross Street when I go through town. The two penny post will not have to go so far as before, it is so fine a day that I must take an amble of the hills, the one on which the British threw up their works is on the north side of the town, the hill is full of holes made by the shells and is covered with pieces of shells as thick as stones in some fields, the forts thrown up near the town are very weak. I think it is a very poor fortification, the houses both in the town have a very war like appearance, most of them being full of shot holes and numbers of balls are laying about the town.

The Salop deserves the title of 'China Regiment' now, as they have been so long in the citadel, a march would be as new to you as to the

---

55. Private Joshua Beedle, who was invalided home to the 2nd Battalion on 24 August 1812.

Tower Hamlets. How long has Sophia left the north, I was quite surprised to hear about her being at Richmond, the death of the old ladies has made a [shock] in the family, why they have began to move off by *threes* from the left, a common mode of marching in the Light Division. Mr B[etton] will not have so many to take care of therefore. I hope you will benefit by it. I am glad Mrs Andrews is going to Ludlow, I think she is very partial to the family, she will receive my letter I hope while she is there. I wrote a long letter to Mrs Andrews when I was in Lisbon, I have not received an answer I wish she would write I would soon answer the letter for writing and drawing are my only amusements when we are in quarters, on a march they find us something else to amuse us.

I could take a very good sketch of the town from an old convent near this place, but the weather is so cold that I could not hold a pencil outside the house, ask Miss Betton if she has taken a sketch [of] Betton, yet we were to have taken sketches from nature it was too bad of you to quiz us as you did.

30th I am just set down after a march of three leagues to finish this letter, that I may have it ready in case the letters are called for. I read yours yesterday, I am very much obliged to you for writing, I assure you that I shall never be at a loss to fill a letter in this country, although I cannot find lively topics, I could fill two sheets more with tails [sic] of misery. I have finished a letter on foolscap paper to Mr Meyricke without giving him an account of either *bullfights or palaces* and I shall send it off the first opportunity. I intended to have taken a sketch of Ciudad R[odrigo] but our march has prevented that. We expect to remain here all the winter, it is a miserable place. We have 5 officers, 2 of them sick in a room not large enough to swing a cat in, no beds, but pork is pretty cheap which makes up. I hear a fine fellow grunting in the next room that I expect to have a piece of in short time. Any news of the little lady in the north will be very acceptable, she will be of age on the 20 December.

To Mr Meyricke, Vine Court, Spital Fields, London, England

Suburbs of Ciudad Rodrigo, 23 November 23 1812

My dear sir, [His uncle]
I waited until I joined my regiment before I wrote to you and when I joined I found my time sufficiently employed, until this day.
I arrived at Lisbon (after a very pleasant journey) with 16 officers and 200 men of the 43rd. The detachment marched up the country after a week's rest and I was left with twenty men. Soon after I was ordered to

take under my command, a detachment of 47 men with 37 mules laden with money to be taken to the headquarters of the army, which I expected to find at Salamanca. Soon after I left Lisbon the country began to wear the appearance of misery, villages deserted, towns with half of the houses in ruins, not a corn field to be seen, and no other trees than olives, which grew something like what we term a pollard in England.

Santarem was the first town I came to of any note, it is situated on a rising ground between two hills covered with these trees, with the Tagus running in its front, it has been a very good town, but most of the houses are in ruins, and the convents are fitted up as hospitals. It is one of the most healthy places in the country, the next place of consequence is Abrantes which has very narrow dirty streets, I have reason to dislike this place as I was on my feet until midnight (after a march of nearly thirty miles) taking over a detachment of 68 men to reinforce my party, as most of my party had fallen sick from fatigue, the weather was so extremely hot that sometimes I had not eight men up with the mules when I arrived at the end of my day's march. The next place was Sabugal, the country about this place is very wild nothing but mountains and rocks.

We found a great difference in the customs and manner of living of the inhabitants on our entering Spain, the cottages (that were left standing were whitewashed and had chimneys), the people wore shoes and stockings and were much cleaner. The Portuguese are very dirty, wear long hair and feed principally on vegetables fried in oil, bread is very scarce all over Portugal and no butter to be had and if it was not for the rations the officers receive going up they would be starved, and as it is you can but just subsist. In some towns you may purchase a little milk, but there is nothing to be had in the villages except a little wine which is worse than bad small beer.

Spain is more like England covered with fine villages and in time of peace plenty of corn, in some places there are corn fields as far as the eye can reach. Salamanca is spoken of as one of the finest towns in Spain, the square is very good, and the cathedral is one of the finest buildings in the world, there are many convents and churches, now used as hospitals & barracks, one of them held the whole of the Light Division about 7,000 men. The streets are very narrow, the town looks very pretty as you cross the bridge but when you enter the place you are disappointed, for the streets are very dirty. Segovia is like most of the Spanish towns, very old fashioned, the gentlemen's houses look like prisons, strong doors and the windows covered with a strong iron grating, and many of the houses without glass window, but strong doors by way of shutters.

Madrid is a very nice city, clean in comparison to the other towns, the streets are very broad with good houses, several excellent markets for fruit and vegetables, there is an excellent walk called the Prado in which there are some excellent fountains, stone seats and a row of trees each side of the walk. On a Sunday evening this place is crowded, with the inhabitants, the only fault is its being very badly paved. I do not think it is quite so extensive as Norwich, very little trade indeed, everything seems as quiet as in a country town in England. At this place I delivered up the money to the Pay Master General and upon mustering my party I found that out of the 47 men I had brought from Lisbon, I had only 2 that were fit to carry arms, and out of the 68 from Abrantes, I had only 8 left. I found my regiment quartered in a convent and upon enquiry I found that out of the detachment of 16 officers and 200 men, only 1 officer and 12 men were doing duty, the rest like my party were left behind sick with fatigue and the heat of the weather. The most intimate friend I had, that I loved as well as I did my brother, was taken ill after the march and died in 9 days, more than one hundred are dead out of that ill-fated detachment.

On 21st of October we marched to the south on account of the enemy being in motion and on the 25th marched to Alcala [de Henares], one of the prettiest towns in Spain, from thence to Arganda [del Rey] five leagues, on this march we passed through a vineyard that I suppose was at least twelve miles in circumference. That night just after we had composed ourselves to sleep after a long days march, an order came for the division to assemble, and in a short time we were under arms and on our road back to Alcala [de Henares], and after a long night's march arrived at daybreak, piled arms outside the town, where we waited until the middle of the day when we were allowed to enter, this was the first beginning of the retreat that you will hear of long before you receive this letter.

28th. It rained extremely hard and the division formed outside the town and after waiting about an hour marched toward Madrid, passed it and arrived at the camp ground about ten pm, piled arms in a ploughed field and rested until daybreak, then marched back to Madrid to cover the other divisions of the army. As the Light as usual was to form the rearguard, in consequence of which honour we lose many hours sleep, the other divisions getting to the end of the march by 3 or 4 o'clock pm and the Light not arriving until nine or ten when it is too dark to get any wood or water. The whole army marched and nothing happened until we reached Salamanca were we joined Lord Wellington and took up the old position, here we remained some days, but in consequence of the enemy turning our left flank we were obliged to retreat. As soon as we turned our backs the rain began, and the road was worse than any entrance into London in bad weather, as we passed through woods and ploughed fields sometimes wading through rivers and pools of water, and as our baggage was in the rear we never had any dry things, getting up in the morning with clothes as wet as if the person had been soaked in a river. There was some skirmishing on our left on the 16th but only on the morning of the 17th some calvary came near the tree I stood by, and Houlton and Baily [Baillie] went to see what they were as we thought they were Spaniards. They allowed them to come near and then fired, but missed them when our chaps were very glad to arrive back, we then moved off and formed on a green were we waited while the rain was soaking us. The enemy did not come on, we retreated, but soon after they attacked us in a thick wood driving our skirmishers beyond the column, we retreated down a very steep and slippery hill, we then crossed a plain and had to ford a river, just at this time the French brought some nine pounders to bear on us. One poor fellow was wounded near me, he cried for his companions to carry him off, which was almost impossible as we crossed the river with the greatest difficulty as the bank was so steep, just over our heads was a battery of our guns driving back the French, we formed in open column to the right and a little to the rear of these guns, the enemy then got another battery to bear from the hill just left and another to the right of that, a shot from the last guns wounded Captain Macdonald of the horse artillery, who commanded the guns that stood close to us, we ever annoyed by the fire of these guns until night. One shot took off Lieutenant Ridout's leg, another killed Lieutenant Hobkirk's horse and wounded him in the heel and Lieutenant Baily [Baillie] was knocked down by a piece of a shell. Their guns were so high above us that most of the shot passed over our heads, if their guns had been lower we should have lost half the regiment. The rain came down so heavy that it was worse than the shot. We retreated about an hour after daylight, but the enemy did not follow us, this was the worst march, we passed through at least sixty rivers and pools of water and what was worse, we had not received a single piece of bread since we left Salamanca, the only thing I had to eat this day were a few acorns, I was [so] tired at the end of this day's march that I went to sleep the moment I halted, wet as I was. Lieutenant Houlton offered 4 dollars for a loaf of bread and could not get it. Thank God I arrived safe and in very good health, the men say this is the hardest march they have had since they came into the country. On the retreat to Corunna they say they had plenty to eat and slept in houses, we had nothing to eat and not even a blanket to keep off the wet sometimes. Remember me kindly to Mrs

Meyricke and my cousin and give my love to my Aunt Harriet when you see her. I remain yours affectionately John Meyricke

Direct to J M 43rd Regiment, Light Division, British Army, Spain

Pamplona 28 June 1813

My dear father,

I suppose you are rather more anxious than usual to hear from me on account of the fighting. I should have written to you before, but we have been close pursuants of the enemy since the 21st [May]. I have just come in from a tiresome march of only two leagues but we halted so often that it is nearly five o'clock. I am extremely sorry that I cannot give you a list of wonderful adventures and narrow escapes, I had not even my cap knocked off, but I might have had my head broke for the shot flew as is general in all battles, so much for an account of a battle. Dinner is ready and I am afraid of the turkey getting cold, therefore I will put by my letter until tomorrow 29 June. We expected to halt for some days at the place where I began this letter, but we were marched on with very short notice and encamped after four leagues march, we have been on our legs ever since last night's march for we did not encamp until near twelve, it was the most dreadful I have come yet, we are in hopes of halting today, we have now been on the march since the 21 May.

I believe you wish to have an account of the campaign, or at least of my march. I have sent one account to Sophia but it is likely you will not see that letter.

On the 21 May we marched out of our quarters and encamped to the north of Ciudad Rodrigo, where the Light Division assembled in the highest order, about 43 file in the weakest company.

22nd, halted after 4 leagues, on the same ground we halted for an hour on the retreat the day after the action, the country at this time was covered with grain, the marks of the retreat were still visible, that is to say old shoes, dead horses & men.

23rd encamped on the ground where the enemy nearly gave us a thrashing on the 17 November [1812].

We halted on the 24th and we had an opportunity of looking over the ground, it is a wonder we were not [all] taken, at this time the country appeared quite different, this was one of the best camps we have had, the householders joined us at this place. If I go on in this account I shall fill a quill of paper and use an hundred pens.

We left Salamanca to our right and forded the Tormes on the 2 June. We marched 7 leagues through a delightful country, orchards on both sides of the road to a camp a little out of the town of Toro, which stands on a very high hill & commands a beautiful prospect. We could not enter the town as the French had destroyed the bridge over the Douro. I was sent with a fatigue party to assist in making a passage over the river, I was kept there until almost midnight and then returned to the camp. I had about an hour's rest, when the bugle sounded, which made me grumble like a bear with a sore head, we were some hours passing the river by means of some ladders put against the broken arches, we encamped about a mile the other side of Toro. I walked back but did not see of anything of notice except the delightful line of the banks of the Douro. Toro has a Moorish castle fitted up by the French, it would be impossible to take it by the way we came but the rest of the army crossed further up and by that means outflanked the enemy who retired leaving a few of their hussars prisoners of the 10th [Light Dragoons] who charged them.

Arrived on the 11 June and took our old position in front of the army, this was a very long march and we encamped in a beautiful valley near a convent that was destroyed by the French. On the 7th, we entered this city Palencia, the enemy had just left it, the streets were full of the inhabitants who shouted as we passed, the people threw down rose leaves & waved their handkerchiefs, the town was in a bustle. This is a very pretty place, the country improves as you draw nearer to France, we left [Valladolid] five leagues on our right.

12 June. The light moved on with cavalry, towards Burgos where in sight on the town we saw some skirmishing to the right & stood looking on for two hours, then moved on and halted and formed line and waited under the hardest rain until night. The cavalry had some skirmishing, when this was over we moved back and camped in some dirty ploughed fields as hungry as people generally are when they have been starving for a night and a day. The next morning we heard an explosion and soon after heard the pleasing news that Burgos was destroyed, we then moved on a long march to the north on the 15th after marching over the most barren country for three leagues, we came to a pass between two rocks and after groping our way for an hour and a half we suddenly came in sight of one of the most beautiful valleys it is possible to fancy; all the places I have read in [blank] or The Arabian Tales cannot be compared to it, it was covered with the finest grain and fruit trees of all descriptions. The River Ebro runs through this valley, we crossed by a neat bridge, the next morning we expected to ascend as steep a hill as we entered the

145

valley, as it was surrounded by high mountains, but surprised to find a narrow path between two steep cliffs, where the river entered the valley, the side of the river was a road, or rather a track about two yards wide, we observed several barriers destroyed, the enemy could have stopped the passage of 20,000 with a hundred men, but believe they were not aware of our coming by this road. This pass is the most romantic of any I have seen, we marched for a league by the side of this river, we turned a sharp point of rock and entered another valley not quite so beautiful as the first. We found the 5th Division encamped in this valley and on leaving this valley we marched two leagues further and encamped near Medina [de Pomar], which is an old town with a nunnery & a castle, it is built near a river in a fine country. It would have been easier to climb up the side of some houses than go over the rough [ground] we passed that day 17 June or 18th. The division with a squadron of German hussars moved off early in the morning, to the right through a pleasant valley like at [blank], after two leagues march we had the intelligence that Jack [Frenchman] was on our right, marching parallel and soon after we had the first thing like fighting that we saw, was some Germans coming back with their horses tied up bringing in some French hussar prisoners. We then left the valley on a hill to the left of the road, the first thing I saw was the enemy running away through a valley close to us and the 1st Battalion following up. Soon after another body of two battalions made their appearance from behind a hill close on our right, so close that we took them for Spaniards. As soon as we saw the rear and the baggage following when the 52nd was sent along the road to ascend a hill in front of the enemy column, one of the 95th had got on the hill before the 52nd, the French ascended the hill not knowing what was passing on the other side, when the general got on the hill he perceived the 95th, he tried to collect his troops who covered the hill like ants annoyed by the fire by those in the rear, he rode up and down and looked like a mouse in a trap, he then perceived the head of the column of the 52nd, he then turned to his right and galloped with his officers towards a high chain of mountains, both parties going as hard as they could walk up the hill, the British firing and the French now & then firing a shot. We then saw a body of French cavalry creeping amongst the rocks, our fellows then fired at these and then either killed or took the most of the horses & I believe all the baggage of the division, it was night before the hunt was over, some going two leagues after them, when the men were collected, the place looked like a fair for the men had plunder of all descriptions, even the general's coat, the division moved on a league further and the 43rd were left for two hours in the village where the prisoners were brought to, the enemy must have lost in killed, wounded and prisoners at least six hundred men and our division about one officer and twenty men wounded & I believe none killed. We heard the next day that some Spaniards had been let loose among those poor devils who had taken refuge in the mountains & I will answer for it that they sent some to the other world. The next day we had the 4th Division at work all day on our left, we passed the ground, either no person was killed or they had buried them.

On the 27th, we marched through the town of Taffalier [Tafalla], the streets were crowded with the inhabitants, it was a very pretty sight marching through the street in two columns, the heavy brigade on our right. The householders were so drunk that they could hardly sit their horses.

28th We marched out of this camp and had a very hot march, we felt it more because we had had a great deal of wet weather lately and as much cold as in January. This day the sun peeled the skin off our faces, my nose is dreadfully sore. We halted for two hours to cook and then went over a very rough road, as it grew dark the road grew worse, not being able to go more than one or two at a time. Part of the regiment lost themselves in the wood, we arrived in our camp groaning after a very hard march about 12 o'clock pm, nothing to eat and not the slightest prospect of seeing our baggage. Impossible to go further, for on account of fatigue we had only twenty file in the company. Sometimes they would serve us of two ounces of flour after a long march, sometimes meat or horse beans. We heard that our march in this direction was to cost us a division of the enemy, but they being fresh troops continued to make their escape.

30th Marched to the town of Sargenssen [Sangüesa] on the banks of the River Aragon. The idea is that we should return to the neighbourhood of Pamplona and there rest for a short time, this has been the most active campaign ever known in the country. Our papers came today & the first thing I saw was that the Salop Regiment left the [British mainland] with a fair wind for Cork, cheering all the way. I am very anxious to hear from some of my friends, all the officers receive letters but myself.

Cochrane[56] saw Charles [Mortimer] on the 21st, he passed him in the action and I understand he is very well. It will be foolish to send this letter without knowing where you are quartered, therefore I will keep it ready until I receive a letter from you. I should have written before but I was

---

56. This could be either First Lieutenant Robert or Thomas Cochrane of the 2/95th Foot.

in doubt whether you had embarked for service or not. Give my love to mother, my sisters & Robert, God bless you my dear father, I thank God that you are in that part of the world called Great Britain. From your affectionate son. J M

1 July. An order has come to send off letters to England tomorrow, I am at a loss where to direct this letter. I think the best way will be to direct it to London, as the most likely way of finding you.

Captain Meyricke, Shropshire Militia, Limerick, Ireland

In Camp near Vera 4 August 1813

My dear father,
    The last letter I sent to you I directed to Mrs Andrews, and I am afraid it was sometime before you received it as I have not yet received the answer. I am anxious to hear the account of your voyage to the land of potatoes, and an account of that country. I think that I wrote to you last from San Esteban. We marched on 14th to Sunbellca [Sunbilla] and on the 15th we marched towards Vera, the last town in Spain. A short distance from the place, the enemy skirmishers showed themselves and three of our companies were sent out, who after some trouble drove the enemy out of the town. The regiment was encamped a short distance from the town and the picquet was posted at the church, with the advance sentry within about 30 yards from the French sentry. We had wet for two days together and no shelter, with little food, in consequence of which I had a few days illness, which obliged me to go into the house of a priest about four miles from the camp. The first night I got into the house I got better and for 2 days I was [as] comfortable as a little king.
    On 26 July I heard the army was on the move to the rear, I crossed a mountain and got into the road and lodged in a house at the foot of the hill. Next morning I found the division had passed the very door of the priest's house and encamped on the top of the mountain I crossed in the morning. I then moved to a house on a hill under the encampment and went to sleep, in the morning to my great astonishment the birds had all flown, not a tent to be seen, but I perceived some of the baggage moving along the side of the mountain. The man of my house took [me] by a path up the mountain to the road they were marching on and I followed the division to Sobeater [Zubieta] they had marched all the night.
    29th at nine pm we marched again and crossed another high mountain, on the other side of which we slept for three hours. Then

marched until we came into the high road to Pamplona, we got into the camp at about 3 pm [on the] 30th. On the 31st [at] 3 pm the division marched back the same way on the road to Vera, the French had attempted to throw supplys [sic] into Pamplona, but were repulsed by the 4th Division, who obliged their army to retreat. It is supposed they lost upwards of 20,000 in this jaunt, we lost a great many officers and men. On the return the Light Division made a very long day's march in order to arrive at a bridge before the enemy, it was about eight leagues over very bad roads, nothing but up and down steep hills, the day was very hot, they were on the road from daylight in the morning until after dark, it is reported that some men died from fatigue on the side of the road, I saw one I thought was dead with a woman crying over him.

On the 2nd the Fourth Division was sharply engaged driving the enemy from the hills and towards the evening we had to attack a hill or mountain in the form of a loaf of sugar. The 1st and 3rd Battalions 95th attacked in spirited manner and the company I belonged to was supporting with two other companies in our rear. The fog was [so] great that it was impossible to see three yards, the enemy fire slackened and the 95th thought they had left the hill, but just as they reached the top the French gave a cheer and drove them back with their bayonets. An officer threw one of the 95th down the rocks and broke his neck.

They pushed on again and won the hill and remained there until the Spaniards relieved us. The divisions are just in their old places, the French on one chain of hills and the English in another, both strong positions. If we attack them, we are likely to lose 20,000 men and if they attack us they will be almost annihilated, they make such a noise all day and before daylight with their damned drums, and their people are under arms for hours together. The 5th Division is employed at the siege of San Sebastian and we hear them pounding away all day.

I understand from a man of the 82nd that Mortimer was left very ill at Vitoria, the regiment has been very unlucky, they came into the country the same time as we did about 1,200 strong. Since then they have had a detachment of 100 from sickness, for they have been but little engaged, they are now quite reduced not drawing rations for more than one hundred and sixty men and [in] all only five officers. The 43rd and 52nd have both been in the country for five years and they draw for nearly 1,000 rations each. The 82nd notwithstanding they were so weak, behaved in a most gallant manner at Pamplona.

On 31st of August when the day broke, we perceived several columns of the French at the lower part of this position and as it grew clearer we saw their troops filing over the mountain. Our baggage was packed and sent off in quick time and we sat watching them coming down, it was a beautiful sight. They formed columns after columns, in fact we thought we should never see the rear of them. They brought some pieces of cannon to bear on the 2nd Brigade; we were too high to be annoyed by them. They then formed some light troops on the banks of the Bidassoa River and afterwards a column came towards the river with two peasants at the head who pointed out a ford, the army then forded leaving a sufficient force with two pieces of artillery to secure the passage. They afterwards ascended a hill, the troops posted there retiring before them, leaving us quietly on our hill looking on. The French moved on about 3 leagues over the mountains towards San Sebastian but were suddenly stopped by a line posted on a range of hills, this they attacked three times and were repulsed. In the evening it rained in torrents, which caused Jack to recross the river quicker than he came. We moved about two miles towards [blank] where we rested for the night and returned next morning, [with] time enough to see the French move back to the place he came from. The same day San Sebastian was taken by storm, the Light Division sent a storming party; Lieutenant O'Connell[57] leaded [sic] our men and unfortunately fell by [a] wound in the body, 9 men returned out of 30, most of these wounded slightly, the rest killed or wounded. Lieutenant Follett[58] had just come out from England with a detachment. On the road they met with the enemy and had some skirmishing, poor Follett received a ball in his body which killed him before he saw his battalion. The castle of San Sebastian surrendered, our shells played the devil with them, they made a most glorious defence. 1,500 men marched out of the castle, one of our buglers is just going to be shot for deserting to the enemy. Buchanan[59] of ours is going to England for the recovery of his health, and he will take this pacquet for me. Crawford[60] came out from Cork the other day and says that he saw the Shropshire Regiment, but did not know that I had any relation in the *corps* or he would have called. You may judge how disappointed I was when I heard he came from Cork without a letter from you.

The transports that took you to Ireland brought him out to this country. *Long looked for* came *at last*, I received your letter yesterday you may see

---

57. Lieutenant John O'Connell volunteered for the storming party at San Sebastian and was killed.
58. Actually Lieutenant George Folliett, who was killed near San Sebastian.
59. Lieutenant John Buchanan, 43rd Foot.
60. Lieutenant Craufurd, 43rd Foot.

by the first date of this letter that I only waited to know in what part of the world you had taken up your quarters, now I know where you are you shall not complain of my not writing. As you seem very anxious for a letter, and as it may be some time before Buchanan goes from this place, I will send this by the post, tell me if these large sheets are charged double, if they are I will send no more of them. I will send some letters by Buchanan and my watch for Robert, it is out of repair, but that is easily set to rights in a town like Limerick, although I cannot get it repaired in this part of Spain.

I received a letter from you but I forgot the date, I think it must be the letter you speak of but I always burn the letters in case of accidents, it does not do to keep letters long in this country, I am sure it is the same letter. You are always afraid of my not being able to read your cross writing, I have always been able to make out every word the first time of reading, write as much as you like and cross as often as you can I shall be able to make it out.

I wrote to my uncle to ask leave to draw on him in case of accidents and he returned an answer that he would allow me to draw fourteen pounds, but not as a loan. Knowing my uncle's disposition I wrote word back rather in a spirited manner, that I did not want that time any money and that I should not think of drawing on him for any money without I was actually starving and then I should not have asked for more than half what he offered as a gift and asked him at the same time if he ever heard of anything in my conduct that was dishonourable, if I left any of my debts unpaid when I left England. In fact I answered his letter in a manner he did not expect, at the same time thanking him for his kind offer, since then I wrote another letter to him describing the country, the manner of cultivating the *vines*, and the different plants that I should have met with in the country, this letter I think pleased the old gentleman very much. I remember the old saying, the person who is not in want of money is most likely to get money given to him. I know that is my uncle's plan, therefore I think that is one reason why I am so high up in my uncle's good books, he likes people who do not want money, I think that I shall be good friends with him.

Spain is a country where you meet with many crosses, I will send you a few instead of yours. All the wonders I have met with or heard of in this country are completely eclipsed by your voyage to Ireland, in future I must say nothing, or in other words shut my potato trap. Drinking tea without milk and sugar and being starved for a few days now and then are trifles. What work there must have been to fancy myself the groupe, and how you were stowed, our men call being on board ship *marching*

151

at ease, but by your account there was not much ease during the whole voyage. I am anxious to hear Louisa's account of your trip, tell her if she will write I will not require her to read the letter when written, she may write it as badly as she likes it. If I had been on board I would have kept watch, for you would not have seen me below very often. I suppose the troubles of the first voyage to Plymouth was actively forgotten in the increased disagreeables of so long a voyage. But you must have found greater pleasure when you landed. Whenever I am very hungry and have nothing to eat I always console myself by thinking how I shall enjoy the first good breakfast and how greater [a] comfort a wash and a clean shirt will be, people can never know the comforts of this life without a few varieties, besides mother and sisters will have some wonders to talk about when I come home.

Well now the disagreeables of the voyage are over, I am very glad that you have your favourite potatoes. I am very glad that old Rodney[61] has retired on *half pay* or half his costs. I did not expect you would get even that sum notwithstanding his services. I hope that the next time I see you to find you well mounted, and I flatter myself I am a pretty good judge of horses, at least more used to horses than formerly. I might be able to judge as I have a great deal of it, sometimes twelve hours together. I am afraid that I shall have to purchase another, but I shall put it off until the next campaign, after all the fighting, I think it is very likely that we shall have a peace, in which case I am likely to have to come within the lowest reduction. At present I have only fifteen [lieutenants] above me and some changes are likely to take place very soon. I think that I must be within the twelve before so great a reduction can take place, for I have twenty-eight lieutenants below me at present, besides there is not the least idea of a reduction in the 52nd, 95th or ours, as it is expected that these troops will always be kept in readiness in case of any sudden expedition being required, in case of the worst it is if I cannot get three steps in a twelve month. I am very sorry to find that Crighton[62] has such bad health, remember me very kindly to him, and tell him that I hope to have another breakfast with him and a slice of fat roast beef, so delicious, such as he used to give me at Plymouth, *those were the days*. Tell Mrs Fraser I am highly honoured by the compliments of making me a God father and she may depend upon [me] instructing the lad in all I know, that is to drink and smoke, that is all that is expected for a soldier

---

61. His father's horse.
62. Surgeon William Crichton, Shropshire Militia.

to know. I advise other people to admire, other people are to have the pleasure, and I am to answer for the sins, I hope there is some difference between being the father and the God father. For I had plague enough about being called father. Tell James that I should like to have a few lines from him either in one of your letters or by some other conveyance so as not to put him to the expense of a letter. Charles [Mortimer] is quite well, I have not been able to see him but I heard of him from a sergeant who saw him yesterday. I always ask after him when I meet with any of the 82nd Regiment, I met a little commissary who says that he saw you at Plymouth a short time before you sailed, he is a very friendly little man, I came out from England in the same ship with him and saw him frequently afterwards, he was very much pleased to see me and I was pleased to hear that he had seen you. I think that he deserves pension for his services for the good of the state, he is quite a persevering character, remember me kindly to both and tell them to remember me to Bulham when they write to him. I do not think that Cundy will ever be fit for service again from what I heard of his state of health, it is not always the fine rosy-cheeked boys that stand service the best you sometimes find people with faces like dried herrings, stand better than the handsome ones when it comes to hard work, most all that came out with me are either dead or gone home. There are only four with the regiment out of sixteen who came with me, and some are gone home who came here a short time since. I have been as well since I have been in this country as ever. I was in England only lately I had the same complaint I had in Plymouth viz a pain in the bowels, but I have not been from the regiment and have been for the last fortnight quite well, that is the only thing that has annoyed me since the campaign commenced. I hope that poor Frain escaped the order for the reduction, has he extended his services to Ireland[?] I shall send a letter to each of the party when Buchanan goes home, I am sorry to hear that Mrs Andrews is so unwell. Give my best respects to Colonel Gateacre.[63] I am glad he is so great a friend.

With respect to Murphy, the people are quite mistaken in his character, the worst soldier in the 43rd will give him a good name, for he is a complete soldier's friend and it is his manner of speaking only that frightens.[64] I am sorry to say that Pryce is dead, my volunteers go off so fast that I will never get any more. Horton is recruiting and Jervis and Sherry. There are a great number of reports afloat but we cannot tell when we leave

---

63. Actually Lieutenant Colonel Edward Gatacre of the Shropshire Militias.
64. Probably refers to Lieutenant William Murphy, 43rd Foot, who served in the Portuguese service in 1810–13, in the 23rd Line Regiment.

this ground, the night before last my company was on picquet and an officer in the French service came down at night and called out for one person to advance and he then gave some papers, a copy from the French papers of a battle where the French had taken and destroyed 80,000 of the allied armies in Germany, and taken 100 pieces of cannon, this was printed in French, English, Portuguese and Spanish.[65] When he had given these papers he walked back to his own lines, I believe the whole to be a complete lye [sic]. I hope you will give me a new letter very soon, give my love to my mother and sisters and Robert, yours affectionately J M

To Mrs Meyricke

Camp near Vera, 17 September 1813

My dear mother,

I am rather in a bustle, having at this time to settle with two companies, and Buchanan expects to go off this day, which is much sooner than I expected, he will take my little parcel and send it to you by the coach from Dublin. I have a letter sealed and ready to go off to my father as soon as the order comes. I had just returned from paying a visit to San Sebastian when I received his letter. It amused me very much the account of the preparations and the transfer of old Rodney.

I obtained leave to go over to San Sebastian for a day or two and started from this place in the morning of the 13th. After passing Lesaca[66] the road wound through the mountains, trees over-hanging the road on both sides. Afterwards crossed hill after hill, when I had got about half way it began to rain and I could not see but a short distance, at the same time the road was very slippery up to the horses knees in clay, and great thumping stones strewed all over the road as if were sown, besides masses of rocks to be met with now and then, with [nothing?] that prevented the mules from slipping. The people who have been in the habit of riding in the neighbourhood of London would be afraid to ride over these roads. Just as I reached the top of the mountain the day began to clear and I had one of the most beautiful views I ever had in my life, a delightful valley with good houses scattered over it, at a

---

65. This shows that his letters were written over weeks, as this appears to refer to the Battle of Dresden 26-27 August 1813. It was a famous victory for Napoleon but the allied casualties are very exaggerated, allied losses being 40,000 killed & wounded and 40 cannon captured.
66. Modern-day Lesaka.

distance was the castle of San Sebastian with a view of the sea with ships of war cruising, a little to the right was Passages [Passaia] in front of which place an arc of the sea comes up between two steep hills higher than the mast of the vessels. This place was crowded with vessels which appeared to be locked in, as the entrance is extremely narrow. On going further down the hill, in turning suddenly I came in sight of a kind of foundry directly below me, but it took nearly half an hour to get down to it, the road was so very bad, [that] the most unpleasant thing is to meet a brigade of mules, for the path is not wide enough for two loaded mules to pass.

About two o'clock I got to Lezo, where I left my horse and walked on to Passages [Passaia], this place was crowded with people, a new scene to a person from the mountains where there is nothing passing. The sea looked quite charming and how delightful the sea smelt, I fancy'd I were at Portsmouth. I crossed the water and walked about five miles to San Sebastian which stands on an isthmus and at high water is nearly surrounded by the sea. The town is quite destroyed, there is hardly a house standing, the streets was [sic] covered with dead bodies, I never saw a worse sight in my life, the greatest part had been burnt.

It looked very like war, implements of war laying about in all directions, it certainly was a melancholy sight, a beautiful city in ruins, the streets all barricaded and the stink of dead bodies in all directions.

Our volunteers got lots of plunder, a corporal of the company gave me a silver tablespoon and fork which I shall l keep in honour &c &c of the giver, who is as brave a fellow as ever lived.

I wish you would not be always fancying that I am always ill, I have never been unwell without telling you. I staid [sic] in the neighbourhood of San Sebastian for three days and then returned to the regiment which I found in the old place nothing stirring, the 82nd are about six miles to our right on the same chain of mountains, but the road through to the place is a very bad one. I expect to meet some day on the march, as I have met the 7th Division[67] frequently when Mortimer was in the rear.

If I have time I will write to Louisa and Harriet, but I am afraid I shall not have time, I am just giving over a company, and if I was to write until twelve tonight I could not finish my work. God bless you my dear mother, write soon to your affectionate son. J M

---

67. The 82nd had been transferred from the 4th Division on 17 October to the 7th Division.

To Captain Meyricke, Shropshire Militia, Limerick, Ireland.

Near Bayonne, 16 December 1813

My dear father,

I have received your very affectionate letter, I had just returned to my quarters after being employed for a week, during which time we expected to be attacked every minute, therefore could not take off our clothes. Those Irish people generally make blunders and they never made a greater one than when they made me out severely wounded. I would not have had my name put into the list, but the commanding officer wished the names of those who were hit to be mentioned and my captain said it might do good and could do no harm. I am inclined to think that your wound was about two times as bad as mine, for I am as well as ever I was in my life and only feel a little pain when I am tired, the things I had in my pocket prevented the ball from hurting me. While you was writing on the 23rd of November I was hard at it tooth and nail and was near being taken, at last about forty of us got close under the enemy's works, without knowing it. They let us come, but to get away the thing, to retreat it was necessary to pass a cornfield exposed to the fire of a French division, they came on beating the charge, I then thought no time was to be lost, our retreat now sounded and I took to my legs which thanks *to my mother* are *pretty long*, and ran until I got out of their reach. I believe all the men who were left alive and not wounded followed me, Hobkirk was taken, Baily [Baillie] killed, those who could not run fast enough were taken, the man who was next to me was nabbed, they came out as thick as bees after us, shouting as if they had beat the whole army. If you feel so anxious about me you will make me afraid of going into action, and every skirmish I shall be wishing myself at home.

On the 10th [November?] I was on piquet, the whole regiment was on duty that day. About nine o'clock the French attacked, they came on without packs, sounding trumpets, beating the charge and hollowing in the old way, we of course fell back pretty quick to our fighting position which was a gentleman's house and the church both fortified. They pressed so close that they took an officer and twelve men of the 95th and about the same number of ours. One of our companies had to run through them, we got to the church, and they came on as if after a mad bull, but such a fire was opened from the church that made them go back quicker than they came, the whole church with the ground in front appeared on fire. They brought up some guns and levelled as if they intended to hit the moon, the firing continued all day with very little loss to us, we were kept on the alert day and night, expecting they would attempt to take the post by storm, but on 13th they walked back to their old ground. What was done on the right and left will be seen by the papers, our division is in the centre, we have since learnt that before the order came for them to return they had some grenadier companies told off to storm our little garrison.

We had a little siege of our own. Their people desert very fast, they have hung several. Our men picked up several of the French balls that struck the ground or trees and sent them back again, I think I have given you a long account of the war. Considine had his thigh bone broken very high up, but is doing remarkably well, by the death of poor Freer[68] and some more friends I have risen very high up, I have not more than ten or eleven above me in the regiment, the compliment of lieutenants is forty-six.

I told you in my last letter that I had received a *copy of the will* from my uncle and was happy to find that you was so considerable a gainer. I told my uncle that I did not want the money immediately and wished that he would keep my legacy until some other time. I am sorry to hear of your accident, I mean the twist of the foot, for I consider the breaking of the mare's knees of little consequence as she is young, with little trouble the blemish may be hid some time since. I was going very hard over a rough road with my horse and he came down and cut both his knees, but at present it is hardly seen and I think he is every bit as good as before. If the marks remain it is like a gash in the face, looks very ugly but does no harm.

The strain you got is of more consequence. I hope to hear of that being well in the next letter. With respect to flannel I have worn that stuff ever since I have been in the country, when my mother knows this I hope she will be happy, and give my compliments and if ever she takes the trouble of dreaming about me I hope the dreams will not be of horribles, but of good eating and drinking. I think that she has been quite out with respect to her dreams this time, for take one month with another I never have been as well in my life as I have been since I left Portsmouth and if Jack Frenchman will remain quiet I will have such a thumping plum pudding, that is to say if I can get the flower [sic] and the plums. I don't intend starving, instead of being pale from hard work I have got such a blooming red nose the men always take care of their pouches when I come near them afraid of the ammunition exploding. I am glad to find that Robert is going into such good quarters. My uncle will be very fond

---

68. Lieutenant Edward Freer, 43rd Foot, was killed at the Nivelle.

of him, no man likes the name of Bob better than the old man, he was quite pleased one day when he heard me call my brother *Bob*, it reminded him of old times when he used to be called Bob himself. He wrote in a very affectionate manner to me, spoke of great dangers fatigues &c and wished I was with him at his and my cottage at Dinham,[69] said the place was always kept in excellent order and seemed in a great fright of losing it.

Some days back I was sent on a regimental fatigue to take charge of a party who had to carry two men on bearers who got their legs break [sic] in the skirmish on the 28th. We had to go to the General Hospital at Fontarabia [Fuenterrabia].[70] The road before we got to the Bayonne road was infamous, over the ankles in clay every step and some places over their knees, still they persevered in carrying the poor fellows. In all my life I never was so much frightened, talk of shot, no shot ever frightened me as much, I expected every minute to see them come down. After great trouble we reached St Jean de Luz where we waited three hours for the surgeon to come up with the rest of the wounded who were on mules, it was too late to go further that night, the men were put into a miserable old house they called the hospital. After the men were settled I went in search of a quarter but it was impossible to find a place to put my head into, I was therefore obliged to take up my abode in one of the rooms that was a little the worse for the service it had seen, rather too many windows at the top. We got under way next morning after many delays from the medical people, it had rained during the whole march and still continued, the poor wounded men were in great pain not having the wounds dressed, which could not be done as there was no dressing to be had. Every department in the army is well supplied except the medical department and these people are always in want of something, so very much afraid of expense.

About a mile from St Jean de Luz is a small village called Ironia [Urrugne]. This is a delightful country, gentlemen's houses on the side of the road, a thing never seen in Spain or Portugal, all the heights between St Jean de Luz and the river, the French had thrown up strong works with battery's on the road which in some places is quite straight, it would have been impossible to have forced this part of the position.

The French were completely turned out of these strong works by the movement made by the troops on the right and centre. The left had very

---

69. Now part of Ludlow.
70. Modern-day Hondarribia.

little to do, the light troops had some skirmishing (on the 10th) when arrived at the River Bidassoa, we found the bridge had been destroyed and therefore had to go a little further and cross at a bridge of boats, we crossed the river and halted for half an hour at Irun the first town in Spain. This is a miserable old place and full of Spanish troops. After the rest we proceeded towards Fontarabia [Fuenterrabia], the road runs along the bank of a river on a causeway and near the entrance of the town the causeway has water on both sides which I should suppose was something in its favour as a fortified town. We arrived as the sun was setting and I was happy to have the men lodged safely in the hospital. The men bore the journey remarkably well, the company officer was remarkably kind, he ran over the town to procure a billet for me, as he could not get one that appeared comfortable, he took me into his own quarter and although he dined out he made his servant get me an excellent dinner with good wine and a desert and a good bed, it was so very different from the fare I had the night before, that it appeared like enchantment *I had only to rub the lamp* and I got what I wanted.

Before breakfast we took a walk on the works, which have been strong in the old style but they were blown up some years since. The back of the town is surrounded with [an] immense chain of mountains with a view of our old mountain, La Rune [La Rhune] which looks very formidable, in front is the Bay of Biscay, the waves rolling in with great fury, on the right on the opposite side of the river stands Andaya [Hendaye] a French town almost in ruins. Beyond this is a charming view of France, in fact Fontarabia [Fuenterrabia] is one of the most romantic places in the country. After breakfast I marched my party back by the road we came to St Jean de Luz from which place we endeavoured to find a better road to the division, but after walking until some hours after dark, we found ourselves in a wood and the road stopped by a mill. All hands thought it best to stop during the night, but as the party were without arms, we could not get a light. To lay all night in wet clothes in an old house up to our ankles in mud was no joke. I therefore sent out to see if any other house was to be found and after waiting some time in suspense they returned with the pleasing intelligence that they had found the 2nd Battalion 95th. I therefore rode through the mill and went to the house where I found *Tom Cochrane*[71] who told me that I was not two hundred yards from home and through the mill was the road they always went to St Jean de Luz.

---

71. First Lieutenant Thomas Cochrane 2/95th Foot.

Major Napier has given me a detachment for my journey, and the men a double allowance of rum for a week for their trouble. The 82nd were quartered very near, some of their men and some of ours in the same house. I saw David Fraser[72] who was very well, they marched the day of the row and I have not seen them since. Remember me kindly to Crighton, Fraser[73] and his good lady, my Godchild and the rest of my friends. And if you see my name another time among the wounded, for there are a number of wounds returned severe that are not dangerous, a ball through the arm or leg, a hand knocked off they call severe, fat people are very apt to be carried off by a slight wound, but I expect it will be a good respectable kind of a lick that will send me to the other world. No person can be more lucky than I have been, I have not been in the rear once since I came into the country.

Will it be convenient for you to pay Watkins' little bill, it is £2 18s for altering a pair of wings, let me know. I think this is a pretty long letter, I hope there is sufficient for the whole party and I expect to have a few lines from all hands in return. I am glad to hear Bob has got the watch safe, Buchanan was afraid of losing it. Give my love to mother and sisters, God bless you my dear father. J M

To Captain Meyricke, Limerick, Ireland

Toulouse, 15 April 1814

My dear father,

I think now that the row is nearly over and my mother will have the pleasure of seeing her son come with a whole skin. The Light Division crossed the Garrone [at] 1 o'clock on the morning of the tenth, after we crossed we marched towards Toulouse. About eleven some skirmishing occurred on the right and soon after a battalion of the 95th Regiment went out to skirmish. The Light Division was posted on [the] road leading to Paris. The enemy were posted on a hill fortified with redoubts commanding each other, the fight lasted until night, the French threw some very heavy shot and shells. We were not engaged, although posted in front of the town and Lord Wellington would not allow a single shot to be fired into the town. The fight was very bloody, the Spaniards lost a

---

72. Lieutenant David Fraser, 82nd Foot.
73. Lieutenant John Fraser, Shropshire Militia.

great number, I believe that I have not written to you since I left Aroutz [Arrauntz] (a village near Bayonne) which was on the 16 February.

The army moved to the right in order to pass the River Adour, when the Light Division reached Bastide de Clearance [La Bastide-Clairence] and another order came for the 43rd and 1st [Battalion] 95th to return to St Jean de Luz for clothing, we therefore moved to the rear and reached Eusteritz [Ustaritz] the day the rest of the division moved to the front from Eusteritz [Ustaritz], the tent mules were sent for the clothing and Lord Wellington was so good as to lend us some of his private mules, this gave us the start of the 95th but we were unable to follow the army until the 24th, we then went two days in one, on the 25th we marched to Garits [Garris] a very pretty French town situated in a beautiful country. The 26th to St Palais a better town than the day before, at this place we relieved the 57th[74] which regiment moved on. 27th moved on to Sauvetere [Sauveterre-de-Béarn] were we passed a very bad river but crossed without losing a man. At this place we heard the fire of the engagement near Orthez, this made us push on three leagues further, we had no rum for the men and a double march every day.

28th Under weigh early in the morning and passed the 57th the regiment that started a day before us, *sleeping in their beds*, passed through the town of Orthez which is a very good town but the houses in the principle [sic] street were completely covered with the marks of shot, the people were in a most terrible fright which continued for some leagues. The first thing we saw after passing Orthez was one of the 5th Regiment hanging to a tree on the side of the road. Soon after we came up with the 3rd and 6th Division of the army and encamped at night near the town of St Sever where the French army was posted. The morning when the army was under arms, Lord Wellington passed and asked for our commanding officer and desired the 43rd to move on, we were all in high spirits expecting we were going into the road but soon after we found the enemy had retired, we then moved on to the town of Mont de Marsan and was the 1st British regiment that entered that place, the rest of the division came in late at night they came by another road. Mont de Marsan is an excellent town, we halted one day and then moved to some scattered houses to the right. The cavalry had some skirmishing. Harris of the battalion distinguished himself, he has been very kind to me.

Soult retired and took up a position near the town of Tarbes on the 20th he was driven from this place, his men fought well as a number of

---

74. 57th (West Middlesex) Regiment of Foot.

them were knocked over. I never had so good a view of any affair, the army moved on in four columns, the heads of each in a line, both armies manoeuvred beautifully. When it was dark, Soult took up a good position on a hill with a river set in his front, but retired during the night towards Toulouse. We followed next day and came in sight of the town and part of the brigade had a little skirmishing. On the 27th of March we continued in the neighbourhood moving from one village to another until the 10th of April.

We then crossed the river Gione [Garonne] a little above the town, the 3rd and 4th and 6th Division crossed some days before without opposition. The river was very rapid we had a bridge of eighteen pontoons.

The enemy left Toulouse on the night of the 11th next morning the division were sent into houses in the suburbs, my house was rather airy being full of loop-holes. I went into the town where the white flag was flying on the town hall and the bust of Bonaparte thrown out of the window, everybody appeared in high spirits.

At night I went to the theatre which was very much like a country theatre in England, during the performance a gentleman came in who was sent by the *Mayor* with the glorious news that Bonaparte had been kicked out and that the whole nation had declared for Lewis [Louis] the 18th this was received with shouts of joy and at present all the army carry the white cockade as well as the people of the town. The houses of Toulouse are good, the bridge over the Girone [Garonne] is a very pretty one, the town hall is a beautiful building and the Royal Canal of Languedoc which runs close to the town adds much to its appearance, there is a walk on each side of it, planted with poplar trees.

17th We moved to the front in consequence of Marshal Soult not chusing to be quiet and halted about 4 leagues from Toulouse, the French general in a carriage with an escort of French hussars passed as hard as he could go towards Toulouse.

18th Announcement came that an armistice was made, and we moved to a small village called Bastide [Labastide d'Anjou], this I think is the first day's march towards England.

On the road we met the French general on his way back to the army, he appeared in excellent spirits. Nothing is talked of but embarking, I suppose we shall embark at Bordeaux where Mortimer is at present with the 7th Division. I have seen him several times, I suppose that we shall march towards Toulouse tomorrow and I suppose that in six weeks or two months we shall be in England. I do not like parting with my favourite pony, I have two of them to sell, but horses will be so cheap that I shall get nothing for them. We had a detachment joined from

England on the 16th they just came in time to go home, we are very strong, our company is a hundred and fourteen in the country. I suppose we are the strongest regiment in the country and in excellent order, the people of England will hardly think the regiment has been nearly six years in the [foreign] service, and the cutting up they got at Badajoz, this company lost 43 men at the storm. Remember me kindly to my friends Crighton and Meteyard,[75] I shall make a most tremendous hole in the doctor's *sirloin of beef* if *he gives me a breakfast*, if he consults his pocket he will not give the invitation to a hungry fellow like me.

About six months since I asked for some things to be sent out from England, the parcel was to consist of shirts, a new jacket and some other things which I am afraid are gone to feed the fish in the Bay of Biscay where they are remarkably hungry.

The consequence of this said parcel not being received is that I have only two shirts and they are much better calculated for *summer* than winter. Now I should wish (if the coin can be procured) for my mother to buy some of that excellent Irish linen so much talked of and make for her dear boy some excellent shirts against he lands. And perhaps my *lovely* sisters would employ their charming fingers in making delicate frills for the said shirts. And if my sister *Louisa* should be troubled with ennui, she will oblige me in amusing herself by making some of those *strong* socks, of the same kind as she made before, a pair of which I have on my feet at present which are very good, only want a little *washing*, the weather to be sure is *rather warm*. I have an excellent jacket that belonged to my old friend Freer and I have the handsomest sash in the regiment, therefore the outside is good although the shirts are not the best of all possible order. It is possible that I will bring a few things from this country. I should like to know what would be best to bring, that will be of the most value in England, answer this letter as soon as possible, I am afraid it will be some time before I have an opportunity of sending it to you.

28th April. I have been waiting for the post for a long time and now I have only time to close the letter. All is peace here, we are quartered in different towns. The people are remarkably kind. The 43rd is quartered in the town of Montich [Montech], all the officers have houses to themselves. I am just going to spend the day with an English lady at Monteban [Montauban] I have not my for finger which prevents me from writing. I never was more comfortable in my life. God bless you all and may I see you all in good health. John Meyricke.

---

75. Lieutenant William Meteyard, Shropshire Militia.

To Captain Meyricke, Shropshire Militia, Dublin

Plymouth Dock, 3 July 1814

My dear father,
    They have not given me leave of absence yet, and I do not expect leave for more than between the Returns, I think it is likely that I may get leave on the 10th. The plan I mentioned in my last letter is now completely knocked on the head by our battalion being under orders to embark for America, I am therefore sorry to say that I shall not be able to see you this trip.
    I suppose it will be at least a month before we can be fitted out. Five companies of the 3rd Battalion 95th go with us. I certainly should have liked [to] have past [sic] a month or two in England, but it is all the fortune of war, I think it is much better to go to America than stay here under your old General Brown,[76] who wants to put us into apple-pye [sic] order before we had all got on sure [shore?], wished to alter our uniform, get the lay up caps &c, he made us carry our swords, a thing we had never done for a length of time. What is still more disagreeable we have just such another old fashioned soldier at the head of our regiment who gives us two parades in the day and goes through the old thing, wheeling into line with bayonets fixed, this old jockey will join the 2nd Battalion which is on its march for this place between 600 and 700 strong very fine men. We are now more than a 1,000 and we are to pick the best men of the 2nd and give them our worst, all the sickly men, idle &c &c will be turned over to them, we are to be completed to 1,200 men and I rather think it will be one of the finest battalion ever left England, sixty file per company. I am very busy in fitting out the company I belong to.
    Champ my captain went through France to Calais and has not joined us yet, I pay his company during his absence. I am afraid that he will leave us, which I should be very sorry for not wishing to quit the company that I have been so long with, being in a good many rows together, make the men attached to their officers and officers to their men, but if a captain is put to the company that I dislike, I will apply to get into Swinburne's troop.[77] I am afraid that I shall go out with a[n] indifferent kit for I am rather shy in [the] shirt way, it is not likely that I shall be able to get the parcel of cloathes [sic] I lost the [one] which I believe has gone to

76. General Sir George Brown, commander of the forces in Ireland.
77. Captain John Swinburn, 43rd Foot.

Portsmouth, it is a great loss for I shall be obliged to purchase another jacket which is the most expensive article.

Buchanan told me of your being quartered in Dublin having seen it in the papers, I wish you could obtain leave and come by sea in a vessel for Plymouth and we could all live in the same lodging until I am embarked. Mrs and Miss Luckraft are very anxious for your return, I am there almost every night, miss calls me brother. I went to church last Sunday with them and Mr Parson gave us such a long sermon out of his own head that I was quite tired. I hope that he will put his next sermon on paper. My plan was this, not liking the parade and fuss of a soldier's life in England, I intended going on half-pay 4½ [shillings] per day which in my opinion than would be better than 6 with the mess and other expenses of dress &c &c tacked to it besides being independent, and it was therefore my intention to exchange with some second battalion buck and could have obtained a difference in peace time of about £300 which would with care make up the difference of pay for some years. Now things are altered I am going out on service and if I am lucky I shall get my company before I return. I do not think that a yankey will break my head as the French did not.

Remember me kindly to all my friends particularly to Crighton, Fraser, Meteyard let him know that Beckham is quite well and as fat as a pig, he will join the 2nd Battalion. I have brought over some long and short French kid gloves for my mother and sisters which I will perhaps leave in London, and I shall leave my journal in London and my large book of drawings, they may amuse you when you get hold of them. In my journal there is the account of all the skirmishes that I have seen and all the military transactions during the three campaigns, it will perhaps amuse Bob to trace the different marches in the map and he may compare my description of the towns with the Gazetteer. Love to mother, sisters and brother and pray write as soon as possible to your affectionate son, J Meyricke

To Captain Meyricke, Shropshire Militia, Limerick

Plymouth Dock, 26 August 1814

My dear father,

When in London I found that I could not write to you, I was so completely out of spirits that I could not put two words together. And if I do not take care I shall get another fit of the blue devils, and shall not be able to write this morning. You know what preys on my spirits therefore I shall say no more on the subject, and trust to fate.

I returned to the regiment on the 24th my leave being out and found them making great preparations for this expedition to America, we have turned all our weakly men over to the 2nd Battalion and have received nearly 300 lads in the place of them which completes us to 1,000 men. Colonel Wells[78] has the command and a pretty tight hand, he is an old Adjutant and keeps up to the letter of the law, I understand that he has been stirring up all hands, while I have been absent, he has frightened our boys. I could not help laughing at their accounts of him, I don't think that he will incommode me much, he is a very good man, but so very fond of regularity, besides I have got my old captain back who is as good as the shield of Ajax. I feel quite comfortable now I have him back again.

Great changes have taken place in the regiment, most of the officers have been changed from one company to another, and each battalion takes its own officers, I am to remain with Champ.

The 1st Battalion is quartered in the Long Room barracks[79] and the 2nd Battalion marched in on the 23rd and are quartered in Georges[80] and Granby Barracks,[81] they have two companies of the 1st Battalion not being sufficient room in the Long Room, for the whole battalion.

I am at Long Room, I am very intimate with Albert Luckcraft[82] and I pass an hour or two there every day. Miss Luckcraft at present is very unwell indeed she appears very anxious to hear from the girls. They live at Stonehouse at a place called *Navy Bower*, I daresay my sisters recollect two small houses that stand in a garden leading to which there are a pair of low green gates, it is nearer the hospital than the mess and on the opposite side of the street. I understand that my mother went to look at one of them before she went to Ireland, but I know that my mother has not a very good memory with respect to streets and houses &c. When I was in town Mr Hale was particularly kind I supped with him two or three words. Old Mr and Mrs A[ndrews] were at King's Land and I used to go there with Edward almost every evening, most of the time Sophia

---

78. Lieutenant Colonel Joseph Wells, 43rd Foot.
79. The Longroom Barracks formed part of Stonehouse Barracks in Durnford Street, Plymouth. The original barracks had been converted into an officers' mess and a new wooden temporary barracks was constructed for the men in 1805.
80. George's Square Barracks was erected in 1757 near the Main Guard or South Barrier Gate.
81. Granby Square Barracks were also erected in 1757 and were demolished by 1830.
82. The Luckcrafts were a naval family.

was at the Sw[83] who were very kind to me. I called on Coad but he was out and Kelsey is not a man that I like. I paid a visit to Aunt Abbott and got a kiss and a glass of wine, I hope that will please my mother. I have given Mrs Luckcraft the name of mother, I am there almost every night. Edward Meyricke has taken a house at S[outh] Newington for his mother and Jane, but I had not time to see them often. E[dward] Meyricke and I dined together at V Court and he looked on my face all the time like a Newfoundland dog.

After dinner he say'd [sic] 'But there is one thing my *dear* John that *quite grieves me* and that is I was thinking what's the matter now' and after about ten minutes, out it came (you have got into the habit of writing so *remarkably small* that I am obliged to get glasses to read the letter).

My Dear Harriet, I received your letter and for the same reason that hindered my writing to my father, prevented my thanking you for your letter, and mother, Louisa for the shirts, the new fashion may be very neat, but I cannot say there it is an improved plan, except that they are much easily pack as they do not take up the room in a trunk as the old shirts did.

They are made like my friends C[oad] without a back part to them but perhaps they will stretch.

Notwithstanding all these great preparations I do not think that we shall go to America. It seems the general opinion that we shall not go. I suppose that would make my mother quite happy. Mr Crofts who is [in] the Ordnance Department says that preparations are going on but very slowly and you know there is no fighting without ammunition and I think it is very likely that we shall meet in Shropshire in less than three months. It will be a very bad thing for me this peace if there is one with America, for I am in an awkward place in the regiment, I am too high up to go on half pay and too low down to expect my company in any reasonable time as the companies are [told] off, Houlton who is eldest lieutenant cannot get his company although there is a vacancy. Now on the other hand a sharp campaign or two will give me my company. McLean's [Maclean's][84] brother who was at Portsmouth the other day saw a paper parcel directed to me and would have sent it but they would not allow it without an order from me, on hearing this I wrote to the Military Store Keeper at Portsmouth begging him to send it by the coach in about a week I therefore may expect an answer and

---

83. It is unclear as to what location Sw refers.
84. There were two lieutenants named Maclean in the 43rd Foot, John Leyburn and John Livesey. Were they brothers?

perhaps recover my long lost parcel. I shall be very lucky it has got in it a number of things have been lost. McLean [Maclean] has lost his own things.

He here appears to discuss the ladies with his brother Robert.

You say that H Andrews has broke the charm, I am very much afraid that she will not be happy, I do not like him at all, Edward is a very genteel young man when compared to this hero, who has got about 10,000 Reas not £s at his command and these he uses on all occasions, they have no servant and from his shabby appearance they must be poorly off for coin. She had better remain single all her life, besides he did not appear very bright. Edward seems to have made a comfortable match he seems very happy and has got a very well furnished house at Kings Land.[85]

Mrs E A[ndrews] is at Harrogate with the young ones and old Mrs A[ndrews] keeps house in her absence, they do not seem to admire miss's choice especially Edward. You and Louisa must write a long letter to Miss Luckcraft, she is very ill and it will amuse her, direct it to me if you like and put M.L. on the back and I shall know it is for her. Miss is a very *great* favourite of mine, her brothers call her a 'spare Top Mast'. I have seen two very nice girls the Miss Cowells I believe they knew you, I believe I should be inclined to tumble in love with one red hair only they are engaged. Sophia introduced me to some very pretty girls in London, the Miss Rawlings but I could not make the prettyest speak although she had my arm for an hour, she was rather too shy. Your affectionate brother.

He returns to his father

I think that this war with America will end in smoke, if it does we shall soon meet in Shropshire, during the peace would it be a good plan to take a small house near a country town, not in one, as in that case both rent and taxes will come higher. I think that Edward Andrews plan was good, he took a house rather out of repair and he and his father fitted it up. Now I think that with a very little money we could make a cottage look very pretty. I will volunteer to paint the rooms, having painted and fitted up many barracks when in England and I will colour as many drawings as you like. I am going to send a set to Edward if I have time, and I do not sail. Besides the house, which ought to be taken

---

85. Kingsland is now part of central Plymouth.

for some time, there should be a garden which will not only amuse you, but produce sufficient vegetables for the family. As for living near London with a moderate income is out of the question, the taxes alone would swallow it up besides the different appearance to be kept up, I rather think that a quiet life for a short time would give back the years lost by bustle and uneasiness. It is impossible to be comfortable in a lodging, a cottage of your own and you can make any improvements you like, a little trouble will supply the place of money.

You perhaps will say money is wanted, I grant this is the case, a little ready will save a great deal in the end, but by hook or crook I think I can raise sufficient for my plan, and when once you have a house of your own you will find no want of [employment?]. I want you to fix upon headquarters for yourself and your old sabre will serve instead of a hatchet. When once the headquarters are fixed, you may detach parties where you like, for no visitor is so welcome as a person who has a home to return to. You have seen enough of this gypsy life and have met with too many disagreeables. Oh I wish I had been at home when that disagreeable circumstance happened, it sticks in my throat. Your mind is clogged by having a family, with men the case would have been different. Let me see you independent, it is better to live independent even on a small scale than be subject to the whims of others. A boy can jostle through the world and find dry and wet days balancing each other, it is not so for a man having a family, every vexation that happens, attacks the whole and he has not only to think of himself but the family likewise.

I can go through any row without the least fear and let everything turn out as it likes. Would to God I could see you comfortable settled then watch the father take a good bottle of wine with his affectionate son J Meyricke

When in town I bought utensils for drawing to the amount of £1 5s and I mean to attack it in a most determined way. I have got the baggage I left behind me at Brabourne Lees when I went to Spain. Most of my French books are lost, I packed them up in Fidlor's chest, not having room in mine, the consequence was they were sold with his. All the other things I found right. I will give Beckham Meteyard's wish when I see him. Remember me kindly to all that enquire after me, love as usual to mother and Louisa and Robert.

Mrs Meyricke [care of] Mr Lewis, Margaret Street, Cavendish Square, London

Plymouth, 13 October 1814

My dear Sophia,

After being at Ludlow for a few days I received the order to join as the regiment was to embark immediately. We were just going to have a dance at the Willingses when it came and I was very busy in helping the young ladies to adorn the room with laurels. I staid [sic] for the dance, which was a very pleasant one and then put myself into [the] mail [coach] and arrived here before the regiment had embarked. I went on board yesterday with my company, we go out in transports *Sharman* and our company go in the same, she is a good ship and I think that we shall be very comfortable. The weather was too bad yesterday that they were obliged to discontinue the embarkation and the rest of the regiment are now embarking.

I passed my time very pleasantly at Ludlow. I was a great deal out with the young misses to Harriet's great annoyance. Coming through Worcester I dined and spent the evening with Mr and Mrs Weaver, and [on] a pleasant day Mrs Weaver walked all over the town with me and was as pleased to see me as if I was her son. We talked about the little friends at Ludlow, I used to [go] waltzing and drawing there almost every morning, it is by far the pleasantest family I ever met with, yet notwithstanding there is not one I like better than another and I cannot form any plan of happiness without little Harriet.

Call on Mrs Crofts and tell them that I am on board and sail with the first fair wind perhaps tonight and when they hear of my little girl I wish Mr C[rofts] would send the letter to E Andrews in Bread Street as I do not wish for Mr C[rofts] to pay the postage which he must do if he sends the letter direct. I do not wish the letter to be sent to Vintners Hall, you can speak to Edward I have already spoken to [blank] Tell Mr C[rofts] that E[dward] A[ndrews] is in the habit of sending things to me. The long lost parcel has come at last and I am obliged to you and the rest of my friends for the trouble and give my thanks and a kiss to the [blank] for the map. God bless you Sophia I shall see you soon in better health. J M

Mrs Meyricke [care of] Mr Lewis, Margaret Street, Cavendish Square, London

Copy of letter written to Mr Robert Meyricke of Ludlow from M S Champ 1815, Dauphin Island. Gulph of Mexico 18 February 1815

Sir,

It is with the deepest regret I have to communicate to you the melancholy information of the death of your nephew Lieutenant Meyricke late of the 43rd Regiment and of my company, who died on board the *Gorgon*[86] frigate the 17th of last month most sincerely lamented by his brother officers and all who knew him. You have already been informed by the surgeon of the regiment that he was severely wounded in both legs, in the attack made on the enemy lines near New Orleans and that one of his legs was afterwards amputated. He appeared to be doing very well for some days after the amputation had taken place and this induced him to determine on being taken on board ship, though he had previously been advised to remain in the hands of the enemy. Unfortunately, the weather proved bad and he was five or six days coming down the lake in a small vessel, where no medical assistance could be procured and to this circumstance perhaps his death is more to be attributed than to the badness of his wounds. It will be some consolation to you and to his friends to know that his remains were taken on shore the day after his demise, and decently interred in Cat Island attended by his servant and some people of the ship.

With respect your nephews effects they have been all sold, (with the exception of a sash, sword and watch, which I shall endeavour to take care of till I have an opportunity of sending them to you, or to his father) the produce of which with his pay and allowances after deducting some trifling regimental debts, will amount to between 80 and 90 pounds which will be remitted to the agents immediately after the 24th of April.

I understand Mr Meyricke left a large box in charge of Mr Lowcroft [Luckcraft?] a friend of his at Plymouth containing a writing desk, pair of pistols, some shirts, sheets &c. What few papers he had have been carefully examined and destroyed except a letter addressed to you which I have forwarded by this mail, and I am with esteem truly yours M S Champ.

---

86. HMS *Gorgon* was a 44-gun frigate.

Chapter 13

Lieutenant Wyndham Carlyon Madden

Letters

Wyndham Carlyon Madden was born in Madras on 31 August 1793, the son of Major William Molesworth Hatch Madden of the 52nd Regiment of Foot. Major Madden had married Elizabeth Ridewood, widow of Captain Richard Ridewood, who had died in India while on duty with the regiment in 1784. Elizabeth brought into the marriage her son, Henry Ridewood, who had been born in 1781.

Wyndham was educated at Westminster School and was originally designed for the Church. However, when not yet 15 and with his father's reluctant blessing, he entered the army on 18 February 1808, commissioned in the 43rd Regiment of Foot as an ensign. Within a year he was in Portugal with the army led by Sir Arthur Wellesley, later the Duke of Wellington, and promoted to lieutenant on 3 May 1809. All of Major Madden's sons, including his stepson, Henry Ridewood, who was a major in the 52nd, served in the famous Light Division during the Peninsular War: William was a captain in the 52nd, Monson was also a lieutenant in the 43rd and Edward was a lieutenant in the 95th Foot. All were wounded at least once, and two, William and Henry, were killed in action. Edward died soon after the war, apparently from the effects of it. It appears that Wyndham was a good soldier, as were all the brothers. Wyndham served at Vimeiro, Ciudad Rodrigo, Badajoz (where he was severely wounded), the Bidassoa, Nivelle (severely wounded again), Tarbes and Toulouse. Besides his service on the Peninsula, he was with his regiment at New Orleans in 1814, then back to the Continent, landing in Belgium a day too late for Waterloo. He was then in the Army of Occupation in Paris, and finally in garrison in Ireland. This was all excellent preparation for a successful military career. Nevertheless, in 1820 he defied his father to resign his commission and take Holy Orders when on the brink of promotion at the age of 27.

When he left the army he went to Queen's College, Cambridge, taking a degree and Holy Orders in 1823. He held a curacy in Cambridge and then the same at St Paul's Bedford, before getting his own parish in January 1825; Christ's Church, Woodhouse, near Huddersfield in Yorkshire. This was an industrial community that, in the early days of the Industrial Revolution, must have presented many challenges. Here he married Mary Whitacre in 1826, by whom he had two daughters, Anne and Elizabeth. After Mary died in 1844 he was appointed to Holy Trinity Church, Fareham, in April 1845 and married Charlotte Leeke, daughter of Thomas Leeke of Longford Hall, Shropshire, in 1846. Their eldest son, Wyndham, was born in 1849, followed by two boys, neither of whom survived childhood, and five girls, Emily, Clara, Amy, Caroline and Charlotte. Finally in 1852 he was appointed Rector at Bergh Apton, Norwich, where he served until he died in 1864.

Maimao, Portugal, 5 August 1811

My dearest mother,

I received your letter the evening before yesterday dated the 20 June and have taken this opportunity, which is almost the only one I have had since we left Lisbon, of answering it. The one I sent from there of course you have received long ago. We joined our first battalion at Arronches after a march of nine days, and since that have been constantly on the move towards the north. The French having collected there in great force, today we have halted for provisions, and tomorrow we proceed to Sabugal, the scene of honour and glory to our regiment. But we are ignorant as to our destination, although it is generally supposed to be Espeja or Gallegos in Spain where our division lay before they removed to the south. My disappointment was extreme, as you can imagine, to find I had lost the opportunity of seeing Henry before he left the country[1] and partly through my own neglect, for, had I written from Lisbon, he might possibly have managed to have met me on the road. But we did not know the route we should take until a day before we marched. I shall write to him as soon as I possibly can and send him two congratulations

---

1. Henry Ridewood, his stepbrother, had returned home to take up his post as a lieutenant colonel in 45th Foot.

at once, both for his promotion and his marriage which I do not think will be delayed long. William,[2] I am happy to say, is as hearty and wild and merry as ever. I have lived with him since we joined, and but for the inconvenience of our brigades being separated, would still remain in his mess, However, I don't think we will pass without our seeing one another. He has lent me an excellent mule to ride until he can purchase one for me. That which was sent down to Lisbon by Henry to bring up my baggage having been shot on its return for the glanders for which he was allowed by Lord Wellington 84 dollars, the original price not exceeding thirty. Also, an old baggage horse of Henry's, which was returned as his first charger, and for which he received 31 pounds 10 shillings. William's steeds at present consist of three excellent mules and 2 horses, which he will be compelled to curtail as General Craufurd has issued positive orders to officers commanding regiments to see that animals above the number allowed are immediately disposed of viz a riding horse and baggage mule for a captain, and for subalterns a riding horse each and a mule between two. The marching we have lately undergone and little or no forage, has knocked up a great many animals and it is no uncommon thing to leave two or three every day on the road out of our division. The promotion of field officers with us is immense, Colonel Gifford[3] has retired on half pay and has been appointed Adjutant General in Scotland. Colonel Ross has also left the 52nd Regiment[4] to go to India as Adjutant General to Brownrigg[5] who commands at the Island of Ceylon. How delighted my dear father would be to see the high state of discipline of this division. I do not mean their appearance, or good marching, or manoeuvring at a field day, with which indeed they are never troubled, but I mean their readiness at all times to get under arms, to obey orders and to make themselves comfortable after a most fatiguing march, during which not a man falls out unless through absolute necessity. Their conduct in action is spoken of by all the army in the highest terms, and to be in the Light Division is sufficient to stamp a man a good soldier. As I have not always an opportunity of finishing a long letter, I shall leave this open as a kind of journal, and daily mention anything that may occur to me. At present, adieu. I have just heard we are to move at 5 o'clock this evening to another ground.

---

2. His brother William Madden was a captain in the 52nd Foot.
3. Lieutenant Colonel William Gifford, 43rd Foot.
4. Lieutenant Colonel John Ross, 52nd Foot.
5. Lieutenant General Robert Brownrigg.

6 August

We have returned again to our old ground, which is a flat entirely surrounded by mountains, and it being found unhealthy during the nights from the damps which rise from the river, we are taken up the hills to sleep, and in the morning resume our old position. How long we are to remain here, I do not know. I am at present writing this in a snug little hut which my servant and myself have built with oak boughs. We are leading a gypsy life, which is generally the case with this division. We had flattered ourselves we were comfortably settled in cantonments in Castelo de Vide where we continued a week with every prospect of being comfortable for a month or six weeks, as it was the cleanest and best town I have met in Portugal. But a sudden general movement took place through the whole army and headquarters are now within a league of this. By the letter my father received from me at Lisbon, you will have learnt that I am well provided with trousers & shoes. Poor William indeed I found badly off, for he had not a rag to his back except two check shirts & I have given him two out of my stock. With every other description of clothes, he is well provided. His baggage in general consists of silks, satins, gold and silver lace, which I have no doubt came *innocently* into his possession. He has given me sufficient lilac coloured silk to make a very handsome waistcoat. The costume of British officers when they wish to appear gay, would highly entertain you. Forage caps, jackets, waistcoats, overalls of the most fantastic cut and covered with lace with Wellington buttons. Indeed, it is intended to introduce entirely new fashions when we return to England. The officers' messes in our regiment, are in general very excellent, but at the same time extravagant, for every article of food is dear beyond conception. I have not yet entered any, but William's, whose fame for catering is by no means diminished, but the one I intend to join is the best managed of the whole. The army I am sorry to say, are paid indifferently, and we are taught by our paymaster not to expect any pay until November or December next. How I am to perform my promise to Fraser, I am in great uncertainty and it is a matter of much uneasiness to me as the bill that was drawn on him becomes payable on the first of next month. I intend to write to him by this post and inform him of my inability to pay him the balance of my account at present and request him to send a statement of it to Horsham, where I will remit the remainder as soon as I possibly can. I am very happy that my father took Edward to his regiment as I am sure he is comfortably fixed.[6] In a

---

6. Edward joined the 2/95th as a second lieutenant in May 1811.

short time we may expect to see him out here. It will prove of service to him. The 102nd also may in space of time smell powder[7] for they have got in Lieutenant Colonel Napier[8] a most excellent, brave officer and a man of the greatest interest. How fortunate it will be for Monson if he is not yet married!

I have just this instant received a letter from my dearest mother dated 10 July. How thankful am I to her for affording me the consolation of hearing so often of all your welfares. Think not you can write too often, or I too often receive your letters. To me they are the source of the greatest comfort. Thank God my dearest father has recovered from the serious indisposition under which he laboured, and may this letter find his health firmly established. I am disappointed at not hearing from him by this packet and shall look forward for the next. How surprised and delighted I am to find that you are now personally acquainted with Miss Murray, and that you have formed the same opinion as myself. I was convinced she would soon (gain) father's love and esteem. Yours, she was already in possession of. William and myself have just been comparing letters and he has found that a post goes off this evening, so I must either finish my letter or delay it until the next. Most of the officers who came out with our detachment have been taken ill. I thank God, have escaped and have continued in the most perfect state of salubrity [a la Holton?[9]]. William is a genteel slim figure and weathers it out well; lots of brown complexion. He has received a letter today from Lisbon informing that the whole of his baggage which he had left there, had sailed for England and he wishes my father, whatever the expense may be, to get it immediately from Portsmouth, where a depot will be formed, as there are in it many valuable articles and he requested it may not be opened unless wet or damaged for some very particular reasons. It consists of a large red box, the same portmanteau his father gave him, two small canteen boxes and a mattress & pillow in a velise [sic] with a Mr Cray's [Craig's] name on it, late deceased of the 52nd.[10] He would have written by this post but had not time, and sends his love to you all.

---

7. His brother Monson had transferred from the 43rd Foot to the 102nd as a captain on 19 April 1809.
8. Charles Napier had joined the 102nd Foot as a lieutenant colonel on 27 June 1811.
9. Probably refers to Holton Hall in Oxfordshire, built in 1808 by Elisha Biscoe.
10. Ensign William Craig, 52nd Foot, had died on the 13 December 1809.

So, after all, Monson is married and departed with his spouse for Guernsey.[11] May he be happy, and may this change in life benefit him. Give my love to my dearest father, it will be his turn to hear from me next, and also to Henry, Charlotte, Maria and the rest of the family, and believe me, my dearest mother, your most affectionate, Windham Madden

PS Look out for a wife for me by the time I return.

L'Insena [La Encina], 21 January 1812

My dearest mother,

The siege is finished and thank God William and myself are safe and in perfect health. I did not wish to write until all was over as I know you would be uneasy till then. The people of England I know will be surprised (and not without reason) that Ciudad Rodrigo should be taken in twelve days at this season of the year, while the French were twice that time before it with the advantage of summer weather. The difficulties we have undergone have certainly been great, but I hope they will in some measure be repaid by the credit we shall obtain. Four divisions of the army have been deployed in this duty: the Light, the 1st, the 3rd, & 4th. Ours marched on the 12th instant and broke ground on the same evening, although it was necessary first to take possession of a fort which the French had erected on a rising ground which commands the town, for it cannot be approached in any other direction. This duty was performed in a very gallant stile [sic] by four hundred men of our division, with a very trifling loss and by daybreak we had dug a trench sufficiently large to cover a brigade. As only one division was before the place at a time, we were three days off duty, although but two day's rest, for the village we are in is nearly four leagues from the trenches. I'll give you an idea of our work. We marched before daybreak, arrived on the ground about one o'clock. One brigade went into the trenches where they worked until 6 o'clock, relieved by the other brigade which remained five hours, and so on for twenty-four hours when we returned to our quarters. We were very lucky in not having any rain, but the weather was very frosty and we had no cover for there was not a tree near us, not even sufficient to make a fire. I assure you, my boat cloak by the morning had been sufficiently stiffened by the frost almost to stand erect by itself. I however, was always well cloathed in flannel, and

---

11. Monson Madden had married Elizabeth (née Gibbes) in 1811.

did not suffer very much from the cold. We had only been three times in the trenches in our turn, and we marched the day before yesterday for the purpose of taking the place by storm if they did not hang out the white flag. We had battered two breaches, a small and a large one. The Light Division were to enter by the former. The 3rd [Division] who were that day at work in their turn, by the latter. The advance of both were to consist of 300 volunteers. As soon as it was dark our division marched and formed in the rear of an old convent in the suburbs about three hundred yards from our breach without being perceived. The 3rd were formed on our right. At 7 o'clock in the evening precisely, the signal, a fireball from one of our batteries, being fired, we started and advanced so rapidly that they had only time to make two discharges of grape which happily did no execution, being badly directed. They kept up a decent fire of musketry but could not withstand the bayonet with which they were actually pushed from the breach.

Our instructions were for the 43rd when upon the ramparts to turn to the right and join the other division at the other breach, and for the 52nd to clear the ramparts on the left. The advance of our regiment had just reached the other breach, where the other division had mounted, when a powder magazine unfortunately exploded and completely cleared the ramparts. The number destroyed by it is astonishing. Among them is General Mackinnon of the Guards[12] who commanded a brigade. He was missed all night and could scarcely be recognized this morning among the dead. One of our officers, Pattenson,[13] was blown into the town, but is in a fair way of recovery dreadfully burnt. Some other officers are wounded, but none of our regiment killed. General Craufurd is not expected to live, having been shot in the lungs. Colonel Colborne of the 52nd is severely wounded.[14] Major Napier of the same has lost his right arm.[15] Captain Dobbs killed.[16] The loss of the other division is dreadful, I counted seventy-five officers & men lying dead on top of the breach, besides those blown into the town and lying in the ditch below. Indeed, the whole was a scene of horror and plunder and I never wish to see it repeated, although I am not sorry to have been present at such a service. As soon as the place was in our power, I was placed

---

12. Major General Henry Mackinnon of the Coldstream Guards was killed.
13. Lieutenant Cooke Tylden Pattenson, 43rd Foot, was severely wounded at Ciudad Rodrigo.
14. Lieutenant Colonel John Colborne was severely wounded.
15. Major George Napier, 52nd Foot.
16. Captain Joseph Dobbs, 52nd Foot, was killed.

on guard at the breach where I remained until relieved late yesterday. Many of our officers have got horses and mules, William has got two beautiful animals. He has promised to give me one of them. The scene is so fresh on my mind, that I am not capable of writing of anything else, and therefore you must excuse my having dwelt on it so long. William has just paid me a visit. He will write home directly and sends his love to you all. I keep a regular roster of letters, for I know if I wrote twice to one of you the other would be jealous. Maria's wish shall be complied with, she [shall] soon hear from me. I don't think we shall remain long in this place, for we shall be better supplied at Salamanca. I shall be very unhappy if I find Mr Fraser's account is not settled as it has been due for a long time and he will have a very poor opinion of me. I expect to be properly quizzed for having written the same letter both to Henry and my father. However, I did not know you were in the same town. As the post goes out early tomorrow morning, I have not time to say as much as I could wish, but I will soon write again. Give my love to my dearest father and sisters, as also to Harry and Charlotte if with you and with sincerest wishes for the health and happiness of you all. Believe me my dearest mother, your most affectionate son Wyndham Madden

Badajoz, 15 April 1812

My dearest father and mother,

Being unable to use my hand I have got Mr Considine,[17] a fellow sufferer, to pen to you the dictates of my heart. Cooke[18] has already given you an account of the dreadful occurrence which took place on the night of the 6th instant. To repeat them will only be to rake up fresh feelings. As soon as I can move with ease, I intend to move towards Lisbon for the purpose of getting to England, where, under my dear mother's care and attention, I shall recover my strength. My wound may be a tedious one but it is not in the least dangerous. The ball has struck me high on the right shoulder and has caused a small fracture. And now my dear mother I have to request that you keep up your spirits until I arrive when I am sure my endeavours will not be less successful in making you happy and comfortable. You shall hear from me every post, by which I will give you an account of my progressive recovery. My dear father also must take care of his health and not be over affected

---

17. Lieutenant James Considine, 43rd Foot, was severely wounded at Badajoz.
18. Lieutenant John Cooke, 43rd Foot.

at the death of a son who has fallen like a soldier.[19] In prayers for the health and happiness of you all believe me my ever dearest father and mother, your most affectionate son Wyndham Madden

Badajoz, 18 May 1812

My dearest father and mother,

According to my promise to write to you by every post, I have commenced this small note, a larger one I dare not undertake as you cannot conceive how fatiguing it is to write with the left hand. I am daily expecting letters from you as we have received papers with accounts of the taking of this place and am particularly anxious to know how my dearest mother bears her misfortunes. You, my dearest father, must also have suffered much but, being yourself a soldier, you must have been prepared for something taking place among the many sons you have constantly had abroad and in a division which can boast of having partaken in every glory and danger. All that I have to beg of my darling mother is to keep up her health and spirits until I arrive, and I will undertake in a very short time to bring back the smile of pleasure into her countenance and make her look younger than ever. You and I, my dear father, will have our walks together which used to amuse us so much and as I have been absent a year, there will be incidents sufficient to afford us conversation for a long time. Henry is so busy with his regiment, I suppose he cannot afford time to write to anyone but his Charlotte. I have only received two short notes from him since he left me, which is nearly five weeks ago. However, the whole of the army from the north shall be here by the latter end of this month as all the sick and wounded are ordered from Elvas to make room for headquarters. Poor Jones[20] is here, he occasionally sends me the Horsham news. The surgeons do not expect him to live as he is shot through the lungs and he has not been very attentive to their orders. You cannot conceive the improvement I am making within these few days' past. The cough, which has been so troublesome, has nearly left me. I have a most excellent appetite which I take care not to indulge too much and I have a fine, refreshing sleep almost all the night long without the aid of opium &c, indeed I find myself getting stronger & better every day and the doctors are surprised

---

19. Wyndham's brother, William, had been killed in the attack on the fortress of Badajoz.
20. This probably refers to Ensign John Jones, 45th Foot, who died of wounds suffered at Badajoz on 18 June 1812.

at the ease with which I move myself. I assure on my honour I have given you a true statement of my case. The house I am in is a very comfortable one, directly opposite Colonel Muller's[21] who got me removed into it that he might have more frequent opportunities of seeing me. Indeed, I have received every kindness from him and shall like him as long as I live. By the next post or so, I shall be able to give you a letter in full and with better writing. I don't know how you will manage to read this and the last. Write my dear father and mother by every post. It will be a great comfort to me to know you are well. Direct them to Ridewood. He will always know where I am and now, my dearest father and mother, I shall finish the letter with the hopes of soon proving to you in person that you still possess all the love and affection of your dear son, Wyndham Madden

Badajoz, 25 May 1812

My dearest father and mother,

You see I am punctual to my promise to let you hear from me by every post. I am in hopes there will not be occasion to write by many more as I find myself getting better every day. The swelling on my shoulder has at last come to a head and today they are going to let it out, by which means they will be able in a day or two to put my arm into splints, oh, how happy I shall be when I can tell you I am on my way to Lisbon. I shall endeavour to get to England in some man of war which is going direct to Portsmouth, which I have no doubt I shall be able to effect as Charlotte will certainly be acquainted with Admiral Berkeley's[22] daughters, who commands all the shipping in the Tagus. You will perceive an improvement in my writing, I think, as my two last were written in bed. I am now sitting in an armchair at the table. I get up twice a day and nearly remain up two hours each time which I find of great service to me. I will now give you an account of my diet. At breakfast I take my tea and a slice of buttered toast, with a second with honey on it, besides a fine fresh egg, laid by my own hens, of which I have a couple. Between breakfast and dinner, abundance of oranges etc and at dinner either boiled fowl or veal with the heart of a fine cabbage on which I have lived for a long time. So you see I am

---

21. This would appear to be Lieutenant Colonel Frederick Muller, who was in the Portuguese service.
22. Admiral George Berkeley commanded naval operations at Lisbon, helping materially in supplying the army. The admiral had three daughters.

not starving. I wrote a long note to Henry yesterday abusing him for not writing oftener and longer letters. I hope he has been better in that respect towards you as he has received accounts almost daily of my health from Mr Forbes,[23] who is the principal medical [man] here.

26 May

I deferred finishing my letter until today that I might give you an account of the success of the operation on my arm, but they have put it off to today. However, I will not close my letter until it is over, as I know you will be very anxious to know the success of it. General Hill has again been beating the enemy in miniature. His victories though trifling, are generally very complete. He attacked the Bridge of Almaraz on the Tagus which the enemy had fortified with a tete de pont upon this side, a strong fort on the other. Our fine fellows carried them by escalade in broad daylight. The enemy loss was 300; ours about 130. I am become very uneasy at not having heard from you and I can only account for it by supposing you have directed my letters to Harry, not knowing where I should be. Thank God, my dearest father and mother I can not only congratulate myself on the complete success of the operation which by taking a great quantity of matter has reduced the size of my arm and it now is not larger than the other, but I can also give you the pleasant information that the doctor ascertained by the probe that there were no splint[er]s of bone loose but the whole has united of itself by my having lain quiet so long and I hope by a fortnight to have recovered my strength sufficiently to make a move towards Lisbon. Oh God, how I long for the time to come when I can embrace you both and assure you of my affection which you so fully possess. Give my best love to very dear sisters and believe me my dearest father and mother, your most affectionate son, Wyndham Madden

Badajoz, 1 June 1812

My dearest father and mother,

With what pleasure can I now address you, as I can assure you that in about a week or ten days I shall be sufficiently strong to proceed on my journey to Lisbon, which will take me some time in performing as the weather will be too hot to travel far in a day. This I tell you, that you may [not] be too anxious in expecting me. I think at about the latter

---

23. Physician Charles Forbes.

end of June or the beginning of July you may begin to look out for me. Oh, with what delight I shall again embrace my dearest parents and sisters, with what delight, pay them those attentions which they so well deserve from their son. I received your letter to Henry dated 27 April only a day or two ago, enclosed in one of his which gave me the utmost comfort as it convinces me you bear with resignation the misfortunes which the Almighty has been pleased to inflict on us. My prayers are regularly offered up for your health, your peace of mind, I know, cannot yet be re-established but I hope my endeavours, when I am at home, may be successful in restoring it to you. With what pleasure do I think of the walks we shall take together in the charming summer evenings and Marianne and Clara running races on the common. Does she still outstrip Maria in speed? I forgot to mention to you in my former letters about the parcels you sent out by Henry. He left them at Estremoz under the charge of Dr Matthews,[24] your old friend, for when he came to see me he did not bring any baggage with him. They are still there and are no doubt safe enough as I heard of them about a fortnight ago. I have written to request they be kept there until my arrival as it will [be] necessary for me to go there to be present at the Medical Board before I get my leave for England, of which there is not the least doubt as both Mr Forbes who is principal physician and Dr Burnall[25] the Staff Surgeon will give me sufficient certificates to satisfy the several inquisitors. Thank God I have no bones to show as those which have come away were not bigger than the smallest crums [sic] of bread and were too insignificant to keep, the largest splinters having firmly united. What a fortunate dog I am to have recovered so soon from so severe a wound. I am very happy to say that Jones's wound has taken a most favourable turn and the greatest hopes are entertained of his overcoming it. Weakness and an inclination to consumption is what he has to dread. It is very extraordinary, I have never lost my complexion since I have been wounded. I think this is a pretty long letter for so young a beginner at left hand writing. I will finish it with praying God to keep you in health and patience and to grant a quick passage to your most affectionate fond son, Wyndham Madden

Badajoz, 8 June 1812

---

24. Surgeon James Matthews, 3rd Foot.
25. Staff Surgeon John Burnall.

My dearest father and mother,

How often do I blame those winds which have so long detained that pacquet [sic] which I am convinced brings me a letter from my beloved parents. Had I not seen yours to Henry my unhappiness would have been excessive and my conjectures about the cause of your not writing would have made me melancholy; but in it I perceived such fair promises, as I mentioned in my former letter, of your enduring your misfortunes with fortitude, that my uneasiness is greatly allayed by it. I believe I must wait another post before I can tell you the exact day I move, as the doctors are undetermined by what mode I shall proceed to Lisbon. To ride, they say, will be impossible as the least trip or stumble might be of the most serious consequences. I must therefore go to the expense of one of the country coaches by which my journey will be made much easier and shorter as they will travel the distance of four or five leagues a day and will be some protection from the sun which will be a great point gained as it is so excessively hot that at midday I can scarcely draw breath. I received a letter from Cooke[26] yesterday who wrote for me to you the day after I was wounded, in which he explained to me the reason why you did not receive it. It appears Cox[27] knew of some person going instantly to England who took not only my letter but two or three others which never have been received. Our army in the north is expected to advance daily, as those divisions that have been cantoned in the rear have closed up to the front, towards Salamanca is supposed to be the direction. Henry will have a long march of it, as his division has been for some time near Oporto. Major Wells[28] and Captain Oglander of the 47th, who was [a] lieutenant in ours and has lost his left arm,[29] went from here in a spring waggon for Estremoz. I am the last of the 43rd now here but the doctors have promised if possible to move me in three or four days, and as I have some interest with Forbes and Colonel Muller has a good deal with him, I think between us both we can manage to get a spring waggon to myself which will be much better than one of the country carriages, as I shall be able to lay down when I wish and will be more comfortably protected from the heat of the sun, although perhaps, a little more shaking which, thank God, cannot hurt my arm as

---

26. Lieutenant John Cooke, 43rd Foot.
27. Lieutenant John Cox, 95th Foot, had been severely wounded at Ciudad Rodrigo.
28. Major Joseph Wells, 43rd Foot, was severely wounded at Badajoz.
29. Captain Henry Oglander, 47th Foot, had previously served as an ensign and lieutenant in the 43rd.

the fracture is completely united. I am now able to move my arm from the elbow and when I lay down, by taking off the sling, I can almost straighten it. Well, I am happy in thinking in a very short time I shall be getter nearer to you every day and before this day month shall enjoy the society of my dearest father, mother and sisters for whose happiness and health the most constant prayer are offered up by their most affectionate son & brother, Wyndham Madden.

Badajoz, 15 June 1812

My dearest father and mother,

This letter ought to be dated from Elvas, but through the delay of some cars which are to convey the wounded soldiers from here, the same time we go and are not yet arrived, we are still detained. However, if they are not come this evening I shall wait no longer for them but proceed early tomorrow morning to Elvas on my pony, as thank God I am now sufficiently strong. The board of medical men only sits at Estremoz three times a month and the 20th instant is one of their days, so that I shall just arrive in time to obtain my leave to England and proceed without delay to Lisbon where I hope to find some vessel ready to sail, as I wish to delay as little as possible the happiness of being with you all. Since I last wrote I have received your letter and am excessively sorry to hear you have both been so ill, but I am in hopes my letters have given you some relief as you find by them I have been in an improving state ever since I wrote the first. Thank God you were not acquainted for some time with the severity of my wound as that joined to our other cruel misfortune[30] would have greatly increased your affliction.

Alverca [?] 17 June

As the post does not leave until this evening, I was determined not to close my letter, that I might give you the pleasing information of my having commenced my journey to Lisbon. The waggons for which we were waiting not having arrived at Badajoz last night and being informed [by] Doctor Burnall that he did not know when they would come, I was determined to wait no longer for them as I considered myself sufficiently strong to proceed on horseback. I made the attempt this morning at daybreak and succeeded beyond my expectations as I am not much fatigued although the distance is twelve good miles. Tomorrow I shall

---

30. The death of his brother William at Badajoz.

go about the same number. I find the morning gives me a keen appetite and is delightfully refreshing. You must not expect long letters from me while on the road as I cannot yet write with facility. Give my love to Monson, Edward and all my sisters and with increasing prospects of soon embracing you all, believe me my dearest father and mother, your fond affectionate son, Wyndham Madden

Estremoz, 24 June 1812

My dearest father and mother,

I have been here these some days and find my health and strength much improved by the change of air and society which I so much wanted at Badajoz. I passed the Medical Board on the 20th instant, the day I arrived and have got two months leave to England where, they tell me, I must get it renewed. I am waiting at present for the opportunity of a carriage belonging to the paymaster's wife of the 27th Regiment, who intends sending it to Lisbon to be sold and I expect to set off in a day or two, which will save me a considerable sum of money and also be a delightful means of conveyance as I can regulate my stages as I please.

Dr Matthews called on me the day I arrived and brought with him the parcels which I found all right and perfectly uninjured and expressed his sorrow at not being able to show me those attentions he wished as he had just that instant received orders to proceed with all possible dispatch to join his regiment (the 3rd or Buffs) which is in Sir Rowland Hill's Division. Mrs Matthews was out in this country with him but has returned to England about six months ago. I should like very much to have seen her as I recollect I was a great favourite of hers. The rumour in this town today is that Salamanca is in our possession but the French still continue to defend a convent in its suburbs which they have fortified; that Soult who had advanced on General Hill has suddenly retreated and was followed up by our army. I hope when I get to Lisbon to find letters from Henry in which I have no doubt he will give me an account of all the operations of the army in that quarter. I expect also a great number from you both as I have taken care that all letters that arrive for me at Badajoz shall be forwarded direct to that place. I wonder if Charlotte has learnt by this time to support the absence of her beloved Henry. I shall be very happy to see her. She may prove of great service to me for I am in hopes as I said before of getting home in a man of war. I shall take my servant with me if old Peacock[31] who

---

31. Major General Warren Peacocke, commandant at Lisbon.

commands at Lisbon will give me permission, for in the first place I am nearly helpless and cannot do without him and secondly he is so good a man and has attended me so well during my illness that I should not like to part with him. I suppose you begin by this time to count the days until my arrival. [If] I write to you by every pacquet you will be able to judge pretty nearly of the time. How delighted I shall be to surprise you but I give you fair warning not to be too rough in your embraces and particularly to keep Marianne and Clara from jumping on my back as I shall not be strong enough to bear them. Give my best love to them all and believe me, my dearest father and mother, Your fond affectionate son Wyndham Madden

Remember the *warning* I have given you, I am not in joke.

Having returned home to recuperate from his wounds, Wyndham Madden did not return to the peninsula for a year. Having arrived in Portugal in October 1813, he found himself back in action at the Battle of Nivelle very quickly indeed and was soon injured again, thankfully less seriously.

Vera, 11 November 1813

My dearest mother,

I am the most fortunate man in existence. We were heavily engaged yesterday and in the early part of the business I was struck down by a couple of musquet balls, one of which lodged in the fleshy part of the left arm and was instantly cut out and the other struck a little below my left breast. Fortunately for me I had a large biscuit in my bosom, which I always carry with me on a march. The ball broke the biscuit to pieces but from the resistance it met with glanced off, instead of penetrating and has only lacerated the flesh a little. I immediately retired to the rear, got my wounds dressed, mounted a horse and came to this village when I met with a degree of civility I very little expected, for in passing this house, the family to whom I had been introduced by Edward saw me and sent a servant after me [to return?] back again. I am now situated in a comfortable little room, a good bed, and have two pretty girls constantly with me, by whose assistance I hope in a very short time to be sufficiently recovered to rejoin my regiment. Do not conceive, my dearest mother, that I wish to inspire you with false hopes, for I assure you on my honour that I am now writing at a table, dressed and that I suffer little or no pain. Edward, I am happy to say, is quite well. He has not yet been to see me, for our division drove them from all their positions and has advanced a considerable way into France. However, I expect him today or tomorrow.

Our regiment has suffered rather severely; one captain, one lieutenant killed, another captain so dangerously wounded that he must be dead before this and three sub[altern]s severely wounded.[32] The French behaved very gallantly on the first hill where they were strongly entrenched. We soon gained the ridge but they retired into a stone redoubt which they kept until nearly surrounded. Finding their fire very galling, I thought it would be better to run at it, and calling to the men to follow, some other officers and myself started off, but when about twenty yards from them I found myself stopped in the agreeable manner I have before described to you, and am thus prevented from giving my dear father any longer account of the engagement which from the tremendous cannonade and the continued roll of musquetry I heard, must have been very severe. As I know how anxious and unhappy you all will be until you hear from me, I shall make haste and conclude this letter that it may be sent off with the dispatches to England and by every post you shall have accounts of my convalescence. You need not hope to see me in England for this touch, for I have made up my mind for a campaign in France. With my warmest love to my dear father and sisters, believe me my beloved mother, your most affectionate son, Wyndham Madden

---

32. Captain Thomas Capel and Lieutenant Edward Freer were killed, Captain Robert Murchison and Lieutenant John Angrove died of their wounds and Lieutenants James Considine, Wyndham Madden, William Freer and George Hennel with Ensign Rowley Hill were wounded.

Chapter 14

Ensign John Brumwell[1]

Letters

John Brumwell was a member of the Brumwell family of Warden Hill, Weardale. John was born on 14 February 1785 the son of John Brumwell and Sarah (nee Colpitts). John and his brother George initially entered as ensigns in the Royal Cumberland Militia (John on 1 March 1807), then based at Hull in Yorkshire. John then received a commission as an ensign in the 43rd Foot on 14 July 1808, whereas George remained in the militia and it is to him that many of the letters are written. John was sent to the peninsula with the 2nd Battalion, 43rd Foot, in October 1808 and served at the Battle of Corunna before sailing for home with the battalion. He then transferred to the 1st Battalion, which returned to the peninsula in July 1809 and John was promoted to lieutenant on 28 September 1809. He served at the Côa, Busaco, Sabugal, Fuentes de Oñoro, and the storming of Ciudad Rodrigo, where he was severely wounded and he died of his wounds on 27 January 1812.

To Ensign [George] Brumwell, Royal Cumberland Militia
Colchester, 10 August 1808

Dear brother,
    You will perhaps think it strange that I did not write to you sooner, but it was owing to the expectation that we should embark every day, for I intended to have written when we arrived at Harwich, as we have received orders to hold ourselves in readiness for foreign service and

---

1. Originally published as *Letters of a Weardale Soldier,* by William Egglestone, Durham 1912. In many records the name is spelt Bramwell, but the family spelling is certain.

are only waiting for transports to arrive at Harwich for our embarkation. I arrived at Colchester on Thursday last, and with pleasure I inform you that I found the 43rd a great deal pleasanter than the Cumberland Militia. The officers are much more sociable with each other and Colonel Gifford[2] is a very pleasant officer for a commanding officer.

Colchester is a very dull place, but the barracks are very excellent. I commenced drill yesterday. The 43rd Regiment and a detachment of the 95th Rifle Corps are in those barracks. The 76th[3] are encamped about two miles from this place. I will be very much obliged to Captain Gregson[4] if he will have the goodness to write to the Paymaster at Leeds and desire him to pay the money to Captain Gregson. I took my accounts to Colonel Gifford and he told me that he could not pay me any of the money till the men arrived at the regiment and if they did not join I should lose the money which I advanced except the Paymaster at Leeds settled the account. Please to write immediately after Captain Gregson receives an answer and let me know what he says about paying the money. I hope the Cumberland Militia have nearly completed their number of volunteers and that you are determined to go into the line; you will find it much more pleasant than the militia. I should advise you to go into a regiment where there is only one battalion. I have found it much more expensive joining the 43rd than I expected. Promotion is very slow in this regiment and has been for some time past; but we expect an additional lieutenant to the Second Battalion. Our dress in a morning is white belt with trousers and gaiters; to dinner and parade white pantaloons, half boots and white waistcoat, jacket loose, buttoned back and a black waist belt. We never wear breeches nor gaiters. Should you get a commission in the line and Captain Gregson get the money from Leeds it is much at your service. Should you write to my father and mother give my most dutiful respects to them and let them know that I like the 43rd very well; but I shall write to both you and them before we embark.

Give my kindest love to Captain Gregson and my sister and little Sarah. Give my compliments to Major Smith,[5] little Hodgson[6] and all

---

2. Lieutenant Colonel William Gifford, 43rd Foot.

3. The 76th 'Hindoostan' Regiment of Foot.

4. Captain John Gregson had joined the Royal Cumberland Militia on 24 May 1804. He married Elizabeth Brumwell (John's sister) but left the militia in early 1809.

5. Major Ralph Smyth of the Royal Cumberland Militia.

6. Most likely Lieutenant Hodson, Royal Cumberland Militia.

enquiring friends. I am your affectionate brother. John Brumwell Ensign 43rd Regiment

PS I am in great want of my large box, please say what you send it by.

Colchester, 11 September 1808

Dear brother,
I received Captain Gregson's letter of the 3rd instant with pleasure. I see you are well. Please to inform Captain Gregson I received my money from our Paymaster, but he made some objections to pay me; he said that he must have a receipt from the Paymaster at Leeds, which Captain Gregson will no doubt have got by this time. I will thank you to get me a certificate from Captain Harrading[7] stating to what period I received pay as a lieutenant in the Royal Cumberland Militia belonging to the 2nd Battalion there. You don't receive my pay from the Paymaster but from the agent. They wrote to me when I drew for my pay, desiring me to send them a certificate, which you will give to Captain Gregson. I shall write for them both when we return to England. I inform you with pleasure that we have received orders this morning to embark for foreign service and to march at 2 o'clock in the morning for Harwich, as the transports are there. I do not expect we shall go, as we have been under orders to hold ourselves in readiness for some time past. We received two months' pay in advance, so we are paid up to the 24 November, I have got our embarkation money out of that which was stopped, £7 10s for sea stock. We shall have our dinners, pint of wine and two bottles of porter per day besides the allowance of the ship. I shall write and inform you before we leave England what troops are in the expedition and who commands. Perhaps I may be able by that time to inform you where our destination is; we have no idea at present except to the North of Spain.

Excuse haste, for we are all hurry and confusion with packing up our necessaries. I wrote to my father this day. I have sent you the receipt for Captain Harrading. Get the money and give it to little Sarah. I have sent the present in this letter for Mrs Johnson which was so often named before I left Hull. Give my compliments to her and tell her I intended to have sent it when in London, but had not time, but I have much less at present. Inform her I had not time to write and as much more as you like. Give my respects to Captain Gregson and my sister and little Sarah. I have

---

7. Captain E[dward?] Harraden, Royal Cumberland Militia.

not two minutes to spare. I remain, dear brother, your sincere well wisher, John Brumwell.

To George Brumwell Esq, Warden Hill, Weardale, Durham.
Colchester Barracks 19 February 1809

Dear father and mother,

I hope this letter will find you all in good health. You will no doubt be surprised that you have not had a letter from me since I left England. After we left Corunna I never had an opportunity. I intended to have written to let you know before we sailed from England where our destination was, but I had not the most distant idea. The fleet sailed from Falmouth on the 9 October 1808 and arrived at Corunna on the 13 October. After a very pleasant passage being a distance of 450 miles, a thing hardly ever known before, considering that the fleet consisted of upwards of 160 sail. As soon as we anchored in the harbour, Sir David Baird put up a signal in his ship that no person was to go on shore without his permission. The next day he gave leave to the commanding officers of regiments to permit one third of the officers from each ship to go on shore, but not to sleep there. The night we arrived the town was illuminated. A great quantity of sky-rockets were thrown into the air with the ringing of bells the whole night. The ship that I was in being brought to anchor abreast of the town, by that means I had an opportunity to see the whole performance. It had a very beautiful effect. The next day was the Spanish king's birthday. The town was the same as the previous evening. The Spaniards would not permit the British army to disembark at Corunna until they had an order from their commander in chief at Madrid. He sent an express for us to disembark when our commander thought proper. It would have been fortunate for the British nation if they never had landed a single soldier in Spain.

I was on shore several times while we remained in the harbour. Corunna is a very dirty place and the surrounding country is very barren. As for the few soldiers they had in the town they were a most miserable lot of objects, part of them without either stockings or shoes and almost naked.

The Spaniards are the most treacherous and unfriendly set of people in the world, but I cannot describe them bad enough to you, considering how they treated the army in Spain. As for their large armies which they represented to the English nation, it was nothing but most notorious falsehoods; even when we were advancing we were meeting hundreds of the Spanish soldiers running away and likewise officers that were making their escape.

We disembarked at Corunna on the 26 October 1809 and then our troubles commenced. We were encamped near Corunna for a few days. We began our march on the 28th of October, that is just the beginning of the rainy season. We had nothing but torrents of rain for a considerable time. On our march from Corunna to Astorga there was nothing particular. The main road was tolerable good, considering we had so much rain. The country was uncommonly barren and the inhabitants the most miserable set of creatures I ever saw. Their houses had no chimneys in them and were miserable places. As for their bedding I suppose they had little or none. In most places I hardly saw any. We were always very happy if we could procure straw to sleep upon. I took out with me two blankets and a large rug, which I found of great service. I think the weather was equally as cold here as in England. We were seventeen days marching to Astorga. Part of the troops remained in Astorga and the remainder at a small village near there.

For a considerable time it was thought impossible to form a junction with Sir John Moore's army. The information was that the French were between Sir John and us. We had orders and counter orders to march every day until the 25th. There was a report that the French would attack us in a few hours. There was nothing but confusion with the staving-in of rum casks, provision casks &c &c, the soldiers drinking the rum out of their caps. The whole of the troops were ordered to retreat, except General Craufurd's Brigade; we were in it; we were ordered to be in reserve.

On the 2nd of December we commenced our retreat and marched to Manzanal [de Arriba], where we were encamped until the 8th of December. Then we retreated to Valcavado [Valcabado del Páramo] and remained there until the 12th of December. We expected to have gone back to Corunna and to have embarked there. Sir David Baird received orders from Sir John Moore to advance by forced marches, that the two armies might be together. The two armies formed a junction on the 20th of December. Then we commenced our pursuit after the French, General Soult and his army. I suppose we pursued them upwards of 80 or 90 miles. We were always very near them and our dragoons frequently falling in with theirs and giving them a good thrashing, but it was only to entice the English army further into the country, that the other two French armies might get in our rear, when we were in pursuit of General Soult and his army.

The weather was very bad, with a great quantity of snow. The places where we had to sleep were dreadfully bad and frequently we were not able to procure snow and the Spaniards were very uncivil. The morning we marched to Saghagun, General Paget and about 500 of the 15th Dragoons gave the French dragoons a thrashing. They had 950 men; he took and killed a great number of the French. On the evening of the 23 December the whole army had orders to be ready at seven o'clock to march and attack the French. They had entrenched themselves and had thrown up batteries only about 16 or 18 miles from Sahagun. The 95th, 43rd and 52nd Regiments marched from their quarters at seven o'clock to attack them. We got within about six miles of the enemy, when there was an express came from General Moore for the whole army to retreat. We got back into our quarters about three o'clock in the morning. I expected that we should have had some hard fighting.

Fortunately, the English army did not attack General Soult on the evening of the 23 December. There is no doubt but that we should have given them a good thrashing, but the other two French armies would have got in our rear and would have taken possession of all the passes and then we must have been taken prisoners.

Sunday 25 December, we commenced our final retreat. The weather and the roads were both dreadfully bad. On our retreat we expected to be attacked by the enemy every hour. They had an army on each of our flanks and one in our rear pursuing us. The 43rd Light Infantry always formed a part of the reserve. We always kept a party of men on each flank by day to look out for the enemy and at night we had our pickets. On the evening of 26 December, the French attacked our pickets at a small village, near the bridge of Benavente. The regiments were turned out under arms. The French fired a few shots and galloped off for the night. The next morning we were ordered under arms as before; we saw them coming over the hills and the out pickets of our dragoons and theirs were engaged. As our dragoons were over the bridge, it was blown up [and the French] dragoons forded the water to attack ours. Napoleon was himself [present and] sent General Le Fevre [Lefebvre][8] with 800 of his dragoons and [ordered him to continue] until he had destroyed the whole of the English dragoons, ours attacked with about 400 to 500 men, took the general and a number of men and drove [them into] the river, where numbers of them were drowned. We had nothing [further] until

8. General de Division Charles Lefebvre-Desnouettes was captured at the Action of Benavente.

we came to Valcavado [Valcabado del Páramo]. The 1st Battalion 43rd, 52nd, 95th and [both the] Germans, in the whole we numbered 3,000. We [retired before the] French [on our route] by Vigo; it was expected that the French would have attacked the [troops retreating] by Vigo and not Sir John Moore's army, as that was the intention of [dividing] his army. He said after we were gone that he expected nothing, but [they would have been] taken prisoners and the two generals which we had with ours expected [the same].

After we left the road for Corunna we had no provisions for four days [not so much as] a morsel of bread, but you [cannot] form any adequate idea [of the miseries during the] retreat. We were obliged to break open their doors to procure [food, and we had to] march wet to the skin and miserable in every respect. The mountains in the provinces of Galicia, where we had to march over, were dreadful. [We marched] for 16 to 17 days over these mountains without a halt. The [soldiers were] falling out of the ranks sick by dozens together. Many of our men were walking without their shoes [or stockings], for there were hardly anything to be got in Spain. We always had [animals] to kill out of the carts for our provisions. After we got into [them] you may think what sort of stuff it would be. The Spaniards would turn out upon the sick soldiers that were left on the road with firelocks and [other] weapons, and rob them of everything they had [left] but it is no use saying anything more about them.

There are hardly any horses in Spain, but there are mules and bullocks. After calamities unheard of [I may inform] you that we arrived at Portsmouth on 4 February 1809, and then to Colchester. Here was only a part of the regiment, which arrived at the time I did. Out of sixteen officers which we disembarked, we left ten sick on the road. The remainder of the regiment are on their way here. We now heard of four of our officers being dead and a number of sick on the road, and a number of the soldiers there also and I am afraid we shall have a great number [dead].

We had a most dreadful passage to England. While we were laying in Vigo harbour a tremendous gale broke our cable and the ship nearly ran ashore. Afterwards we were ordered to set sail, but for where we did not know. The captain gave sealed orders not to break them open except we lost the fleet. We had not sailed very far [from Vigo] until the signal was given for the fleet to bring to anchor. About three o'clock of 21 January, it blew a very strong gale and broke one of our cables. The ship might have drifted on to the rocks but our other anchor brought us up. The storm lasted that night and until late on the following day. About 10 o'clock the next day we [set sail again]. The captain was afraid to remain any longer at anchor. He expected the other cable to break every moment.

Fortunately the wind came round, which enabled us to run back into Vigo, with the intention to run the ship on the sands, but we put up a signal of distress and the frigate sent us an anchor and cable.

On the 24th the fleet set sail once more with a fair wind and the weather continued fine until the 28th, when it began to blow hurricanes and continued until the 30th. The ship sustained much damage, our sails were much torn, some of the yards broken; the sea breaking over the deck, a great quantity of water got into the hold and both our pumps were choked up; therefore you may imagine our feelings at this critical period. One of the officers in the forecastle, who was dreadfully alarmed, came running up on deck, calling out that the ship was sinking, there being a great quantity of water in the cabin.

Give my love to all my brothers and sisters, please write and let me know where my brother George is and tell him I should be very happy to hear from him and likewise where my brother Thomas is and Longcake.[9] I hope you are all in very good health, as I am. I remain your ever affectionate son. John Brumwell

PS Please direct your letters for Ensign Brumwell, 43rd Light Infantry, Colchester, Essex.

To Lieutenant Brumwell, Royal Cumberland Militia, Hull, Yorkshire
On board of the *Sea Nymph* Transport, 27 May 1809

Dear brother,

I arrived safely at Colchester on the 13th of May, after being told in London that the regiment had embarked, which gave me much uneasiness. On my arrival at Colchester to my satisfaction I found them all very comfortable in barracks, but daily expecting an order for embarkation. When the order did come it was very sudden and only came about eight o'clock on the Sunday evening to march in the morning. The order from our commanding officer was only given out about 12 o'clock at night, and it was to march in the morning at nine, which we did. After having a most unpleasant march, the day being dreadfully hot and the roads full of dust, we embarked at Harwich and on our arrival there the transports were all ready. We went immediately onboard and we should have sailed in the morning if the wind had

---

9. William Longcake, an Excise Officer, had married Sarah Brumwell (John's sister) in 1802.

been fair. We sailed the following day and arrived in the Downs after having a very pleasant passage, only being about 24 hours going from Harwich to the Downs, which were very pleasant, except that I was a little squeamish the morning we left Harwich, for I do not feel so much at home at sea as when on shore. After being a few days at sea, however, I got accustomed to that kind of life and therefore think nothing of it. I always endeavour to make myself as happy as possible. We have a very pleasant party aboard the ship that I am in. I applied to the commanding officer to be transferred to another ship, which he was so good as to do and to appoint me to the company which I applied for. I think that I shall be much more comfortable this expedition than what I was on the last. We are under the same general as we were in the last expedition; with the 95th and 52nd first battalions in our brigade. It is supposed that we are going to Portugal first, but that is only conjecture, for some say we are going to the north of Spain. For my part I am perfectly easy where we go, only I think if we should go to the north of Spain, we may look out for lots of promotion, what with the hard fighting and things that we shall meet with. I hope you will excuse my not writing you before I left Colchester, but upon my word I had no time, for after we received the order we were nothing but hurry and confusion, having all our things to pack up.

My recruiting expenses came to £34 18s 0d and the loss of baggage was given in at £19, all of which were certified for by the commanding officer of the regiment and all of which I shall have to receive of the paymaster. Should I not return to England I appoint you as my sole executor of my personal effects and you will settle all my accounts, but they are not many at present. I have not time to write to my father, but I hope you will have the goodness to let them know that we embarked in such a hurry that I had not time to write. You may let me know that I will write to them as soon as ever we land. I shall likewise write to you on our arrival and let you know the news, but at present we are perfectly happy for we have lots of things and in general drink our bottle of port per day. I shall be very happy to hear from you. I will thank you to be particular in looking in the army promotion, for I expect my promotion very shortly, for I stand third. When that takes place, I shall expect a letter.

I have just returned from store, where a party of us went to buy in what was necessary for our voyage. The town is a very stupid place and quite small. In the night we had great difficulty in making out our ship as the surf in general at this place runs very high. I hope you will excuse the imperfections of this letter. I am now laying in my berth and the signal for sailing is made with the firing of guns, therefore I have not time to say more, but God bless you and I remain your dear brother. John Brumwell

NB When you write home give my compliments to all our people and to enquiring friends at Hull. Should you happen to see Miss Pearson, give my compliments to her. When you write let me know how things are going on in general.

Onboard the *Robert Taylor* Transport, Lisbon Harbour, 30 June 1809

My dear brother,
    I wrote you a letter when we were at anchor in the Downs and which I hope you received. I had not an opportunity to get to the Post Office. Just as I finished my letter, the signal was given to weigh anchor and put to sea. As there was a boat alongside I gave the letter to the man to put into the Post Office, which he promised to do. We did not sail for some days after, as the wind came round and prevented us. We sailed from the Downs on the 3rd of June, arrived at Spithead near Portsmouth. On the 4th we sailed down to Cowes harbour. On the 5th we changed our ship, as the first we were in was a very bad sailer. We set sail from Cowes harbour on the 11th and were obliged to bring up to anchor in Yarmouth Roads the same day. We sailed on the 18 June with a fair wind, the weather being remarkably fine and on the whole we had a very pleasant passage, the one great consolation. We made land on the morning of the 25th of June. We ran on the coast most part of the day and on the following morning we were in sight of Oporto. It appears to be rather a pleasant place and a large town for we had an opportunity to see the place as we were part of the day becalmed. The houses appear to be tolerably good and it is strongly fortified both by sea and land.
    With great pleasure I inform you that we arrived at Lisbon on the 28th of June. For several miles on the coast it is very strongly fortified by sea; it was a very beautiful sight all along the coast. Lisbon is a very large town and I have been on shore this day. The houses are very good and all built of stone and the shops are good, but the streets were miserably dirty. The people are remarkably secret. There is plenty of all sorts of provisions in Lisbon. We were informed that after we leave this place there is nothing to be got for money. The right wing of our regiment leaves the ship this evening of the 2nd of July. They are to be carried up by water in large boats for 40 miles to a place called Valeda [Valada] and to remain there until the left wing joins them; the remainder are to go up the river [Tagus] on the 3 July, when it is expected the whole of

200

the brigade will be there and then we shall immediately commence our march and form a junction with Sir Arthur Wellesley, as he is waiting near Abrantes for us. As soon as the two armies form a junction, it is expected that we shall proceed on to Spain and endeavour to turn the French out of that country, which I hope we shall be able to accomplish. I cannot pretend to give you any information for we never see a paper. In England you have all the news long before we have any and you know much more how things are going on in Spain and Portugal.

When here we shall have nothing but marching and I hope plenty of hard fighting that we may distinguish ourselves, General Craufurd's Brigade is supposed to be the finest that ever left England. It consists of the following regiments: 43rd, 52nd and 95th First Battalions. I suppose that each regiment is not less than eleven to twelve hundred strong. After General Craufurd's Brigade joins Sir Arthur Wellesley, they will have to take the advance duty as they are the light infantry and rifles.

The climate is very different in Portugal to what it is in England. It being so much hotter, I think we shall suffer very much from the fever and heat when we commence our marching. It is reported here that two of the French armies have formed a junction near Astorga and are advancing. If that is the case we may very soon expect to have an engagement. The Portuguese troops that we have seen are very much superior to the Spanish troops. We are told that the Portuguese troops are very much improved since they got so many of the English officers into the service.

The country around this place is very beautiful. Most of the harvest is all reaped. Here is plenty of all sorts of fruit and almost everything that you can buy in England. I expect my lieutenancy very soon and will thank you to look in all the 'Gazettes' and should you see it in any 'Gazette', I will thank you to write immediately as I am the senior ensign on service and that means I have the Colours to carry. When you write to my father and Captain Gregson let them know that I am very well and shall write to them as soon as I have an opportunity. I wrote to my father before I left England. When you write to me you must pay the inland postage and direct your letters for me in General Craufurd's Brigade, with Sir Arthur Wellesley, Spain or Portugal, and I shall be very happy to hear from you as soon as possible. Give my compliments to all enquiring friends. When you see Miss Pearson give my love to her and tell her I shall be very happy to hear how things are going on.

There are five more infantry regiments arrived here and two cavalry regiments. It is reported that they have to be encamped about two miles from Lisbon and not to join Sir Arthur Wellesley until further orders. Most of the transports that are in the harbour have got orders to return to England to bring out more troops. I think we shall see some very sharp work this summer. I shall write and let you know all the news when we join the army. You must excuse this hasty scrawl and the deficiency which you may observe in this letter for we are nothing but hurry and confusion. I remain my dear brother, yours truly, J Brumwell.

Malpartida, 15 March 1810

My dear brother,

Your much esteemed and highly valued letter I received when we were laying at Campo Mayor [Campo Maior]; you may judge of my happiness better than I can express it on the receipt of your letter, for I had almost begun to think that you had forgot there was such a person in existence. I was likewise happy to see that our family were all in good health. I feel myself extremely obliged to you for the trouble you took to inform me of my promotion. I wrote to you when we were in the woods near Talavera.[10] At that time, to all appearance, things were in a different way to what they are at present, for it was generally supposed that we should have driven the French back and in a short time to have been in Madrid. After remaining at Talavera for five or six days we then commenced our retreat, to my very great surprise and sorrow, as I should have liked very much to have seen Madrid.

I shall now commence to give you a small detail of our retreat, for I have no news. You hear much more of the expedition than we do. We generally receive the principal part of our news from the English papers. The morning that we began our retreat it was intended that we should go and attack the French army at Plasencia commanded by Soult. They had got in our rear, therefore we were between two armies. I believe that General Cuesta promised to defend Talavera with the Spanish army. We halted one night at Oropesa. To our great surprise General Cuesta broke his promise and the same night he had his headquarters at Oropesa. I have no doubt, had Cuesta kept possession of Talavera but that our army would have drove the French from Plasencia. When we left Oropesa we left the main road and marched by the bridge of Arzobispo when the river was not fordable and remained on the opposite side for that night. From thence we marched some days over the mountains: the roads were

10. Not extant.

bad and we were very much in want of provisions. We remained at a place called Almaraz upwards of twenty-four hours.

In the daytime we were under the trees upon the top of a large mountain and in the dusk of the evening we were marched down with two pieces of artillery, near to a river and remained there for the night. On the opposite side the French had an army. It was supposed they would cross the river, it being fordable at almost every place. The sentries that were on each side of the river were but a small distance from each other. You have no idea of the misery that we suffered when we were in that miserable place, what with the heat of the sun and the scarcity of provisions for both man and horse. There was only one division at the place under the command of Brigadier General Craufurd and which consisted of the following regiments: 95th First Battalion, 52nd First Battalion, 43rd First Battalion (that was the Light Brigade), the 88th, 45th and 87th (the Heavy Brigade).[11]

From thence we proceeded to Campo Mayor [Campo Maior], where we got into quarters. I assure you it was a great change, for we had not been in quarters for upwards of three months, living continually under trees. I think I was hardly in a house for that time, Campo Mayor [Campo Maior] is a small fortified town; it would not be able to hold out against an enemy for two days. It is commanded by the heights all around. The Spaniards raised a siege and took the place nine or ten years ago.[12] We were upwards of three months there and were very comfortable. We had a regimental mess equally as well as in England. The only amusement we had through the course of the day was shooting and coursing, it being a fine country and plenty of game.

On the 9th of December 1809, we again began to march; it was supposed by the knowing ones that we were going to take a position near Lisbon; in that many people were deceived, for we arrived at a greater distance from Lisbon than when at Campo Mayor [Campo Maior]. We had a very pleasant march. It is not worthwhile to give you our destination, as the country and the small towns and villages we were in were nothing particular. I shall only mention Leon [?], where we halted for two days. It is a large town and I think I may say rather a pretty place. From there we proceeded to Pinhel. It is a poor miserable

---

11. Following the death of General Mackenzie at Talavera, Robert Craufurd commanded the Third Division consisting of the Light Brigade and Mackinnon's Brigade of the 2/87th, 1/88th and 1/45th.
12. Campo Maior was besieged by the Spaniards in 1801 during the War of the Oranges.

place. It was headquarters for the Light Brigade for some time. The 95th and part of the 43rd Regiment were sent out in front near the enemy, later the whole of our regiment was sent out. We have been marching about from one miserable village to another for some time past, still near to the enemy. We have not been much troubled with out-pickets.

The 95th Regiment having been still in front, we are now within about two days of Almeida and expecting daily and hourly to move forward, for we do not stay long at one place. I believe it is almost certain we are going to move to the front to defend if possible, the River Agueda, which is about four miles from Spain. It plainly appears to me that nature has intended this river to divide Spain and Portugal, for it is the most difficult to pass you perhaps ever saw and at this time I suppose the river is hardly fordable, owing to the quantity of rain we have had of late.

I must now date my letter on the 24th of March, for the above was written some days ago at a place called Barba del Puerco, where part of the 95th Rifle Regiment have been stationed for some time to defend the bridge of St Felices [San Felices de los Gallegos], where the French have between three and four thousand men and a fresh general, just arrived from France, who took the command. It is reported he is a German and a dashing young man.[13]

On the evening of the 19th of March 1810, about eleven o'clock, the French crossed the bridge of St Felices [San Felices de los Gallegos] with 500 of their picked men, the general at their head and attacked four companies of the 95th Regiment, which were about 340 strong. After a smart engagement for about an hour and a half the 95th drove them back killed two of their officers, a great many of their men, besides several wounded and some taken prisoners. I am sorry to say the 95th had one officer and five men killed and some men wounded. You may perhaps wonder why they had so few men near to such an army of the French.

I shall now inform you of the particulars between Barba del Puerco[14] and St Felices [San Felices de los Gallegos]. There are immense ridges of mountains and a very rapid running river on each side. The water bed is nothing but rocks and immense stones. The bridge is 75 yards long and five broad; it is a very strong pass and a most difficult position on each side; it was thought advisable to send more men on the evening of the 20th. The company which I was in were ordered to march to support the 95th Regiment. We were about seven or eight miles distant

---

13. The French troops were commanded by General Claude Ferey, who was a Frenchman.
14. Now known as Puerto Seguro.

from them. On our arrival there, all was quiet; they were expected to make an attempt in the night. It was nearly as light as day, therefore at early morning two officers and myself went down to see what was going on. Our curiosity tempted us to go to the bottom of the bank and then to cross the bridge. Immediately we returned they commenced firing upon us. We were not more than three hundred yards from their sentries. Their balls came very near but they did no damage. The same day the French general and several of his officers were reconnoitring the river and all the places around and from that circumstance we expected them to make another attack, but I am sorry they did not. In the evening the general ordered four more companies to come to the bridge. We had there between eight and nine hundred men and very ready to meet them, but they knew better than to try us a second time.

The next day our company was ordered back to its old quarters. The way the French made their attack was this; their general kept it quite a secret and let his men go to bed in their usual way. Between ten and eleven he had the whole [of his] men turned out and marched with some of his horsemen as quick as possible across the bridge. The men scrambled up the rocks like as many rabbits and tumbled and run down like as many devils. While they were crossing the bridge in the advance, they had all the opposite side lined with the remainder of their troops who kept up a constant fire on our side of the hill until their own men were a certain way up the hill firing quite over their own men's heads.

I cannot pretend to give you any particular account of the French army. They are continually moving about from one place to another. They have a large army at St Felices [San Felices de los Gallegos] and the country around. We had an English soldier deserted the other day from the French at Salamanca. He said they had fifteen thousand men at that place. I think it is very probable they have and will march them as quick as possible towards St Felices [San Felices de los Gallegos] and drive us out of this part.

The old patron of the house where I am now billeted, informs me that the French are marching their armies by three different ways into Portugal; one by Badajoz, another by Salamanca and a third by Oporto. I think it very likely to be the case. You may depend upon it their armies are very strong. As for us I look upon it as a most complete conquered country, for they have no army. As far as the few men they have they will take good care never to stand to be shot at. I think I shall not be very long in the country, but I think we shall have some very hard fighting before we leave it.

The Light Brigade is reported to be engaged every night and we shall get it some of those nights. At present we are always on the alert and ready to receive them. We have had two Portuguese regiments attached to our brigade, but we have never yet seen their pretty faces and I am beginning to think we shall not see them in this part of the country.

I was glad to see that you were sent back to your detachment, for I think that you would have charming amusements, what with hunting and shooting and divers other little harmless amusements. I am very sorry to see that my friend Nixon[15] has fallen a sacrifice to the dreadful disease that raged so severely at the Island of Walcheren.

I have a very fine Spanish pointer bitch, which is very much at your service. I shall be very glad to hear from you at your very earliest opportunity and say, whether you would like to have the bitch or not, and all the news you have. When you write home let my father and mother know that I am in as good health as ever I was in my life. When you write to Captain Gregson give my best love to him and tell them I have not forgot them as I have a letter underway. I have nothing more to say. I am dear brother, with best wishes for your health and happiness, your truly affectionate brother. J Brumwell

PS I have just received information that the general has marched the whole of our troops from Barba del Puerco, to a village but a small distance from it called Villar de Ciervo, which is now headquarters for the Light Brigade. St Felices [San Felices de los Gallegos] is now more completely open to the French and they have nothing to do but cross there. The Light Brigade will have an opportunity to distinguish themselves and drive the French back to their old position. I have not time to say more John.

Portugal, Valdaseras [Valdeiras], 15 August 1810

My dear brother,

I have written to you two or three times and am a little surprised you never answer my letters; my last was dated from Gallegos 19 June 1810,[16] with a letter enclosed for Captain Gregson likewise. I enclosed an order for you to draw my claim for loss of baggage on the last expedition to Spain. Some time after I had sent my letter off and directed

---

15. I have been unable to identify any officer this could refer to.
16. Not extant.

it for you in the Cumberland Militia laying in Hull, I happened by chance to get hold of an Army List that one of our officers had brought with him from Lisbon, in which I was very much surprised not to find your name; from that I concluded you had left the militia. If it should be the case, which I hope it is not, I am greatly surprised that you should not have written to me on your leaving the Militia. Should you not have received the letter dated from Gallegos, you must immediately write to some of your friends in the militia and they will send it to you.

I must give you an account of our transactions since we left Gallegos. On the 4th of July we commenced living under trees for we were in a state of continual alarm, we were sometimes turned out two or three times through the course of the day. We were always under arms at daybreak, which is a thing of course with the advance of the army as we were and have been, ever since we came to this part of the country, with some cavalry and some flying artillery. Our own pickets were very frequently having little skirmishes with the enemy but of no great consequence. On the 12th of July the enemy attacked our dragoons who skirmished with them for some time. The infantry was then advanced to form up on a piece of rising ground, which we did, fully expecting to have a little brush with them, when it was observed they were sending a large body of cavalry to turn our right flank and get in our rear, when there was an order came from the general that we were to retreat to a place called Fort Concepcion which was about four miles in our rear and there take up a position where we remained for some days. Fort Concepcion was built by the Spaniards when they were at war with Portugal.[17] There is only a small river which divides it from Portugal; it is a beautiful place. I suppose it would contain eight or ten thousand men.[18] When we first came to it, the place was quite in ruins, for the French had blown a part of it up when they were in this part of the country the other year. We had a governor appointed to it and a great number of guns planted around the ramparts and the place repaired likewise. Some Portuguese troops are in the barracks but for what purpose I do not know. After the place was put in a state of defence it was then supposed to be [of] very little use and it was thought more advisable to have blown it up, for when the French should make another attack it would only fall into their hands and be of great use to them as a place for stores, ammunition &c.

---

17. The fortress was completed in 1758.
18. It was built to hold about 1,500 men and 200 cavalry.

On the morning of the 16 July the enemy drove in our pickets and immediately Fort Concepcion was blown up according to orders. It made a very fine explosion. There was skirmishing with them for some time, but little loss on either side. We were ordered to take up a position by Almeida, where they let us remain at peace for some few days. This was about five miles in the rear of our old position. We were expecting an attack daily which kept us a little on the alert. We halted in an open plain about one mile from Almeida.

On the 23rd of July there came on a most dreadful thunderstorm and what with the rain, hail and other little things, I assure you it was very uncomfortable. We were as wet as if we had been drenched in a river all night.

I shall now begin to inform you of the particulars of the engagement which we had on the 24th of July. I should suppose that you have seen an account of it in the papers, before you receive my letter. On the 24th of July we were standing to our arms as usual at daybreak, all drenched with rain, when we heard a very sharp firing a little way in our front. At this time the French had attacked our cavalry, our own pickets with a determination to drive us on to the other side of the Coa (river), which was about two miles in our rear and invest Almeida which they did that day.

I shall now give you an account of the action to the best of my recollection just as it took place. I am afraid it will be a little long. Some time after the firing had begun in front, the infantry, which consisted of General Craufurd's Division were then ordered to take up a position about one mile in rear of the place where we were then standing. After we had formed there and remained for some time, all anxious to have a little brush with them, a thing that we had been expecting daily for the last six months past, there was an order came for five companies of the 43rd Regiment, five companies of the 95th Regiment and also some companies of the 52nd Regiment, but how many of them I do not know. Our left wing was ordered out and I am in the left company, therefore I had an opportunity of seeing the whole. We were ordered to extend our companies and move on at 'double quick' and meet the enemy which was coming on at 'double quick' and in a very large force. We skirmished with them for about half an hour in which we both lost a good many men. They sent cavalry and infantry to get round our flanks, which was soon observed and we were immediately ordered to retreat. The French pushed on in a very dashing way, the situation then became general, the whole of the troops were then keeping up a very sharp fire but still retreating.

I must now tell you what sort of ground we had to retreat over. There was a number of stone walls, which were very high and we had to scramble over them and grape fields and all sorts of disagreeable places to pass through before we could reach the bridge. The enemy were pushing in very close and their balls flying round us like hailstones; at this time we were retreating for the bridge across the River Coa, the enemy endeavouring to outflank us on all sides and they got nearly round us. When we had got near to the bridge there was an order came for us to charge the enemy up the hill, by that means it gave more time for the remainder of the men to cross the bridge and form on the opposite side which the general was determined to defend and I assure you it was defended in a very gallant style, but with the loss of a great number of brave fellows.

I shall now endeavour to point out to you the position on each side of the bridge. There are very large mountains [hills] on each side of it and both the enemy and ourselves had each side of the bridge and the hills lined with troops. The enemy attempted to cross the bridge three or four times and at each attempt they always marched by the beat of the drums. Each time we drove them back with considerable loss after strewing the bridge with their dead bodies. To the best of my recollection, we began to skirmish with them between six and seven o'clock in the morning and from that time until about four in the evening there was one continued fire. We had three pieces of light artillery placed on the top of the hill, which annoyed the enemy very much, but they had theirs in return, which of course, annoyed us a little, as the shots and shells came quick all the time that we were marching to the bridge. The enemy retreated from the bridge at about four o'clock and left us master of the field for the present. After that we had our dead buried and our wounded taken away to the rear.

I shall now inform you as near as I can how many we had killed, wounded and missing. We had a Lieutenant Colonel, one captain and one lieutenant killed and eleven other officers wounded, many of whom are gone to Lisbon as their wounds are very bad. We had 140 men killed, wounded and missing, but I cannot inform you of the particulars. The 95th Rifle Regiment had 4 officers killed and eleven wounded and some of those since dead, and about the same number of men. The 52nd Regiment had one major and one captain wounded and several men wounded, how many I cannot say.

On the evening after the engagement there was an order come from Lord Wellington that we were to retreat immediately. That night we marched about seven miles and got to a place where there was some straw and laid down for the night. The following night we began our march for Celorico [da Beira], expecting the enemy to attack us every hour. As we marched through villages the people were all deserting them and running into the mountains. When we came to Celorico [da Beira] the town was very much deserted by the inhabitants and hardly anything to be got. The people are now very much coming back, and there is plenty to be got. Lord Wellington's headquarters are still at Santarem. We are in villages about two miles from the town, driven in by bad weather, we expect every day to go under trees as the weather is now taken up. I assure you we live quite at peace here. We see nothing of the enemy. Our dragoons have had some little skirmishing with the enemy, but of no consequence. The enemy are erecting batteries and getting up their artillery to bombard Almeida. It is reported their batteries are just finished. There are a great number of French deserters coming in daily, who all say the French are very much in want of provisions. Ciudad Rodrigo surrendered to the enemy on the 12th of June. I believe they behaved remarkably well to the inhabitants of the place. General [Marshal] Massena commanded the French army in this part. It is supposed he has got a very large army. I cannot say what number. When Lord Wellington intends to fight the French I do not know. I suppose that will be near to Lisbon. It is surprising to me that the French do not march on quicker. I should almost suppose they will not trouble us much until they have got possession of Almeida. Yours much in haste, for you know I always put things to the very last. I have not got a moment more to spare, for the sergeant is now waiting for my letter. I remain, my dear brother, yours truly, John Brumwell. Adieu, God bless you all.

PS Give my love to my father, mother and brothers and sisters. Write to Gregson, tell him I am in good health and spirits and I hope to live to see you all again. But there is no saying what a piece of lead or cannonball may do. After the scenes that I saw the other day, both men and officers shot on each side of me, I am now beginning to think that the ball is not yet cast that is intended for me, but there is no saying for the chances of war. There will nothing give me greater pleasure than to hear from you or my father or Gregson.

The next letter received by the family was not good news. Lieutenant John Brumwell had volunteered for the forlorn hope at the storming of Ciudad Rodrigo and was killed.

Espeja, 25 February 1812

Sir,

I trust you will ere this have received from Lieutenant Colonel Macleod[19] the letter which, as commanding officer of the regiment, he felt it his duty to write you, to apprize you of the melancholy though glorious fate which has awaited your gallant brother, the late much lamented Lieutenant John Brumwell.

It becomes now my duty as acting member of Committee Paymastership to transmit for the information of his relatives a statement of his effects and credit. This I have done on the other side by which it will be seen that a final balance of ninety-one pounds two shillings and fourpence is due to the deceased from the regiment and which balance Messrs Greenwood, Cox and Company [Army] Agents for the regiment, are authorised to pay over to the legal representatives of the deceased.

I ought to be favoured with an acknowledgment of the receipt of this and have the honour to be, Sir, your most obedient servant, Jos Welles, Major,[20] Acting Member Committee of Paymastership, 1st Battalion 43rd Regiment Light Infantry

---

19. Lieutenant Colonel Charles Macleod, 43rd Foot.
20. Major Joseph Wells, 43rd Foot.

Chapter 15

Private John Timewell

Journal

Macmillan's Magazine, **November 1897**

The following is from the original diary kept by Private John Timewell of the 43rd Light Infantry during the campaigns in the Peninsula between 1809 and 1814. The diary is superscribed, '1st Battalion 43rd Captain Sherwin's company, No. 6, Private John Tymon, his book'.

John Timewell was born around 1780, the son of Joan Timewell and was baptised in Milverton Church, Somerset, on 10 October 1782. Mrs Timewell, apparently lived to the ripe age of 104, whereas her son died when only 68.

Timewell appears to have enlisted in the 43rd Light Infantry on 10 April 1805, under the name of Tymon; and he is described in his Army discharge documents as such. He is described as being 5ft 4in tall with black hair and hazel eyes, with a sallow complexion and he was a labourer by trade.

On 24 April 1816, he was discharged from the service on account of ophthalmia after eleven years and twenty-five days service. He was granted a pension of sixpence per day on 19 September 1816, which was later increased to nine pence per day on 1 July 1845. He died on 31 May 1849 at Taunton aged 66. He was buried at St Michael's at Milverton on 5 June 1849. His account is often confused and many of his statements of losses are very questionable. The reader is referred to Chapter 1 for correct figures.

Journal

1809

We received orders to march from Colchester to Harrige [Harwich] on the first day of June 1809, and embarked for Lisbon with a fair and prosperous gale; nothing extra [occurred] during the passage. We landed on the 3 July at Santarane [Santarém], eight leagues from Lisbon and remained there for three days, when we got orders for to advance to Castle a Brank [Castelo Branco].

Forced march of from that place to Talavera in Spain, fifteen leagues we marched in twenty-four hours, which is sixty English miles and never a drop of water all the way, only a hole [pool] we spied in a field about twelve at night. We drank it very hearty; when daylight appeared there was all sorts of dead animals in the same hole and [the water] as white as milk. We arrived at Talavera on the 29 July, but the battle was over. Then we were ordered on duty as piquet, and remained several days till they could bury the dead and of wounded there was a great number. The dead bodies was gathered in great heaps and burned, for the smell was so great that no soldier could stand it.

The forces of the enemy being so superior to ours, and for want of provisions, we were forced to retreat, and had no provisions, to a place they called Lascases [Las Casinas], in Portugale [Portugal], and [there] we remained for seven days. The price of 3 lbs of bread at this place was 4s 6d; we had 2 lbs of beef for three men for one day, without salt, and nothing else. Then we got orders to march as quick as possible, for the enemy was almost surrounding us, to a place they call Castell de Vide, sometimes receiving rations and sometimes none, hundreds dying on the road for want. We would get 2 oz of wheat, 2 oz of peas, 1 oz of rice, 2 oz of beans, and was happy when we got that small allowance.

We retreated from that to Camp Mayo [Campo Maior], and remained there for eleven weeks, very comfortable: we got our rations very regular.

1810

Then our route came on the 9 May, and we marched down [up] all Portugale [Portugal], to a place they call Almeda [Almeida], a garrison town, and encamped about a quarter of a mile from the same on the 23 July 1810, and when night came on, it began the most terrible rain and thunder that I think ever came from the heavens, and having no tents, nothing but the open fields, next morning we were most pitiful creatures to be seen, all running wet. We fell in to be mustered on the plain, and had mustered two companies when orders came that twenty thousand of the French were just at hand and was making for the bridge. Then we made all speed to get there before them, their shot coming as hail from their small arms, and our force was only the 43rd, 52nd, 95th, and the 1st and 3rd Caskalores [Caçadores] of the Portuguese. We fought from

214

five in the morning to six in the afternoon; they charged the bridge three times, but was always repulsed with a great loss. We lost our Colonel Hull and 11 officers, 276 men killed and 96 wounded of the 43rd and the other regiments was equal [in their losses]; the French lost about 1500.

You may think [of] our condition after the horrid night and then was obliged to retire all night to Castenia [Castanheira] and there we destroyed all our stores to hinder them to fall into the hands of the enemy. We still continued our retreat to a place they called Mount Saca [Busaco]. Then the French came down on us in great numbers not knowing that Lord Wellington had any great number of troops, but they were greatly mistaken. On the 27 September 1810, we formed our lines for battle, which reached four leagues, that is, sixteen miles, and then the 95th Regiment was sent out to scrimage [skirmish], and our British cannons roaring like thunder. Dreadful was the slaughter made among the French, when our British heroes gave them a charge, they fell as thick as hail; we drove them from our guns down a large hill into their own lines in great confusion, many thousands lying behind. This engagement held for two days, the loss of the French was 6,430 [and] of the British 4,729. But the next morning, the French getting round our right flank, for their number was three to one, we [were] forced to retreat to Alenca [Alenquer].

It being a very foggy day, they came on us when we were cooking, and [we] had to leave all behind us and they took a great number of us prisoners. We had to be on the run all that night, forcing the inhabitants to fly with us, to hinder them to give the French provisions and many a brave soldier [was] walking half dressed, not having time to put them on.

This retreat was to Ruda [Arruda] heights. This mountain we remained on encamped for six weeks, and it reaches from the River Tegas [Tagus] to the sea, where we made strong works [so] that all the force of the French could not hurt us, though they tried several times, but all was in vain. But on account of an order from Lord Wellington to the inhabitants to leave their houses, the French was forced to retreat for want of rations as far as Santaran [Santarém]. The intelligence of the French [retreat] came to Lord Wellington in the close of the evening of the 3 October 1810. Then we followed them to Santarem, they getting the bridge before us and planting heavy guns to hinder us to cross, and to ford it was impossible. Then we were told off to cantonments at the quinta for two months, planting strong outlying piquets every morning, two hours before daylight, them at one end of the bridge and us at the other.

1811

Provisions began to be hard with the French and they were forced to retire, no inhabitants to give them any relief, and leaving on the bridge a straw sentry about the hour of twelve at night. Our sentries soon found it out and made the alarm; then immediately the blockading of the bridge was cleared off and us after them. We found in their houses, as we passed through, horses hanging up, dressed as same as bullocks for their victuals, and Indian corn made in[to] porridge. We followed as far as the plains of Bumball [Pombal] where they were ready to receive the British; but as soon as the English steel made among them, off they went like deers, leaving many thousands behind both killed and wounded, besides a great number of ammunition-wagons and guns.

In two days' time we fell in with them again on the plains of Conditia [Condeixa] in the morning, and before evening [we] took 3,000 prisoners and a great number of officers' baggage. The plain next morning was covered with English and French soldiers, stripped naked, some not dead.

We still pursuing them as far as Savagal [Sabugal], on the 3 April 1811, in the morning at five we crossed a large river [the Côa]. Then they opened the fire from their guns on us; but we advanced through smoke and fire up the hill, and in forty-five minutes was in the French lines. In spite of all their shot and shell we charged their cannon three times. The first time the 43rd Light Infantry had the honour to take two guns, one howitzer, but with a great loss. The enemy's wounded that lay on the ground they burned before they would let them fall in the hands of the Portuguese. The number [that] engaged us that day was 21,000, and our division, that is the 43rd, 52nd, 95th, two Portuguese regiments, Captain Ross's Flying [Horse] Artillery, and King's 1st German Light Dragoons, all only [a]mounted to 7,000 men; and those 21,000 men was the rearguard of the French army that could not get out of the way. The loss of the French that day was 3,000 killed and wounded, 2,000 prisoners and many mules of officers' baggage. Our loss was very great, out of only a handful, 2,099 rank and file, 27 sergeants and 15 officers.

Then they made to a garrison town in Spain, the name of Roderigo [Ciudad Rodrigo]. Leaving 2,000 to keep the garrison of Almeda [Almeida] till the rest could get away, there we halted for ten days. Then the whole of the French joined, which consisted of 150,000. Coming early one morning on us in camp, and our whole strength of British and Portuguese was only 80,000, [they] drove us out of our camp and we went as far as Fountis De Nor [Fuentes de Oñoro]. Then Lord Wellington formed his lines for battle. We then began on the 2nd of May in the morning very hot on both sides from daylight to dark at night. Then they and us drew back to daylight and morning. But God was King that day! We totally defeated them; the plains was horrid to see, covered with killed and wounded, them crying for mercy from the Portuguese. They lost that day 4,000 killed in the field, 1,520 wounded, and 500 prisoners. The British and Portuguese loss was 3,600 killed and wounded. They retreated in great confusion, not being able to accomplish the design of releasing them out of the garrison town of Roderigo. About three nights after the engagement there was two strong regiments sent to watch them from getting out [of Almeida], the 4th, or King's and 2nd, or Queen's Regiment and through neglect of those two regiments the French made their escape [by] the crossing at Barbry Pork [Barba del Puerco] where their main body lay. A great number was drowned, and a great number of prisoners was taken that missed their way. The colonel of the 4th or King's Own, shot himself: the colonel of the 2nd or Queen's, resigned his commission on account of the neglect of their regiments.[1]

Then we advanced as far as Roderigo [Ciudad Rodrigo] to begin the siege. On the night of the 7th of January, we begun the works, the weather being very cold with frost and snow. We had to cross a river every morning up to our middle, the ice fit to cut us in two, and remain working in that condition for twelve hours under the heavy shot from the town, where many a brave soldier was killed.

On the 19th January the Light and 4th Divisions had orders to be in readiness at the hour of nine o'clock at night for the storming of the town. We begun the assault and made the town in two hours, but with great slaughter. The elements appeared to be on fire for that time from their guns. We entered like lions, took 1,500 prisoners, and had orders to kill man, woman and child, but the English is more generous. We lost our noble General Crawford [Craufurd] who was afraid of no Frenchman. The 43rd Regiment lost in that two hours eight officers, 255 killed, 109 wounded and all other regiments nearly the same.

We halted in a small village, two leagues from the town, for eight days. Then we received orders to march for another garrison in Spain, about two hundred miles, the name is Badahos [Badajoz], and had several skirmishes with them on the way. At length we arrived on the

---

1. The crest of the 4th Regiment is a lion, and of the 2nd a lamb. The following squib was current in the Light Division at the time: The Lion went to sleep, And the Lambs were at play; The Eagle spread his wings, And from Almeida flew away. Lt Colonel Charles Bevan 4th Foot took his own life following the incident.

ground, and on the 16 March 1812, had orders for another siege; and on the 17th at night, the Light Division opened the ground in front of the garrison, under heavy fire from their guns; and we ended the works on the 5 April, all this time under the fire of their heavy guns. And many a brave soldier fell at those works. On the 6th, at the hour of nine at night, the 3rd, 4th, 5th and Light Divisions received orders for the storming. It then began and held to two in the morning. We were beat back twice, but the third time made it good, but with a great slaughter. We lost our noble Colonel McCloud (Macleod), which every soldier much lamented his loss, for he was a father to them, besides 14 officers, 10 serjeants, 425 killed and wounded, in the 43rd Regiment. The elements appeared in flames; during that time it was the providence of God that any man escaped that dreadful siege.

The next morning it was a most dismal sight to behold, some wanting legs, some arms and heads, some drowned; and to hear the cries of those brave soldiers for a drop of water, it would have melted the heart [of] stone. Then Lord Wellington give [sic] orders for every soldier to have four hours' plunder in the town. They rushed in like lions, sparing nothing before them, and took money, clothes, victuals and drink, which made them amends for the sufferings of the dreadful night. The prisoners we took in the town was 2,530; and the loss of the British and Portuguese that night was 3,790, besides what fell in the works. We halted for a few days to bury the dead and remove the wounded, then came [on] as far as Campmao [Campo Maior]. [We] remained there one night; next morning [we] begun our march down Portungale (Portugal) and they advanced after us to Salamanca with their whole forces. Then we received orders to cross the river [Tormes] and to attack two forts [Forts San Vincente and San Caetano] that was in the town, but the fortification they had made we could not touch it; but we starved them out.

Then we advanced to Rueda, within eight leagues of Madrid. There the enemy received a reinforcement; on account of the Spaniards giving way we were obliged to retire, on account of superior numbers and turning our right flank. We made a halt for a few minutes to get a little water, the road being so very dusty and the weather so warm that the men were almost choked; but the enemy coming so rapid down, we could not get a single drop, which caused a number of prisoners to be taken. We had an engagement at Fraka Combat of [Castrejon], but could not do any good. The 11th Light Dragoons was ordered to make a charge, but them failing, Lord Wellington and his whole staff was forced to fight themselves. We then retired as far as Salamanca and lay there for a few days.

Then we received orders on 18th June [22 July] for a general engagement, which begun about five in the morning and held till setting sun. There the brave Wellington gave them a total defeat. In the evening the Light Division was ordered to pursue a heavy column to [sic] daylight, but could not fall in with them. The remainder of the French was all this time on the retreat; the total loss of the French that day was 21,000 killed and taken prisoners. The loss to the British, Portuguese and Spaniards was 11,000 killed, 2,213 wounded. Then fresh orders was for us to advance again as far as Madrid, where we lay for four months and the French retired to Burgus [Burgos] for their winter quarters.

Then we received orders to advance to Burgus [Burgos] castle to take it by storm, but before we reached there, the French blew it up.[2] which was good news for us. Then we were forced to retire by the misconduct of the Guards selling their ammunition and the Spaniards giving way.

We retired as far as Tammas [Alba de Tormes]; there we encamped that night in a large wood and very swampy ground. Early next morning, the enemy coming on so rapid, we were forced to retire in square for three miles resist their cavalry, rushing out of the wood on us in heavy columns. But in a short [time] their infantry and artillery appeared as motes in the sun. They drove us down a very steep hill, their guns playing on us all the time, and at the bottom of the hill there was two large rivers to cross. We forded them up to [the] middle in very cold weather and remained all night in that deplorable condition, and not a morsel to put in our mouths, only the oack corns [acorns] we gathered from the trees. They took most of our sick and several women prisoners. We had two officers wounded, four men killed, and the 20th Regiment of Portuguese was mostly all taken, not being [able] to keep up for want of provisions; this was five days wanting bread. Then early next morning we marched to Roderigo [Ciudad Rodrigo] [on] most cruel roads, over ploughed fields up to our middle in dirt, barefooted and hungry bellies; you may judge our condition. When we came to Roderigo [Ciudad Rodrigo], we had a day's biscuit; it was a glorious sight after being so long wanting. Here the French came no farther. Then we went to a town two leagues farther; the name is Galagus (Gallegos). Remained there six months, very comfortable.

On the 20 May 1813, the whole of the British got orders to advance, and on the 21st, in the morning, marched, falling in with the enemy very often and having a few scrimmages [skirmishes]; but on the 20th of

---

2. This clearly mixes in events from 1813.

June we came to Victora (Vitoria) and in the morning of the 21st about four o'clock begun the action. They had 190 pieces of cannon playing on us. Tremendous was the fire from their guns and musketry; the elements appeared in smoke and fire. We took Napoleon's lady[3] and all her equipage, and were very near taking Nap[oleon] himself,[4] two of our dragoons riding up to him; but he was rescued by a squadron of the French, who got him away.

This battle held [lasted] from four in the morning till setting sun, the longest day in all the year. We took six waggons of money, forty of shoes and all the provisions they had for 250,000 men, clothing, officers' baggage, and other stores, besides 190 pieces of cannon. Most horrid was it to be seen next morning, the plains covered with killed and wounded of both sides, both man and horse. The loss of the French was computed 9,716 killed, 6,019 wounded, and 17,000 prisoners.[5] That was a glorious day and gave them a fatal blow which made these take to the mountains like so many goats, without arms or accoutrements. They left in Pampeloney [Pamplona] 10,000, the rest made good their retreat to the Pyrenees mountains. Then the [soldiers] left in Pampeloney [Pamplona] was forced to kill the cavalry horses for [want] of provisions, thinking they would be set free, which the French [tried] several times but never could succeed. They gave themselves up prisoners of war; the loss of the French at Victoria [Vitoria] was 42,776.

We received orders to advance to the mountains after them; these mountains goes by the River Vera. The British encamped on one side and them on the other; they kept there for three days, but we routed them with a great loss. They made then to the highest mountain in Urup [Europe] which goes by the name Laron [La Rhune]. There they made strong works and us finding outlying piquets every day on it. I never suffered so much cold and hardships as was there; nothing to shelter us from the cold and being so very high. Here we stopped six weeks.

We received orders on 9 October to advance and drive them [from] their works, and on the morning of the 10th made the attack. In this attack we suffered much. We drove them into France to a place they call Arance [Arrauntz]. There the French remained and us remained for two months, finding strong outlying piquets every day; their sentries in one side of the field and us in the other, our piquets and them scrimaging [skirmishing] every night. Never did I spend a more happy Christmas

---

3. General Gazan's wife was taken but sent safely back to the French army.
4. He refers to King Joseph Napoleon, Napoleon's elder brother.
5. This is a great exaggeration of the losses.

night than we had there. But the French got a reinforcement and drove us to a large chapel.[6] There we kept our ground and went to work to fortify it night and day for six days. We had most laborious fatigues, digging [among] the corpses and the headstones to shelter [us] from the shot of the enemy; drinking the water out of the graves, for we could get no other relief.

Then orders went to Lord Wellington of the deplorable situation of the Light Division. He sent a reinforcement to us; then we advanced on their piquets and drove them as far as Bayouhn [Bayonne]. There they made another stand for seven days, but we made round their right flank [and] took them unawares with all their tents and stores and made 700 prisoners, without firing a shot.

Then off they went as far as Tarbes, falling in with them again on the 20 March, had another battle but the British steel made them fly as far as Tolouse [Toulouse] leaving 300 killed, 157 wounded, 1,000 prisoners, besides all the officers' baggage, which was a very good prize. We followed them as far as the Sand village [Samatan] two leagues from Tolouse; there we halted for ten days. The inhabitants of the village all was fled when we came to it. There we had puncheons of wine in every house, as good as you pay in England five shillings a bottle. If you had but seen the soldiers in glory there with fifty glasses on their table all full from morning to night and even washed potatoes in it, it was so plenty.

On the 2 April, about the hour of twelve at night, our route come for Toulouse, where we arrived at daybreak and encamped for two days about two miles from the town. The morning following the Spaniards came up; their strength was 10,000 chosen men for the engagement. They remained in camp to Easter Sunday 10th April, 1813 [1814], when at six in the morning the battle begun with the Spaniards and French till midday. But the Spaniards was beat back twice, though they fought like lions for seven hours. But the General of the Spaniards, seeing these brave soldiers fall in such numbers, that he went to Lord Wellington for a division or two of the British which was granted in a[n] instant. Then they made a most desperate charge, fearing nothing, [and] made the French to leave their works in the greatest confusion, leaving many thousands behind, killed and wounded. The loss of those brave Spaniards that seven hours they were engaged [was] 4,732 killed, 700 wounded. The English [lost] 2,520 killed, 964 wounded. The French lost in the works 6,000 killed and wounded; 8,000 prisoners was taken, 2,552

---

6. The chapel at Arcangues.

taken in a fort a small distant from Tolouse [Toulouse]. The engagement held from six in the morning to four in the afternoon. This was the total defeat [at the end] of [the] long and tedious war of Bonapart[e]. Then the French retreated ten leagues from Tolouse [Toulouse] and the British halted three days to get refreshment, and well they were used. Then orders came for us to advance after them again, but we only [were] about five leagues on the march when the dragoon came to General Alten with the joyful news of peace between France and England. This was the joyful news for the whole army, to think hardships was at an end. Then we returned to Tolouse [Toulouse] and remained there for eleven days; never was men used better than the inhabitants done to the English soldiers.

Then we received orders to march to Mountage [Montegut], where we stopped for two months in quarters; the friendliest people I met with in all my travels; never was soldiers used half so well in England. A loaf of ration bread in this town was 76 lbs and white as your quartern loaves in England. Then we got the route for Blamford [Blanquefort]. We remained there for twelve days in camp, and in this camp a bottle of brandy was only ten pence, one pint of wine two pence halfpenny, and seven pound of bread five pence.

Orders came for our embarkation for England. We then marched to Conahac [Cantenac] and embarked on board His Majesty's ship, the *Queen Charlotte*, of 120 guns. Was on board for eleven days, very comfortable and nothing extra during our passage. We landed at Plymouth and went into quarters. This gives you a small sketch of my travels through the continent.

His story was continued in *Macmillan's Magazine* of March 1898, as he served in the New Orleans campaign.

On the 13th of October 1814, we received orders for our embarkation, which took place on the 14th at Plymouth at Divels Poynt [Devil's Point] on board His Majesty's transport *Ocean*.

We set sail on the 26th with a prosperous gale: nothing extra till the 18th of November, about one o'clock, [when] we crossed the Traffic Line [Tropic of Capricorn]. Proceeding on our course until the morning of the 4 December, we perceived the islands of Dominico [Dominica] and Mantainico [Martinique] to our larboard. We sailed past them; they seemed to be very mountainous. There we met with the *Venerable* [74] who is stationed there. Nothing extra till the 9th instant; then we passed the island of Gardlop [Guadaloupe] and Sandemengo [San Domingo], very high lands; I cannot give you any more [information] about them being a great ways off.

On the 11th we came in sight of Jemaca [Jamaica]; it is very mountainous and the climate very warm. We met with a frigate on her return home [wards] after conveying the troops to their destination. We ascertained from her that the Portsmouth and Cork fleets passed fourteen days before us and is on their way to join the army.

We lost sight of the island [Jamaica] on the 15 December, when a storm arose and held to the 17th in the morning; then the weather becomes more temperate. [Here it was] where we first seen the flying fish in great numbers; they are about the size of a herron [herring] and flies only when the dolphin pursues them, and they fly about two hundred yards, the same as a swallow; then the dolphin leaps six feet out of the water after them.

On the 27 December we passed the island of Cuby [Cuba]; it is of great descent [ascent?]. On the 30 December we cast anchor where the heavy line of battle ships lay and in the afternoon sailed down [to] where the remainder of the transports lay.

On the 31st, [we] received orders for disembarking and landed about nine at night within ten miles of [New] Orleans and encamped on the banks of the river Missipia [Mississippi], and on the morning of the 5 January [1815] joined the army [at] about eleven o'clock within three miles of [New] Orleans.

Then we furnished working parties to cut a canal for our gunboats to proceed up the river; both soldiers and sailors and marines were employed on this laborious occasion, and on account of the ground being so marshy we were forced to build our batteries of shugar [sugar barrels] instead of sand [bags].

When we joined the army we understood from the 95th Regiment [that] there was no opposition on the morning of their landing. We then marched and encamped under the enemy's works near the lake leading to New Orleans. The enemy had stationed in this lake a frigate and several gunboats for the protection of the town, and on the evening of the same day the enemy sallied out [and attacked] unawares and rushed into the camp whilst the soldiers were busy in cooking and refreshing themselves. But the 95th and 93rd Regiments got under arms and with little or no loss on their side, soon made the enemy retire in great confusion, leaving many dead on the field. I am sorry to regret the loss of a few brave officers and soldiers on the above occasion. Nothing else happened during this night, but the next morning the enemy kept [up] a constant fire from their batteries; and the frigate and gunboats was standed [stationed] on the River Misipia [Mississippi] which greatly annoyed our working parties.

All necessary regulations being arranged for the general engagement on both sides of the river, the commander of the forces, Lieutenant General

E M Peckingham [Sir Edward Pakenham] give his orders for the different regiments to form [for] the attack on the enemy.

On the night of the 7 January 1815, [we] finished a battery of nine 24-pounders, and all was builded of barrels of sugar. Then the order was issued that the army was to be drawn up in close column [as] near as possible [to] the enemy's works, the whole moving from their camps so as to arrive at their appointed station about eleven o'clock at night [ready] to commence the engagement a little before daybreak on the morning of the 9th. A rocket was to be thrown up at that hour as a signal to engage in all quarters. The 85th Regiment, with sailors and marines, crossed the river Misipia [Mississippi] before daybreak in armed boats and landed before they were perceived by the enemy, and took possession of two forts without any considerable loss, whilst the remainder [remaining] part of the army was engaged on the right bank of the river leading to [New] Orleans. Close to the banks of the river they had two batteries which commanded the left angle of the enemy's position. A storming party, consisting of 400 men with a proportion of officers and non commissioned officers, first made the attack and took one fort, but afterwards was repulsed with a great loss for want of a sufficient support.

The troops in front of New Orleans was the 4th, 21st, 44th, 93rd and 95th Regiments; the [latter] led the attack; the 43rd Light Infantry and 7th British Fusileers formed the reserve line. A part of the 44th and 5th West Indian Regiment were employed to carry the scaling-ladders and bridges [fascines] for the purpose of ascending the enemy's works, which proved in vain on account of the depth of the ditch that was thrown up in front of the enemy. There was a tremendous fire of cannon kept up from their works.

The commander of the forces observing the misconduct of the 44th Regiment, who was employed in carrying the ladders and bridges, rode up immediately, but before he could reach the spot he received his death wound. He immediately despatched an order to General Kain [Keane], a few minutes before he expired, to withdraw the army, but before General Kain [Keane] could complete this order he was also wounded, which rendered him incapable of taking the command. Major General Lamboth [Sir John Lambert] being the only one left, obeyed his orders, leaving entrenched the 43rd Light Infantry and 7th British Fusiliers, up to their middle in water, the 95th covering the retreat. I cannot bestow too much praise on the above corps for their mistorious [meritorious] conduct of the day.

About eleven o'clock at night, we spiked a nine-gun battery and then we retired in regular form to the encampment of the 21st and 44th

Regiments, who was ordered to the rear, about five miles. Here we remained in front of the enemy, under a constant fire from the enemy for ten days, always accoutred and ready to stand to our arms, as we did not know the minute we [might be] surprised by the enemy. Day and night we had strong outlying piquets posted for that purpose, so you must consider our uncomfortable situation when we were not allowed to uncouter [dequip] or shift ourselves. Indeed we thought every hour a day whilst we remained in this wretched state, besides, the coldness added more to our miseries. Every day we were issued out half a pint of spirits per man, which was of great service to the health of the troops.

On the afternoon of the 18 January 1815, about the hour of ten, the piquets was [sic] ordered to be drawn off, except the sentries, who remained to three o'clock the next morning to take off the attention of the enemy whilst the remainder was retreating, which was performed in the most solitary manner along the banks of a lake, thirteen miles of swampy ground and on the morning of the 19th we encamped among a thicket of canes. This is a small island which was enclosed [separated] from the enemy, where we had strong outlying piquets, so that we rested secure until every necessary preparation was arranged for our embarkation, which took place on the 2nd of February.

After setting fire to our camp [we] went down the lake in boats to our different transports; we remained on board for five days, then we weighed anchor and sailed for the island of Daughin [Dauphine Island] and disembarked on the 8th.

The length of this island is ten miles in breadth, in some parts two miles. It is a complete wilderness; at the upper end of it are a few shabby huts, the residence of a few Spaniards who were fishermen. These huts were occupied by the generals and Staff of the army. Round the shore of this island are great banks of white sand as fine as flour; besides a great variety of trees to be seen, such as Black and Green Tea, great number of Saxafax [Sassafras], Cedar, and Bay trees. The climate is extremely warm besides; [we were] greatly tormented by miskeaties [mosquitoes], flies and a number of alligators of a great size. The head is like a calf, the under jaw never moves, the tail like a fish and its fore paws is like a Christian's; hardly anything can pierce its scales; they are about fifteen feet long; we killed one of them. The turtles is plenty and very beautiful, and several others too tedious to mention.

We remained there to the 4th of March 1815, when we weighed anchor and left sight of that island with a fine breeze. On the 21st [we] came in sight of Cuby [Cuba]; nothing worth noticing; it has chiefly Spaniards [for] inhabitants. The capital is Havana; it has strong walls for its fortification, mounting 360 pieces of cannon besides several forts of great strength. This intelligence we had from a native of the place.

On the 25th and 26th crossed the Gulf of Florida. On the morning of the 3rd April, a dreadful storm which held for two days and many of the ships lost their foremast and sails torn to pieces. We lost the fleet the same night. On the 27 April the weather gets very cold; we enter on the Banks of Newfoundland; at 12 o'clock pm we are 1,541 miles from England.

On the 29th, to our great astonishment, we perceived prodigious mountains of ice floating on the sea, they reached to our sight about four miles in length. This night we lost our latutud [latitude], which is very dangerous; but on the 30th the captain told us we were 1,244 miles from England. The weather becomes a little warmer, and on the 1st of June we comes in sight of England and cast anchor at Spithead. On the 3rd weighed anchor and sailed for Dail [Deal]. On the 4 June arrived, and on the 5th disembarked and marched to Dover.

16 June: Embarked for Holland. Disembarked at Hostend [Ostend] 6 July: joined the army. 7 July: Lined the walls of Paris. 8 July: King Lewis [Louis] XVIII enters Paris. 24 July: Reviewed by the Duke of Wellington, Emperor of Rusha [Russia], King of Prusha [Prussia] and the Emperor of Ostria [Austria].

You must think it very wonderful when we were in three summers and two winters in the space of ten months, and which is more curious, we have been twice in the West Indies, once in America, twice in England and twice in France, all in ten months. I am to incence [acquaint] you with the summers and winters and the different countries. We landed from France, the 5 June 1814; that was one summer, and once in France. Embarked on the 28 October for America and it was winter as far as the West Indies, there we were forced to cover the decks with sails to shade us from the sun; that was two summers. Passing the Bay of Newfoundland, we were almost frozen to death; that I reckon as two winters. Disembarked at Dail [Deal] the 5th of June, that was the three summers. Embarked on 16th for Holland and all in the space of ten months. So this finishes my small book. My wife died on the 17th of May 1825.